Effective Software Engineering

A guide to building successful software products

Author: John Svart

Reviewed by: L.F.P.

ISBN-13: 978-1481176231

ISBN-10: 1481176234

To H & M, may their future shine...

Preface

Having spent the vast majority of past 20 years building software products in different software houses, thus enabling a wide array of clients from many different countries to build their own systems, I decided that it was time to use all that knowledge and experience to create a fast, direct and concise blueprint of the major features, traits and processes that must be accounted for in order to create successful software products.

However, before jumping into the discussion and analysis of such features, traits and processes by dissecting the reasons for their relevance, let us start by understanding, from a software engineering perspective, the criteria that can be used to define successful software products.

Successful software products, from a software engineering perspective, are simply those software products which, on top of implementing the stipulated requirements and beyond satisfying the financial rationale of development cost versus generated revenue/value, are built in such a functional manner that they can be effectively:

- **Deployed to production environment,**
- **Managed by operation teams,**
- **Maintained by software engineering teams,** whose members take up the burden of ensuring that the solution continues to evolve after its initial developmental phase.

These three concepts should be looked upon as the irreplaceable foundation of truly great and effective software engineering, as they will be the measure by which true enterprise capable software is evaluated. Given this, nothing will be more important for mission-critical software than answering effectively the following three questions:

1. How easy is it to deploy the solution to a production environment, including initial installation procedures and subsequent upgrades?

2. How easy is it for operation teams to properly use, configure, manage and troubleshoot the production system once it is up and running?

3. How easy is it for software engineering teams to create new versions of the solution, including bug fixes as well as adding new required features on top of an existing codebase?

Interestingly, with these three questions focusing on key elements that go well beyond the effort of building the initial version of software products, it means that medium to long term sustainability must be viewed as essential for products to be successful.

However, despite this apparent straightforward rationale, herein lays the problem. Unfortunately, many software development teams focus almost solely on the tasks that enable them to create the product itself, and, quite often, lose sight of key components that are vital to the product's usage and maintenance over the years.

I cannot underline enough that I mean absolutely no disrespect for product groups and software engineers who build products, as I've been on their side for many, many years. Nevertheless, though a critique is definitely implied, it originates from self-analysis since, over the years, I have seen that what I either built, or helped to build, usually ended up in the hands of many other IT professionals who would then inherit my creations with all their inherent shortcomings. Overall, this means that, as I moved on to create a new product, these other IT professionals had to endure a colossal battle as they struggled to keep up with systems that sometimes seemed to have a will of their own. And on top of all, they did this with very little knowledge of the system itself!

Consequently, the heart of the matter is:

While IT professionals who create the original versions of a product have a very good knowledge of the product and its inner workings, other teams who later on need to somehow interact with it (either in development or support functions) usually suffer from only barely understanding what they are dealing with.

Product groups have source code, great development environments and virtually no pressure when compared to the drama that usually comes about when a production system malfunctions.

Conversely, operation teams have little knowledge of the system, and usually no source code access or relevant skills to analyze it as they try to identify the origins of a problem. Quite often, they also have to handle crowds of users that are not so understanding and fail to comprehend both why the system is not working to perfection and, even worse, why operation teams simply cannot fix all problematic issues in a split second.

Furthermore, software engineers who maintain the code are usually unaware of all the history that led a specific software to be built in a certain way and, faced with the inexistence of proper detailed documentation[1], they struggle to understand the inner workings of the system and, hence, fail to quickly identify the reasons for the system's failure, and the path and implications of the required fix.

---

[1] Yes, proper detailed documentation on the specifics of why and how products were built and coded in a certain way are nothing but an urban myth…something that simply does not exist!

Thus, the powerful combination of all these elements have driven me to put in ink a set of principles that I have, not only adopted for myself, but also recommended to many others over the years, so as to breeze through the creation of truly easy to **deploy**, easy to **operate** and easy to **maintain** software products.

As such, this is not a book that focuses on the merits of development teams and development processes *per se*. Instead, it is a book directed to those who are indeed building software products and wish to ensure that they have included all the features which will allow all other IT professionals who will interact with these products, over the years, to do so in an effective way. Only through this path will they be able to claim that they have created, from a software engineering perspective, a successful software product.

Interestingly, history has shown me that these critical features are not exclusively related with coding skills or with development processes. It takes a mixture of many factors to really create a successful product, so the items that are included in this book look to reflect that exact mixture and have, thus, been divided in five distinct sections:

1. Coding and execution runtime.
2. Development environment and technologies.
3. Development process.
4. Deployment and supportability.
5. Miscellaneous.

Naturally, I expect that readers will agree with some points and disagree with others. However, I believe that even the intellectual process of reflecting and disagreeing with portions of this text will enhance readers' preparation as well as their chances to successfully build better software products. If you analyze some of the presented guidelines and find that they are not to be followed, you will then have, at the very least, contemplated their reason for being and decided that they would not enhance the product you are building. Such systematic review of these guidelines will ensure that you have thought about all the presented features and understood where the added value exists and where it fails to show itself.

Enjoy and have fun while building successful software products!

Table of Contents

Section I – Coding and execution runtime

This section will present and discuss fourteen items that are directly related with coding practices and execution runtime elements. Along these items, I will review what I consider to be the most crucial elements on how to craft great code, how to ensure that great code can be effectively maintained and the specific pitfalls that should be avoided to ensure that you can produce effective runtime components.

1. An unavoidable reality: errors and exceptions will happen

One of the most important features of any software system consists of error and exception handling, since it is when errors and exceptions occur that everything comes crumbling down. Software engineers will routinely invest a significant amount of time to properly conceive their data structures and their data crunching algorithms. Some will even spend a vast amount of energy coding an efficient and appealing user interface, as laid out by their designers and user experience teams. However, how many delve for countless hours into the different ways that can be chosen to handle errors and exceptions? And how many actually consider each point of failure individually by conducting:

- An analysis of what makes up the information required to identify each particular error or exception point,
- A thorough diagnosis of their origin,
- A systematization of the main guidelines that will ensure the correct approach is taken to overcome the situation.

Sincerely, I know of very few software engineers who view errors and exceptions as first class citizens, on the same level of importance as data structures or algorithms. Furthermore, those isolated cases, in which considerable thought is put into error and exception handling, are usually within the realm of user interfaces, more specifically errors messages, of which many tend to inform about error conditions while failing to direct users' actions towards the appropriate solutions.

Simply put, errors and exceptions must be given significant and detailed thought, so that products can ensure the existence of consistent strategies to handle all these deviating situations. Given this, here are a few guidelines to help you address error and exception handling:

1. **Ensure that all errors and exceptions are registered in a uniform way.**
   Unfortunately, there are too many cases out there where we find that some errors that occur in a system are registered in log files while, others, are simply not registered at all. Additionally, in other situations, logs are scattered in different storage targets according to non-uniform criteria, while in yet other scenarios, some errors are only shown in debug builds and others are simply ignored (from a registration perspective).
   It is also quite common to see products where different components use distinct logging options which vary in terms of persistent storage, formatting information or intrinsic organization of logging data.

This kind of diverse approach makes it extremely difficult, as well as time consuming, to troubleshoot problematic scenarios, since it forces IT professionals (most often a member of the operation team) to go through distinct files in order to correlate entries that often fail to present a consistent method of identifying related items/information.

Furthermore, in some extreme cases, the timeline between the events registered within distinct artifacts is not even prone to a clear cut analysis, mostly due to either varying timestamps that result from out-of-sync resources, or due to the adoption of an asynchronous pattern that drives registration of data[1].

These scenarios, where information is not handled in a consistent way, and which bring about scattered information that make detailed analysis extremely difficult and time-consuming, are simply a nightmare to those managing and maintaining the system, and should therefore be avoided at all times.

2. **Ensure that each error or exception is registered by containing information that enables IT professionals to identify the origin of the problem, as well as what happened, and what the context was.**

   Usually, this means more than a simple error message, especially one that sheds little light on the error itself. Instead, error messages should clearly identify three things: what happened, in which context it took place, and what could potentially fix it.

   Do not underestimate the importance of a complete piece of information and do not hide behind performance issues or storage limitations when logging information on errors or exceptions. Being as complete as possible will always be of great benefit when, later on, production issues emerge.

   Consequently, carefully register information about any relevant internal data structures (namely memory variables, exact point of execution and stack traces) in order to ensure that, once IT professionals read the error messages (and all associated information), they are able to comprehend the specific context of the intrinsic execution environment that led to the occurrence of the errors or exceptions. Only such detailed information on errors and exceptions will enable their effective diagnostic and correction.

3. **Ensure that no security sensitive information is logged as clear text.**

   Despite the need to produce a logging system with all relevant information required to understand any issues that may arise, do not fall into the trap of logging security-sensitive information in clear text. All too often, logging information, after being collected by operation teams, is passed through different channels and, eventually, is relayed to development teams for further analysis. This is obviously problematic, since

---

[1] As defined in item **9 Maximizing efficiency**.

there is simply no way of ensuring the safety of a system when secure data is simply made available to many different parties[1].

As such, it is advisable to either forgo entirely the registration of restricted data[2] or, at the very least, encrypt this important data before logging it. Naturally, only the sensitive part needs encrypting and, obviously, you cannot forget to provide a way of reversing the encryption to those with appropriate clearance, should this part of the information be relevant to the troubleshooting effort.

Finally, keep in mind at all times that protecting a piece of information through encryption always has its limits, as any encrypted piece of data can be decrypted by an untrustworthy party should they have the appropriate tools and a broad enough window of opportunity to do so.

4. **Handle errors and exceptions consistently in code.**

   Modern systems are built by many different software engineers, and an even higher number of engineers end up being involved during the many stages of a software product's lifecycle. As such, it is imperative to create a standardized way of handling errors and exceptions in code. This will ensure that development tasks can easily be assigned to different engineers on the team, while still allowing for consistency to be achieved throughout the product's codebase. Furthermore, all the available resources from the chosen development environment/language should be optimized in order to create (or use) some sort of template code-like feature that enables software engineers to easily and quickly use the stipulated error and exception handling policy. Modern development languages have so many features available that it is extremely easy to make use of templates, code snippets, class inheritance or, simply, some base functions, to allow software engineers to consistently handle errors and exceptions with no more than a few lines of code.

5. **Ensure that all third party components that issue a distinct error handling output are wrapped to create a consistent experience.**

   To provide a consistent error and exception handling experience you cannot overlook whichever third party components that have been integrated into the solution. Naturally, these components will rely on their error and exception handling strategy and, as such, it is almost mandatory to wrap them in a way that the solution produces a coherent and consistent experience under two different perspectives:

---

[1] Often, security issues can even be raised when sharing information with a single party.

[2] Though passwords are the most common example, other items may be equally important, and a context-dependent analysis must be conducted in order to ensure that no undue data is inadvertently exposed.

- **In logging**, we must ensure that the logging repository target, its content and formatting rules, are in line with whatever is produced by all components built for the solution. Otherwise, we would fall into a situation similar to what would happen if we simply failed to implement such a common procedure within our own components.

- **In coding**, should software developers be forced to use different error and exception handling techniques when calling into third party components, engineers will, ultimately, make mistakes by will applying wrong techniques to these distinct scenarios as, sooner or later, they will fail to abide by the specifics of each scenario (handling errors and exceptions that emanate from third party components versus handling errors exceptions that emanate from our own components).

  Given this, it is a far better strategy to wrap third party components in your own layers of code. In doing so, you can be certain that the time spent on this task will be more than compensated by the time gained, as all developers will be using one single coding technique to handle errors and exceptions throughout the entire codebase, not to mention the benefits attained when analyzing existing logs whenever problems do occur.

6. **Ensure that the logging level can be changed dynamically, while preventing the exclusion of basic error and exception information from being registered.**

   Traditionally, logging systems have adhered to switch-based configuration to define how much information is registered. Unfortunately, though systems usually see this feature as a way to specify which events are registered and which are not, most do not allow operation teams to specify which pieces of data are to be registered within each specific event. As an example, consider that many web servers provide a logging configuration feature that allows you to specify, for incoming requests, which pieces of data are registered. This approach often produces an enhanced support experience, namely by supplementing the sheer ability to select which events to log, with the ability to configure which pieces of information will be registered for each log entry.

   On top of this, one must carefully consider how to combine these approaches, so as to ensure that the system is able to be changed without any sort of downtime, even **bypassing simple process recycling**. To achieve this, you probably need to ensure that detection of changes in system configuration is an event-based notification feature, as you do not want to be checking for changes each time a log is to be produced, since it would significantly hurt performance (more will follow on this topic).

   Lastly, and although many systems support a configuration level that completely inhibits any sort of logging, it is not recommended to do so. Such procedure inhibits gaining access even to the most basic information pertaining to any issue taking place within the system, which would be a move in the exact opposite direction of what is required in order to have healthy and maintainable systems.

7. **Although performance and storage are always to be considered, errors and exceptions are not expected to be too prevalent. Hence, you have a lot of leverage to produce code that is slightly detrimental to the overall system resource consumption.**

   Errors and exceptions, by their own nature, will not be the common trend at runtime. Therefore, you can safely implement systems that do not perform optimally when handling errors and exceptions and use slow computing resources such as persistent storage and inherent IO.

   Though errors and exceptions are critical and must be handled appropriately, it is important to resist the immediate temptation to resort to asynchronous techniques in order to optimize system flows. It is highly inadvisable to delegate the process of registering errors or exceptions to lazy-writer threads[1] in order to allow the main execution path to move on, as you risk losing the logging information altogether. As such, it is far safer to look at error and exception registration as a component that requires transactional semantics. Despite this, you should not confuse, mix or integrate it with a detailed tracking/tracing of system behavior (which might also produce logging similar to whatever is produced when registering errors and exceptions) with error and exception handling[2].

8. **View operation teams as any other user of your system, and ensure they have a smooth and agreeable experience.**

   Operation teams will be keen to support software products that cater to their needs and will, at the very least, frown upon software products that seem to go out of their way to make their lives miserable.

   Therefore, it is fundamental to ensure that your software product development cycle includes, within its deliverables, the production of all required tools that, quickly and efficiently, extract all relevant information from error and exception logging.

   Doing so implies that you should avoid having an unwelcomed extra load being put on operation teams, forcing them to manually review scores of logged data as an alternative way of compensating for the absence of feasible tools that quickly search and correlate entries. Such case will, quite often, lead to the usage of scattered and rudimentary tools that fail to bring a full understanding of the complete logging picture and, in turn,

---

[1] As defined in item **9 Maximizing efficiency.**

[2] As defined in item **30 Strange unexplainable behaviors are inevitable: create a detailed and systematic tracing** feature.

condemn operation teams' efforts to fall short of delivering the required analysis of available logging data. In extreme cases, you will find that important pieces of logged information will simply fail to be timely reviewed, putting extra and unnecessary strain and risk on the system. Thus, the obvious and straightforward bottom line is simple: supplying the adequate tools to explore, analyze and review error and exception information must always be a top priority.

9. **The ultimate dilemma: which errors and exceptions should simply not be handled?**

Software engineering literature is packed with advice on this dilemma, with the resounding truth being that there are errors and exceptions from which a solution cannot simply recover from automatically. This, however, does not mean that you should not log such situations nor does it mean that you should allow whichever process harbors the event to simply crash, as the exception is bubbled upwards towards the operating system's handling mechanism.

From a logging perspective, no error or exception is too serious to the point of forgoing its registration, unless of course the logging system itself is failing. Barring this exceptional case, you should strive to log all errors and exceptions.

Interestingly, this raises a further dilemma, which is that of what to do if the logging system itself fails? While some systems see this as too critical to continue and simply halt, others ignore it and continue as though nothing happened. Given these options, which one should be looked upon as the most appropriate path to take? Simply put, this really depends on the solution but, for modern mission-critical solutions which run on redundant hardware architectures without single points of failure, it is probably more appropriate to consider halting part of the system.

Considering the example of a load-balanced scenario with several servers, halting part of such system would entail halting one of the servers – the one that would be failing in the logging actions. In turn, this would ensure that subsequent calls would be redirected to the other servers. This action would inevitably spur warning cues to operation teams, who would then act upon the halted server in order to resolve whatever problems are preventing the error and exception logging feature from working as expected. This example, and its inherent strategy, assumes that there isn't a single point of failure in the logging system itself, which enables other servers to continue running smoothly, including logging any additional issues in appropriate fashion.

Conversely, within cases that differ from the previously laid out example and where single points of failure do exist with the logging system, halting may not be the path to take!

Item recap:

This item's fundamental guidelines can be succinctly systematized as follows:

- ✓ Ensure that all errors and exceptions are registered in a uniform way, using the same target repositories, the same formatting options and the same level of detailed information.
- ✓ Ensure that you can effectively correlate entries if required. Timestamps are not a feasible way of achieving this goal.
- ✓ Ensure that each error or exception is registered with information that enables IT professionals, faced with the responsibility of managing the situation, to identify the origin of the problem, what occurred and what the context was.
- ✓ Ensure that no security-sensitive information is logged as clear text and, quite naturally, provide adequate tools to process encrypted information if so required.
- ✓ Ensure that all third party components that issue a distinct error handling output are wrapped in order to create a consistent experience.
- ✓ Handle errors and exceptions consistently in code by using the same pattern to treat errors and exceptions throughout the codebase. This should preferably rely on easy to use templates, code snippets or other coding encapsulation techniques.
- ✓ Ensure that the logging level can be changed dynamically while carefully preventing basic error and exception information from being excluded from registration. Ensure that changing the logging level does not force any sort of downtime, while still ensuring that the new options are respected.
- ✓ Although performance and storage are always to be considered, errors and exceptions are not expected to be too prevalent and, as such, you have a lot of leverage to produce code that is slightly detrimental to the overall system resource consumption.
- ✓ View operation teams as any other user of your system, namely by ensuring they have a smooth and agreeable experience. Always provide adequate tools to ensure that information can be easily analyzed and reviewed.
- ✓ No error or exception can go without proper registration. Carefully contemplate what to do if or, better yet, when the logging system itself should fail.

2. Juggling the retry logic conundrum

Exceptions are usually a subject of much heated debate[1] and, regardless of both how you decide to register them and, eventually, recover from them, there is one particular nuance that deserves a dedicated analysis: the ability to apply retry logic.

Not all exceptions need to be immediately handled through some retry logic, since many errors are deterministic to a degree that will warrant the repetition of the same operation useless, given that it will always return the same result. However, there are many actions that, quite often, result in exceptions which can be easily resolved or overcome by the inclusion of some retry logic.

Nevertheless, it should be noted that, in many cases, the exception that results from a specific action, needs to be analyzed with care, given that, depending on the root cause of the problem, it may or may not be appropriate to attempt to use retry logic.

So, applying retry logic is both possible and, sometimes, recommended, but it is fundamental to be aware of the following guidelines:

1. **Apply retry logic consistently in operations that are time sensitive or that rely on weak infrastructure points, such as intermittent connectivity.**

   A significant percentage of exceptions that occur within an application are related to some time-sensitive actions that sporadically fail. Likewise, errors related to temporarily loss of connectivity are also pervasive and most of these occurrences can be easily handled by introducing some retry logic into the application. Although many solutions fail to adopt such recovery actions, which condemns them to merely propagating the exception as any other error and leaving users with the difficult task of having to decide what to do next, implementing retry logic in such cases can often resolve the issue.

   In these situations, retry logic needs to be bound by some upper limits, which define the amount of time and number of attempts that we should perform such repetitive recovery actions. Although no boilerplate value can be given for these thresholds, it is almost inevitable that, to overcome the exception, one needs to follow two complementary solutions:

   - Repeat the recovery action for a short number of times which, additionally, span over an equally short amount of time, before notifying the user that such a recovery attempt is being executed.
   - Repeat the recovery action while informing users (and eventually requiring their direct approval) that such an attempt is under way. Avoid going beyond a certain

---

[1] As reviewed in item **1 An unavoidable reality: errors and exceptions will happen.**

time frame for its execution, as it can induce users to think that the solution is blocked or hung.

Eventually, upon reaching the upper limit for these repetitions without successfully recovering from the error, one will need to propagate the exception while ensuring that it is handled like other similar problems.

2. **Beware of libraries that do not implement retry logic.**

Sometimes, implementing retry logic can be a real nightmare, especially when working with libraries that expose a set of operations which, when individually executed, result in a series of distinct chores. In such cases, in which a single operation hides the complexity of a few distinct actions, it may be extremely difficult to implement retry logic, as you may not have the information that is required in order to determine exactly what caused the exception and whether it can be resolved through retry logic.

Most often, these libraries fail to implement retry logic, including situations where it could be the appropriate course action to take, which leaves you in a position that might force you to contemplate whether or not you are able to do it on a higher level. Nevertheless, achieving this requires ensuring that the library forwards detailed information pertaining to the exception as well as the policy it adheres to in terms of exception guarantee (more on this later in the next item). Thus, and assuming you have detailed information on the exceptions, you will only be able to safely implement retry logic in a higher layer if, and only if, you have transactional semantics applied to these operations.

3. **Carefully evaluate situations where retry logic may create problems due to previously failing non-transactional actions.**

As stated in the previous item, having transactional semantics in an operation may be a requirement so as to safely implement retry logic. Without having such a guarantee, it will be very difficult to repeat operations automatically as an attempt to recover from certain types of exceptions. Just imagine attempting an automatic recovery of an operation by repeating certain actions that may have been partially completed! What would this result in? The answer is simple: it would be totally unpredictable. It could be the case that those partially executed actions could be safely repeated as they implied no state or, even if they were to be stateful, it could be the case that re-executing them would produce no additional results. Nevertheless, the most likely scenario (especially for an operation that failed to implement transactional semantics) would be that the partially completed actions would have left an inconsistent state, therefore effectively preventing any automated recovery.

Consequently, and in order to be on the safe side, do not implement retry logic unless you know that you are either executing stateless operations that can be repeated time and again without side effects (such as simply reading static data), or that you are executing operations that truly guarantee transactional semantics upon the occurrence of errors and exceptions.

4. **Apply retry logic on actions that depend on dynamic environments.**

   In some cases, there are environments that are dynamic in nature to the point that you can have very short periods of downtime. Some scenarios where this can happen include solutions that are installed on top of load-balanced infrastructures, in which case, there is the possibility that an operation fails due to the fact that one of the several servers went down without being immediately detected by the load-balancing system. In these cases it is possible to have an incoming request being sent to the load-balancer and forwarded to a server that is already down, but whose unavailability has not yet been detected by the load-balancer. In these scenarios, it is very common that a request coming in a few milliseconds later will be then forwarded to an available server, as the load-balancer will eventually detect the existing issue with the failing server and, hence, prevent such routing to take place.

   These types of problems, as well as others similar in their resulting outcome, are rare but, nonetheless, can occur, therefore making up another type of candidates to retry logic. Cloud services[1] often fit within this realm, where a few requests may fail because part of the redundant infrastructure failed and incoming requests were processed just before the failure was noticed by the controlling devices. As such, you should also contemplate applying retry logic to these requests, though, without losing site of the issues revolving around transactional semantics, repetition thresholds and usage of distinct libraries.

---

[1] As defined in item **19 Shoot for the sky: leverage cloud-based services to provision temporary environments**.

Item recap:

This item's fundamental guidelines can be succinctly systematized as follows:

- ✓ Apply retry logic to operations that have an outcome that is not deterministic, as it may change due to external conditions. Within this set of operations you should include time-sensitive actions or actions that are based on (potentially) intermittent connectivity support.
- ✓ Restrict automated retry logic to operations that provide true transactional semantics, or to operations that imply no state and that can be repeated without any sort of side effects (such as reading static data).
- ✓ Beware of libraries that do not implement retry logic and do not attempt to support it at a higher level, unless you are absolutely sure that, either these libraries deliver transactional semantics, or the operations you executed from these libraries can be repeated without side effects.
- ✓ Some dynamic environments, like load-balanced solutions, may showcase an extremely low rate of failures, as a result of server related problems not being detected by the load-balancing/controlling devices. Consider retry logic in these scenarios, while still looking out for transactional semantics and repetition thresholds when so required.

3. Coding rules: are we back in elementary school?

Coding rules are a matter of hard fought debate amongst software engineers. As with most things in life, many love them while others hate them. However, most of those who do love them do so conditionally: they love them as long as they follow suit with what they believe to be the best practices to follow and, additionally, as long as they do not go against those few principles that each engineer feels are just non-negotiable. In other words, people are willing to accept rules as long as they are aligned with those items that they regard as unquestionable dogmas and, therefore, simply cannot even consider that a better way might exist!

Interestingly, this type of discussion has already lasted many years (more likely for decades) and, for the most part, it has led to an unwarranted focus towards insignificant issues that clearly bring no added value to a project[1]. Instead, what really does matter is whether you apply the correct patterns in concrete coding techniques that can and do improve your overall code quality. Here are just a few examples:

- Are you correctly releasing unmanaged resources?
- Are you using the appropriate algorithms to process a standard data structure?
- Are you using any illegal API calls?

Though these are but a few samples of items/rules that every project should look into, these are the kind of items/rules that you should look to enforce, just as if you were back in elementary school. **Coding rules are not about style and formatting**, albeit those are issues on their own that you may or may not feel that require any sort of attention and standardization. Instead, they **should be about applying specific patterns** that are applicable to whichever technology you are using and which, if used, **will generate correct and robust code**.

By correctly conveying this message to software engineers you will have a happy crowd on your side, as they will hail the benefits of reducing bug-chasing time by reusing proven and tested techniques. Furthermore, using adequate tools that run against your source code, or against your binaries, and which check whether certain patterns are in place, will not undermine the creative freedom of your engineers and, additionally, will even make their work far easier, less prone to errors and, in the end, more productive.

Hence, the fundamental message to take home is that using this type of coding rules is beneficial to everyone. Apart from the positive effects on your bug rate, you will also gain in consistency and, possibly, in coding time as well. As many of these rules reflect the usage of standard and boilerplate code, many development environments give you the ability to configure these rules in

---

[1] Yes, it really does not matter whether you open curly braces in the same line or in the line below!

"ready to be used" code snippets that can be imported into your source code on demand through the easy use of a few orchestrated keystrokes.

Using code snippets is a preventive technique that ensures that certain coding rules are observed. Code snippets output boilerplate code that reflect the exact best practice that a certain rule wishes to uphold and, in doing so, save software engineers precious time by allowing them to reduce the amount of code they type while also doing a bit of "fill in the blanks" coding spree.

It makes nothing but sense that, when these snippets are in place, every single engineer should embrace this help, just as they embrace the usage of a debugger to test out their code. Additionally, by doing so, they will, in all likely-hood, avoid failing most validations performed afterwards as a result of using a **coding rules verification engine**.

Such engine is, usually, an autonomous tool which, in many scenarios, can run from within the development environment. Furthermore, it runs against source code or against binaries, validating these same rules by searching for specific patterns.

By using these complementary techniques you will, not only, guarantee that certain best practices are followed but, that they are applied in a consistent manner as well. After the common initial distrust, most software development teams will find themselves in a position where they recognize the value brought by these tools. Therefore, many of them end up extending their tool of choice to validate even more rules, adding a personalized touch to their development project.

Ultimately, this means that the more rules the better! Many of these tools come with a limited set of rules that validate common constructs and common patterns, which are widespread and are not derived from a specific context. By extending these tools you will, usually, not only be able to create a set of new rules that improve on what you get out of the box, but you will also be doing so in a way that is specifically tailored to the type of code you are producing. Over time, as your product evolves, so will the tool, with more and more cases being covered. Eventually, you'll reach a point where new team members are easily integrated, in the sense that they can code without too much guidance, as they rely upon these automated processes in order to ensure that they are following in the right footsteps.

In fact, onboarding new software engineers into the development team of a product that has a long and vast history is usually a time consuming affair. There are many tricks of the trade to learn, many concepts to absorb and many rules to follow. Plus, many of these rules stem from the need to code in a certain way so as to ensure that you do not fall into erratic situations which have been uncovered over the years, thus constituting a layer of general wisdom shared informally by those who have been working in the development team for some time. Given this, there is no better way to have these rules sink in than by semi-automating them through code snippets and automatic rule checking.

Finally, let us wrap up this item with a word on code reviews. **Code reviews are a great way of sharing knowledge and code ownership amongst team members**. On top of this, they are also a great way of getting input from those who have been busy doing other things and, therefore, manage to sometimes bring a fresh look into a battered subject. The analysis of alternative routes for solving specific problems is, by itself, always an interesting intellectual process but, from a practical standpoint, this can also unravel better paths to reach one's goals. Whenever this happens to be the case, there should be no hesitation in adopting these different approaches, independently of whom their author[1] might be, as this is exactly what the code reviewing process is all about.

Code reviews should not be about syntax details or coding styles and formats. Instead, they should be about robust software development. Simply put, they should be about writing better code and about improving your product by upholding overall product quality, spreading knowledge and creating a sense of collective code ownership[2]. This can be achieved by using the above mentioned rules engines which places the focus on specific coding patterns as well as driving code review sessions from the output produced by those same engines. This way, you can ensure that no small mind will be held by petty details on syntax and style and, ultimately, that your software engineers will focus on true and effective brainstorming regarding coding rules that implement the best design patterns, which ensure great software quality and which are geared exclusively towards improving the product you are building. Furthermore, by adopting such policies/methodologies, you also ensure that, from these discussions, new rules and patterns will emerge from time to time, meaning that the extensibility features of code snippets and rules engines will be leveraged once again so as to add new items that further enhance your source code.

Final note: Although pair programming is often defended as a programming technique that can stem collective code ownership, as well as improved code quality by enabling code validation in flight, it rarely works. In reality, since no two engineers work at exactly the same speed and no two engineers think exactly alike, pair programming ends up being a burden that makes different personalities clash. Overall, it brings about little to no added value and, inevitably, results in

---

[1] In order to naturally use any new and better strategy, it is crucial to avoid holding any sort of emotional/intellectual grudge against those who, momentarily, seem to have showcased the superior mind. If needs be, take comfort in thinking that the reverse will, eventually, also happen and your day to shine in front of your peers will also come.

[2] As defined in item **22 Store and share know-how: create an internal global knowledge depot**.

having one engineer coding with the negative impact of having an overshadowing counterpart, while another engineer simply floats away in personal thoughts, which hinder his/her concentration given the lack of direct involvement in the task being pursued. Code reviewing is a much better technique and, by focusing on technical patterns and avoiding styling confrontations, it generates real added value.

Item recap:

This item's fundamental guidelines can be succinctly systematized as follows:

- ✓ Ensure that coding rules are about design and coding patterns, and not about styling and formatting rules.
- ✓ Try to automate as many of these patterns as possible through features of your development environment, such as code snippets.
- ✓ Extend these rules over time, as new and better practices are defined by the team.
- ✓ Use code checking tools which can perform either source code or binary analysis, in order to verify usage of these design and coding patterns.
- ✓ Invest in code reviews so as to share knowledge and code ownership, as well as to improve code quality. However, ensure that code reviews are about design and coding patterns, and not about styling and formatting.
- ✓ Do not rely on pair programming, as it is often, not only, a waste of resources but, additionally, a step towards growing animosity within the team.

4. Document you source code: follow the proximity rule

If there is one thing that manages to be far worse than having no source code documentation, it is to have wrong source code documentation! A pretty good analogy that accurately depicts this is that of, when lost, not being helped at all or being helped by someone who is simply pointing towards a random path, which will do nothing but mislead those who are already lost! It won't help the querying party and it will definitely not give you any credits!

Likewise, with source code documentation we have the exact same scenario. Wrong documentation simply misleads software engineers who will make certain incorrect decisions based on assumptions instilled by the existing documentation, leaving them completely oblivious to the fact that they are actually creating chaos as a result of supporting their decisions on false premises.

If, on one hand, we will probably tend to believe that no one will deliberately write incorrect documentation, on the other, we must acknowledge the fact that all documentation tends to be left behind during (as well as after) the initial product building phase. Plus, and even worse, it often fails to be correctly updated as the codebase simply evolves as a natural consequence of the process that brings about new features, refactoring and bug-fixing.

Additionally, this scenario is, usually, made even worse whenever the documentation sits far from the subject, which implies having source code documentation anywhere but within the source code itself. By introducing any sort of distance or barrier between source code and its documentation, we will inevitably create far greater conditions to increment the risk of having things just fall out-of-synch. Whenever software developers go about changing source code, they will, not only, naturally browse through any comments and general documentation that sit intertwined with the source code, but also be prone to updating it, as long as these pieces of documentation feel as a natural extension of the coding language itself.

However, on the opposite end of the spectrum, very few engineers[1] will be as diligent as to change a few lines of source code scattered through different files and, after completing their coding and testing tasks, still have the ability to create a perfect parallel between the changes they made and whatever is registered on the documentation set (should it be kept under different files, or under distinct persistent storage or even in some other external system).

Given this, the crucial message to take home is quite simple: software developers will only be thorough in reading the existing source code documentation if, as they read existing source code, it feels as a natural extension of the source code itself. Furthermore, it is highly likely that, even without added incentives, they will update the source code documentation within the natural

---

[1] To be honest, I have never known of, or come across anyone, of the sort.

flow of updating source code. Hence, do not create any sort of unneeded distance or barrier by placing these complementary elements in distinct places.

Does this mean that we are limited to having technical information mixed within the source code? Does this mean that we will not be able to rip any of the extra benefits they usually come about by having detailed technical documentation elsewhere? Not necessarily so, nevertheless, be sure that you use an automatic tool that, at any point in time[1], is capable of re-creating the standalone documentation from its origin[2] and, therefore, ensuring it is updated for a specific release or build level.

By using this type of approach you will be able to get the best out of both worlds: documentation within the source code, along with appealing documentation that is beautifully formatted and presented in an alternative support[3].

Nevertheless, beware of automatic tools and how they will adhere to the above-referred principle: documenting source code should feel as a natural extension to the coding flow! Consequently, be sure that the automatic tool of your selection does not impose complex grammar for documentation stuff, since this increases the complexity of software engineers' tasks pertaining to writing documentation as they create or change source code and which, ultimately, slows down their productivity.

Should the rules for adding source code documentation be too elaborate, forcing software developers to use or memorize strange tag-based patterns (oddly enough, software developers will happily do this for obscure programming languages syntaxes, but not for documentation idioms!), the desirable functional source code will fail to have the appropriate level of documentation within its boundary. Additionally, you will often be confronted with existing documentation which is not properly updated whenever changes are brought about.

However, assuming that you have indeed found a tool that allows you to use a balanced approach to source code documentation (where the few tags it imposes are easy to remember and add virtually no overhead that would turn off a typical software engineer) make sure you remember to pass along to your team the correct guidelines as to what should be documented as well as how it should be placed within source code.

Essentially, you should strive to achieve an intrinsic documenting spirit within your software development team that emphasizes the following items:

---

[1] For instance, within the execution of a build process.

[2] Which is the properly documented source code.

[3] Which can be used, searched and read without the complexity of having, in parallel, to jump over source code.

1. **Add detailed source code documentation of all algorithms that have any complexity.**

   Though attempting to define complexity is highly subjective, in order to keep procedures as down to earth and functional as possible, here are a few pointers that usually pinpoint the existence of complex source code that should be properly documented:

   - Any breadth of monolithic code that spans over more than the size of a standard display screen.
   - Any breadth of code that induces state changes that are not local to itself by relying and changing variables, or any other memory structures that are defined in some enclosing scope.
   - Any breadth of code that has any sort of computation that relies on a mathematical or scientific formula that is not apparent to the common mind within a few seconds of analysis.
   - Any breadth of code that contains nested loops and intertwined function calls (including direct and indirect recursion) that prevent experienced software engineers from understanding the code flow within a few seconds.

2. **View source code in the broad sense.**

   It seems that people tend to be just a bit too simplistic in their interpretation of laws, rules and general guidance, and even more so when it suits them. Furthermore, the definition of what is both understood by and included in source code, is one of those scenarios where one can sometimes be just a bit too narrow minded. Source code can be, and usually is, a lot more than just lines of code, as its direct meaning would imply. Source code can be seen in a wider realm, where we include items such as:

   - Scripts that are written to be executed by external products,
   - Configuration files that are used to define and tweak the solution's behavior,
   - Auxiliary scripts that command the development process steps, such as build scripts,
   - Diagrams of relational database systems or other external components that are used to generate or automate the generation of code,
   - Project settings that constrain the compilation tasks.

   With all these items being, indeed, source code in the wider sense, its intrinsic documentation should be kept within its own boundary, regardless of whether it is (or isn't) processed by an external tool meant to generate a more user-friendly and eye-appealing documentation item.

   Finally, special care should be put forth towards **documenting any changes that are made to generated code**, as these changes must be extremely well documented and fully automated in all cases since, as failing to do so, will entail, sooner or later, the risk of losing them upon any re-generation tasks.

3. **When coding for others be a good citizen.**

   Of all code that needs thorough documentation, public (or private) APIs that are entry points into some software layer are definitely up there within the list of things that need to be accurately documented. Nothing is more frustrating for software developers than consuming any type of API[1] and, after banging heads with what turns out to be gravity defying rationales, reaching the conclusion that the existing documentation is incomplete, incorrect or simply unusable, turning the API into a foe instead of a friend.

   When software engineers set out to consume an API, they do it because they expect to get in return a more productive experience than the one they would achieve had they decided to write it from scratch by themselves[2]. Hence, nothing is more infuriating than using an API whose documentation fails to correctly state:
   - What actions are performed by each call,
   - Which call order dependencies exist, should there be any,
   - Which values can be passed in as arguments,
   - What types of return values may be expected,
   - What errors are produced[3], under which conditions, how they can be averted, and how they can be further analyzed.

   Though most APIs are very decent in their behavior and inherent documentation when it comes to the first group of items[4], most APIs will, unfortunately, fall short, or even very short, when it comes to troubleshooting errors[5].

4. **Use the vacation test to know what to document.**

   When you go on a vacation that is, at least, one to two weeks long, your mind will naturally reset some internal pointers. Who hasn't returned from vacation to find that:
   - They have forgotten a password they used routinely,
   - Some daily tasks that were previously automated, now require your full and undivided attention to actually be accomplished?

   I'm sure that everyone has experienced such things. However, the relevant issue here is that going on vacation and returning to write documentation[6] is, actually, a very good

---

[1] Regardless of its underlying technology.
[2] I'll concede that, many times, there is simply no other option, but I'm sure you get the gist of it!
[3] With this being the most relevant element of this list.
[4] Purpose, call dependency order, parameters and return values.
[5] As defined in item **13 Do's and don'ts of APIs**.
[6] Source code documentation.

strategy, and one that easily enables you to single out which items need documenting and which ones are just plain vanilla stuff that is just self-documenting.

The sheer act of being away from the source code on a daily basis will make your mind less aware of it and, hence, you will be better at judging what needs documenting upon returning. Thus, even if you cannot precede all documenting sessions with a two-week vacation, at the very least try not to document source code that you have been looking at for the past five days. Leave a gap between coding and documenting so as to ensure that your brain is not synched with your code to such an extent that makes it almost impossible to realize what needs documenting.

Furthermore, do not document obvious stuff! As previously stated, document things that you wouldn't understand within a few seconds of analysis, especially after having not looked at the source code for a few days.

Item recap:

This item's fundamental guidelines can be succinctly systematized as follows:

- ✓ Source code documentation needs to be within the source code, or it will easily fall out of synch.
- ✓ Source code documentation needs to follow some rules, so as to ensure it is homogeneous over the codebase.
- ✓ Source code documentation must also be guided by a simple set of features that enable automatic documentation generation without, however, becoming an overly complex burden for engineers.
- ✓ Source code documentation needs to focus on complex algorithms, areas of code that provoke side-effects, complex formulas, as well as nested and intertwined loops and function calls.
- ✓ Source code documentation must be broad enough to include elements that sometimes are not seen as source code (in the strict sense), which includes scripts, configuration elements and changes to generated code.
- ✓ Source code documentation must ensure that those who did not write the code are indeed able to read and understand it.
- ✓ APIs must be extremely well documented, including their behavior, inputs and outputs, and all possible error conditions.

5. Beware of abstraction layers that generate code

Code generation is, for many, the holy grail of software development. A few clicks here and there and you get a ton of ready-to-compile source code[1]. However, we need to focus a bit on what exactly we are building and what has been really generated for us.

Most code generation naturally takes place through template technology, where boilerplate code is used in a way that makes it an overall fitting recipe for all situations, regardless of their specificity. Alas, with there being no way that such specificity can be relayed into the code generation layer, herein lays the real problem: is the generic solution we are getting a functional and effective one? Or is it merely acceptable? Plus, should we be pleased with incorporating into our product anything that is just good, instead of really going full throttle to achieve greatness?

This is, obviously, an extremely difficult issue to handle. On one hand, code generation will save you thousands of hours in learning a specific issue, writing the required code and going through all the process of debugging it and building a stable version. On the other hand, you will be taking it on faith. You will be using thousands of lines of generated code without having even a glimpse as to what the code does.

Naturally you will have a general idea of what the code's purpose is as, if that weren't the case, you wouldn't even be using it. Nevertheless, the objective reality of this issue is that you don't really know a lot about it, which includes being unaware of data structures that are used and of the algorithms that were employed, as well as of any imposed runtime restrictions and unnecessary overhead. Thus, before using massive amounts of generated code, and especially if you are using it on a critical layer of your product, you should, at the very least, consider the following guidelines:

1. **Review the generated code.**

   With most code generation being done through templates, once you start using a specific code generating technology it is very likely that you will find existing patterns in it. As such, you won't need to review every single line of generated code, especially if it is being used to generate similar code for analogous entities/scenarios. You should, however, identify all the different entities/scenarios where you are applying code generation and, afterwards, review one sample of each case.

   Reviewing each sample should be a task undertaken by experienced engineers with a keen eye to detect both problems and situations where clearly better solutions could be attained by adopting alternative paths. Often, these generated lines of code have

---

[1] Contrary to what happened in many cases back in the 90s where the generated code often failed to compile without a few manual fixes!

significant space for specific optimizations that could have been easily introduced by an engineer, had the code been manually crafted. Over the years, I have identified an absurd quantity of database access generated code that simply failed to generate efficient SQL statements and, often, users of these technologies were totally unaware of what type of code was actually being created by the tools they had chosen to use.

By this, I am not stating that we should go back to the days of writing every single piece of code but it cannot be ignored that we need to understand what the tools are delivering, as well as successfully being capable of identifying what needs to be re-written, so as to achieve our goals.

Within this analysis do not rely only on a manual code review. Instead, when wondering about performance of the generated code, it is wiser to use profiling tools and, if possible, look to compare the output of two or three distinct code generation tools that deliver the same features. By reviewing and comparing what the generated code is (from these two or three distinct tools), you may easily detect alternative patterns and, consequently, end up setting a good baseline for what you deem to be the best solution.

2. **Research what others have found when delving into it.**

   One of the most interesting things about the internet is its capability to easily provide information on people who have already gone through what you are currently struggling with. Hence, it makes nothing but good sense to use this wealth of knowledge to your advantage by trying to discover what others have uncovered when reviewing the code generated by a specific tool that you are contemplating using. Although you should not rely exclusive and entirely on these third-hand reports, and much less on one single opinion, the bottom line is that many of the reports that are out there, and usually available in the form of informal blog posts, do present some good hints about these tools.

   You will usually find specific information about situations where the generated code was either incorrect or recorded negative performance due to the genericity of the algorithm that was used.

   Often, you will find analysis of specific situations that either became problematic under heavy load or simply failed to function when a concrete element of the underlying execution stack[1] was updated. Many of these situations will effectively serve as good general awareness about the tool and, though you probably won't encounter all of them while using the code generating tool, the simple research process will give you a better picture of what:

   - The tool is,

---

[1] Possibly due to a version change of some underlying component.

- Others are currently struggling with,
- Kind of maintenance and evolution the tool has had over the years.

In fact, and because many of these tools are open source projects, it is critically relevant to understand who exactly is driving the tool and, additionally, what source code access you might have to it. Essentially, you should try to know whether you are able to have source code access to it in case something catastrophic were to take place, forcing you to do a dire fix in it. Furthermore, you should research the market to verify whether the industry backing of these tools is good enough to guarantee the required level of supportability.

By reviewing what others have found along these lines, you will be better equipped to handle the decision process of selecting the appropriate tool for your own usage.

3. **Replace generated code that imposes unnecessary overheads.**

Having gone through a phase of code reviewing and, thus, being armed with the added input of what others have learnt in the past[1], you will have a better picture of the complexity and quality of code that the tool is able to create. However, even when using tools that have proven to be worthy, you will still be confronted by occasional circumstances that force you to either change the behavior that is implemented by the generated code or, alternatively, tweak it so that the execution pattern and the outcome being produced remain unchanged, while optimizing some stretches of code that simply do not live up to the performance requirements.

Whenever being confronted with such scenario you need to understand two crucial and related issues:

- How do you change the generated code in a way that safeguards future code re-generations from destroying the elements that you changed?
- When changing the generated code for a specific situation that may repeat itself in similar scenarios, can you incorporate both these changes and their binding rules into the code generation mechanics?

These items are extremely important and, often enough, good code generating tools will allow you to adapt the generated code by adding new templates, tweaking existing ones or, alternatively, by setting the changes in specific files that are preserved, regardless of how many subsequent re-generations are executed.

Interestingly, not all code generation outputs source code to be used during the building stage. In many circumstances the generation of code happens at runtime, with a straightforward example being that of tools that are used while building websites. How many tools are used to build websites and, thus, generate HTML and JavaScript at

---

[1] While analyzing and troubleshooting the same tool.

runtime? In this sense, the HTML and JavaScript is source code and, despite not being truly compiled by the browser in most situations, it is, nonetheless, still generated, and often requires tweaking.

Additionally, how about SQL generating technologies that generate statements on the fly? In these situations it is, sometimes, more difficult to know exactly when you need to change the generated code but, once again, the same steps should be used. You can use profiling tools to inspect the generated code and you can also look up what others have found about it but, as always, you basically need to learn how to change the generated code so that you can meet whichever thresholds you have set for your product.

4. **Subject the generated code to the same quality control techniques.**

   Simply because the code is generated it does not mean that it will not suffer from the exact same problems that any other piece of source code may suffer from. Therefore, the generated code needs to be included in your overall code quality control procedures, which include test cases[1] and code analysis.

   Setting up testing procedures for generated code is just as important as doing it for code that was written by any of the team's engineers. Simply put, you need to assure your clients that every piece of software that composes your product is of the highest quality. Clients will not be the least bit interested in knowing that a specific bug had its root origin in some generated code. A bug is a bug, nothing more and nothing less, and it needs to be bashed away, for the potential harm it may cause is independent of its origin. Therefore, be very careful when defining the test cases for generated code, as it is even more difficult to do so than for any other piece of code. The reason being that, in many instances, there is little knowledge about the full actions that the code is executing and, thus, test driven development[2] becomes all the more difficult.

   On the other hand, you should include within the scope of whichever code analysis tools you are using the source code that was generated by any code generation tool. Again, the focus of code analysis should not be styling issues, but rather detection of code patterns that relate purely to quality of code. Given this, these patterns need to be upheld, regardless of whether the code was written by an engineer working within the team or whether it was generated by a tool.

   Being this careful, by subjecting the generated source code to the same stringent quality criteria, is the only way to really guarantee that it will not puncture holes into your own armor.

---

[1] As defined in item **26 Testing and quality assurance procedures**.
[2] As defined in item **20 Nothing works better then test driven development**.

Item recap:

This item's fundamental guidelines can be succinctly systematized as follows:

- ✓ Review generated code so as to ensure you have good insight into what was generated.
- ✓ Ensure that you subject generated code to the same level of quality control practices, including testing, profiling and code reviews.
- ✓ Review what others have found about the code generation tools you are using and, if possible, compare the quality of the generated code from two or three equivalent tools.
- ✓ Understand the supportability and maturity of open source tools used for code generation.
- ✓ Detect which situations force you to replace generated code due to functional or performance reasons. Understand how re-generation might affect specific changes you introduced.

6. Minimize the impact of slow operations

There are a few set of operations, present in all enterprise capable solutions, which, due to their inherent features, will be far less efficient than your mainstream computing calculations. Within this group of slow performers, we usually find the same common culprits:

- Storage access,
- Network connections,
- General IO tasks.

As such, this item is not about comparing good algorithms with bad ones[1]. Instead, it is about all those standard operations that any solution needs to execute here and there and, over which, control is usually lacking. This lack of control, even if it is just partial lack of control, dictates that a hit in performance is not entirely due to a choice that the development team made. Within this group, you will find most IO operations which will naturally perform far slower than common CPU instructions, even when requiring general memory access.

IO operations are inherently slow. They need to interact with a physical device[2] that is limited in its own speed and, therefore, no match for the CPU's internal power or for the speed at which internal buses can be accessed. Furthermore, modern operating systems impose a controlled access to devices which also adds some overhead to these operations. Considering all these issues, the reality is unavoidable, in the sense that IO is slow and needs to be tackled carefully in order to ensure that it does not hinder the application's performance altogether.

Considering that we cannot really forgo using IO altogether[3], how can we minimized the resulting impact? Here are a few guidelines:

1. **Minimize IO operations and reduce them to the bare minimum.**

    Have you ever tried to resolve any version of the travelling salesman problem? Just to make sure that we are all on the same page, the travelling salesman problem is a problem in combinatorial optimization studied mostly in operations research. It consists of finding the shortest possible route that allows a travelling salesman to visit (given an initial list of cities to visit and their pairwise distances) each city exactly once, while ensuring that, ultimately, he returns to the city of origin.

    Hence, how does this relate to IO? Well, though only remotely, the essence is that, during the execution of your product's code and for a specific timeline, you will be

---

[1] As defined in item **8 Algorithm complexity and optimizations**.

[2] Many times an external physical device.

[3] Since, in most solutions, we do need to interact with physical devices for, at the very least, storage and network purposes.

performing several IO operations that warrant the need to understand how to organize them best so that you minimize their number and, therefore, avoid executing those which, somehow, can be eliminated (possibly through alternative mechanisms such as caching[1]).

Overall, just like the travelling salesman needs to see the travelling costs being minimized while still visiting each city once, in IO, you need to be sure of minimizing your costs[2] while ensuring that each specific task is only performed a single time. Honestly, how many times have you been troubleshooting an application, only to find out that, just because calls weren't aggregated or because no cache was in place, some tasks were repetitively executed for no reason whatsoever?

Therefore, at least in theory, the recipe is fairly straightforward. All you need to do is analyze which distinct operations you are performing and, consequently, define a plan that will reduce them to the bare minimum. This should be accomplished by ensuring that you are not duplicating repetitive operations, thus enhancing overall performance.

2. **Aggregate calls whenever possible.**

   One of the most common problems with web-based APIs, which have become prevalent due to the adoption of service oriented architectures, is that the granularity of these APIs is usually too fine-grained for many enterprise scenarios. Many of these APIs provide an almost atomic way of executing very specific actions through individual calls, often leading to a situation where you need to perform several distinct calls to actually execute a complete business function.

   This is a perfect example where aggregating calls can actually be very useful in optimizing performance and reducing IO. By creating a composite version of these same web-based APIs you can, in many cases, reduce the number of distinct individual calls to a bare minimum[3], which will also do wonders for the implementation of transactional semantics. Such reduction will drastically cut down on the overhead that each IO operation implies and this sort of reasoning isn't exclusive of network IO. Even storage IO can sometimes benefit from this type of optimization, although features like read-ahead or delayed writing[4] are usually more viable options.

   Regardless of the specific solutions adopted, the fundamental guideline should simply consist of analyzing which operations make up the bulk of the IO in your solution so as to aggregate distinct calls whenever possible, under the overall strategy of cutting down on

---

[1] As defined in item **16 Use in-memory distributed caching systems to enhance performance and scalability**.

[2] By performing different tricks, such as caching or aggregating calls.

[3] Ideally of one.

[4] As defined in item **9 Maximizing efficiency**.

the number of individual operations and, thus, reducing the overhead that the IO itself imposes on the system.

3. **Use an asynchronous model.**

For a wide array reasons, IO operations are usually ideal candidates for asynchronous patterns, including being relatively slow when compared to other actions your product will naturally support. This difference in pace really calls for an asynchronous model that allows the IO to be performed in the background, while your application continues to execute other tasks, such as running number-crunching calculations or updating the user interface (which is just as noble as any other computer chore)!

Naturally, whenever an asynchronous model is used, the need to establish some synchronization points will arise. Nevertheless, in the vast majority of the cases, you can really gain in terms of responsiveness. Furthermore, you will also improve in terms of usage of the computing resources that are made available to the solution. Hence, IO operations are the perfect example where you should carefully consider using an asynchronous pattern, while taking into consideration the options and constraints presented in the following item.

4. **If possible, execute delayed writing and read-ahead features.**

Many IO operations involve persistent storage devices that possess some type of mechanical features. It so happens that these devices, and their intrinsic mechanical features, are usually slow to execute the initial location of data[1]. After the execution of that first hurdle, the amount of time that is required to read either a few contiguous elements or a bit more than a few contiguous elements is practically the same. As long as you do not need to reposition the reading spindle you can pretty much read a few bytes, or a bit more than that, in almost the same amount of time. Therefore, you can indeed gain a lot by placing related information in contiguous blocks within storage devices, as this enables you to retrieve it in one swift operation, even if you currently do not require it all. Chances are that, soon enough, your application will be crying for that exact piece of information, giving you the ability to really gain from having in place a read-ahead feature whereby you read from the storage device more than was needed at a specific point in time, following such action with the complementary task of placing that wealth of (currently unneeded) information in an in-memory cache. This cache will then serve this information to its consumers as soon as requested, therefore minimizing the chance of bringing about slow IO operations.

---

[1] Most of which is related to the mechanical movement required to position reading spindles.

Although this presents a clear benefit, you need to incorporate into your solution all the aspects that will deliver the appropriate level of cache-coherence, thus avoiding serving stale data when such a situation would constitute a functional and logical error.

Inversely, by caching or buffering data that is required to be written to storage, and performing only a limited number of effective writing operations, you can also streamline your performance. Instead of writing a few bytes each time into the slow performing IO device, you write them to a cache/buffer-based mechanism which, later on, performs the actually physical IO, thus reducing the overall number of requests and delivering a far better performance.

The pitfall surrounding the optimization of write operations pertains to the transactional semantics issue, more specifically, since you do not actually write data synchronously during the logic processing flow, should a subsequent failure happen before the actual writing operation is executed, it can lead to loss of information. Given this, you need to balance delayed writing with the need for pure transactional semantics but, if you analyze the spectrum of operations that your product needs to perform, I am sure you will find many situations where you can trade transactional semantics for better performance based on delayed writing techniques[1]. On the other hand, and when we are dealing with read operations, the real pitfall consists of maintaining cache coherence, particularly whenever it is crucial, for business reasons, to avoid serving stale or incorrect data.

5. **Use caching whenever possible.**

   To finalize this item, let us just recap what we have seen about caching. Simply put, either due to read-ahead techniques or to support lazy-writing, caching can do wonders to reduce your IO. Since it is an essential technique in order to improve performance in many different scenarios, you should look to use it whenever possible. Nevertheless, do not just go about starting to build your caching system, as there are plenty of solutions already waiting to be used. Instead, make the most of them, as you should with pretty much every component that already exists. Reinventing the wheel is hardly effective software engineering!

   Over the years, I have personally worked on several applications that were made considerably faster simply by introducing the right layer of caching at different levels. As an example, just consider that there are many applications out there that constantly read the same configuration information over and over again, either in the form of true configuration items or in the form of metadata elements that rarely change, with the

---

[1] Most tracing features are a great example of an element that can survive the rare event of a subsequent error.

worse thing being that they end up being read, several times, by different components, often in the course of the execution of a single processing flow. I have actually debugged a solution that read the same configuration parameters up to 10 times during the execution of a single request, with some of these repetitive actions being done by distinct binaries, while others were executed by the same binary (which just happened to read the information for a specific decision process while failing to store it in memory and, then, just went back to re-reading it again). Do try to avoid these situations, since they will definitely contribute towards giving you a negative reputation, once a field engineer starts poking around the system with tools that capture the IO operations being executed.

A final word on this item: although many modern operating systems do supply some sort of intrinsic IO caching that minimizes scenarios like the one described, this is neither a full-blown guarantee nor a way to build a great application. Never create bad code while relying on other components to solve your mess!

Item recap:

This item's fundamental guidelines can be succinctly systematized as follows:

- ✓ Minimize the number of distinct IO calls by reducing them to the bare minimum.
- ✓ Prevent duplicated or repetitive IO calls, and aggregate atomic calls when possible. Beware of web-based APIs that are too fine-grained and force you to make innumerous atomic calls in order to perform a single logical function.
- ✓ Consider using in-memory caching and buffering techniques to reduce IO.
- ✓ Use an asynchronous model to perform IO operations when possible.
- ✓ Consider using read-ahead and delayed-writing patterns to improve overall performance and responsiveness. Use caching with read-ahead and buffering with delayed-writing.
- ✓ Maintain a sense of the required level of cache coherence and transactional semantics. Do not overlook transactional semantics in delayed-writing and cache-coherence/stale data within read-ahead patterns.

7. Interfaces and mock objects

Isolation and well-defined boundaries are one of the key elements to achieve a robust software design and, a robust design, will allow you to drive forward loads of different things, including:

- Ease of maintenance,
- Low-cost troubleshooting,
- Effective evolution.

Therefore, one thing that can really do wonders for the development of a robust software architecture is a preference towards interface-based design.

Should you drive both your software components and your codebase to be defined and guided by a dictatorship of interface definitions, you will ensure that dependencies between classes and components are limited to a behavior defined by a contract. This principle will enable you to easily replace components and classes, as long as you uphold the interface and its implied contract. Essentially, interfaces are your new best friend!

Every distinct and unique component must present the outside world with nothing more than an interface that, not only isolates all outsiders from implementation details, but even isolates all outsiders from programming language concepts such as classes. Having your entire codebase running on the sheer boundary of an interface will allow you to easily plug in new components or classes, which can be used to great advantage in different situations. One of those situations is the ability to test a portion of your codebase without requiring the whole underlying suite of external systems, which the solution usually depends on to fully run.

Understandably, this is where mock objects show their value. A mock object is nothing more than a stand in object that implements a specific interface[1], but which differs in its internal implementation from the real runtime object. In this specific case[2], the mock object would implement the desired interface without depending on the external system, therefore easing the task of running some tests, without really needing to bind to the previously referred to external system.

Considering this pattern, it is safe to say that mock objects can be used in a variety of scenarios, such as providing a base for unit testing or allowing developers to write and test their code without relying directly on other external systems. Therefore, there are very few enterprise capable projects that can be effectively created without using interfaces and mock objects.

---

[1] As it would be implemented by the real runtime object.
[2] Of using interfaces to extract benefits while executing tests on some part of your solution.

Consequently, let us try to summarize their main uses and benefits:

1. **Support testing.**

   As previously discussed, both interfaces and mock objects that implement them are vital in allowing you to run unit testing[1] whenever a dependency on an existing external system is just impossible to use.

   Over the years, I have worked on several products that simply depended on systems for which there really wasn't a viable testing environment. Given this, and quite naturally so, running tests against the production environment was either impossible or, at the very least, not viable[2]. Since one simply cannot expect a development team to be bound to such limiting scenarios, by creating mock objects that simulate the real external systems, teams were able to move along and test their code without ever requiring direct access to such a scarce and constrained resource.

   This type of reasoning can be applied not only to these types of systems, for which there are significant constraints in general access, but also to limit the complexity of having a testing environment, whenever you need to focus on small sections of your product, without wanting to be dependent on any external components.

2. **Isolate developers.**

   Following suit with the previous item, developers are usually more productive if they can have full control over their development environment, which allows them to run things at their own pace and, especially, execute their daily tasks without any imposed constraints or security risks.

   Nevertheless, isolating developers from different parts of the system, with some occasionally being too complex to be individually assigned to single developers, should be a key concern. On top of that, isolating developers from external resources through mock objects may also help you minimize management and security issues.

   Whenever you have a dependency on an external system you will need to consider all sorts of overhead in terms of management, such as guaranteeing access to the system or assigning and managing permissions within the system. To avoid all these issues, you should use interfaces and mock objects so as to simulate these external systems and, thus, allow developers to implement their code and carry out their tasks without ever having direct contact with them.

---

[1] As well as other types of tests.

[2] With the exception of a few very specific windows of opportunity which were limited by very severe constraints.

33

3. **Allow for distinct implementations of a specific contract.**

Interfaces can do a lot more for you than just allow you to use mock objects with the purpose of development and testing. Defining interfaces can also be critical in allowing you to create distinct implementations of a specific contract, while still maintaining the coherence of the remaining parts of the solution.

Interfaces can be successfully used to change implementation details without causing a broad trickle down impact on the whole codebase.

By adhering to an interface-driven design, every class and component will know nothing more and nothing less about the items it interacts with other than the formal contract they sustain. With this in place, you will be able to easily change different parts of your code, either to fix problems or simply to support natural product evolution, without any major disruption to other elements.

4. **Create the base for dynamic component usage.**

Long gone are the days where a software product was immutable to a level that everything could be hardwired, as well as statically linked[1] when leaving the development shop.

Nowadays, things are a lot more dynamic and interfaces are usually the basic cornerstone that supports dynamic component usage. By being interface-centric, you will be able to change components whenever either new versions of the product are available or when desiring to support extensibility features. Within this latter scenario, it is quite common to allow certain entry points to be used, either by clients or partners, which can leverage those extensibility points by implementing either new runtime classes or entire components that hook into the processing flows by virtue of adhering to the defined interfaces.

This kind of practice is well established at all levels and it is definitely one of the best practices to deliver a high level of isolation and flexibility between all elements that compose your product. Without this approach you will simply be unable to support extensibility points, and the whole maintenance and evolution of your product will be severely hindered.

---

[1] As defined in item **12 Linking code: the static vs. dynamic option**.

Item recap:

This item's fundamental guidelines can be succinctly systematized as follows:

- ✓ Being interface-centric and using mock objects can support testability without full dependency on external systems.
- ✓ Doing so also allows developers to have an isolated environment, without directly accessing all system components. It reduces the complexity of setting up development and testing environments which, in turn, reduces management issues, such as provisioning resources or configuring security permissions in external systems.
- ✓ Interfaces allow you to easily change implementation details without trickle down effects that have broad impact on the codebase.
- ✓ Interfaces provide the best mechanism to support extensibility points as well as to build on the advantages delivered by frameworks that support dynamic component usage and loading.

8. Algorithm complexity and optimizations

Search algorithms are the perfect academic example of how you can create a myriad of distinct algorithms, all of which execute the required task, though being vastly different in performance and inherent complexity.

Along with all other optimization techniques such as caching[1], optimizing algorithms or, at least, choosing the best possible one for the task at hand, is a must-do for every engineer that wishes to create effective code. It is unwise to rely on modern day compiler magic, delivered through aggressive compiler optimization techniques, in order to ensure that you get the performance you want. There are goals that simply cannot be attained unless you choose a good, or at least, not a bad algorithm.

Analyzing and understanding algorithm complexity is one of the key tasks that engineers must undertake in order to deliver high performing code. However, there are more caveats hidden within this task than most initially expect to find. Here are a few pointers that you need to be on the lookout for:

1. **Understand both the data structures you choose to use and the complexity they impose on the algorithms that operate on them.**

    Whenever you pick a specific data structure you need to take into consideration the complexity that it imposes on the algorithms that will later execute all the required operations on it. Data containers[2] are perhaps amongst the most recognizable data structures that vastly differ in the complexity of their inherent algorithms. Such containers are well known to provide distinct access times in key operations, like insertions, deletions and searches. Furthermore, understanding one's data structures does not resume itself to the task of comprehending what they can do. Instead, it is much more about how they actually go about doing it! Hence, whenever you need to pick a data structure, make sure you look up its corresponding documentation, for only this will provide a solid understanding of what the algorithm complexity is for each key operation that you will be performing on it.

    Going back to containers, it is quite common to find implementations of typical lists that provide linear access time[3], whereas arrays typically provide constant access time[4]. Given this, not only can complexity be measured, but it is usually done so and presented in qualitative terms such as constant, algorithmic or linear complexity. Therefore,

---

[1] As defined in item **16 Use in-memory distributed caching systems to enhance performance and scalability**.
[2] Such as lists, vectors and arrays, to name just a few.
[3] As you need to transverse the list, from item to item, to reach whichever element you need to access.
[4] As you simply and directly access the item you want.

understanding the complexity of algorithms is critical to reach a decision on which data structures are best suited for the task at hand.

2. **Understand the different complexities that are implied in each distinct API.**

   The abstraction power of APIs is absolutely great. An easy to remember method name together with just a few parameters[1] is all that development engineers want, isn't it so? Well, though at first it might look that way, it is actually not that simple! With any abstraction comes ease of usage and concealment of complexity, but, contrary to this, knowing the inherent complexity should be something that a good API directly presents us with within its documentation.

   Despite this, and unfortunately so, the world is filled with APIs that are almost unusable by those needing to deliver high performance systems[2], as a result of internal workings that are contrived and poorly implemented.

   A very well-known example of such a poorly implemented API is what I call "the case of the misleading array-like API". Consider an API that, internally, manages a collection of items, and presents an operator[3] or a method[4] that seems to directly access one element. From the initial startup point, most software engineers would imagine that such an API call would be cheap in performance terms while providing constant access time. However, this is not immediately guaranteed, as it really depends on the inner workings of the API, and we have all seen products that supply such APIs. In the end, such APIs do all sorts on unexpected things, such as retrieving the whole list of items and going about either only selecting the required one or using an internal data structure that does not provide constant access time, which completely mislead software engineers through its method name or overloaded operator syntax!

   As such, you need to be aware of what exactly APIs perform underneath and, when in doubt[5], do not be afraid to spend time profiling APIs' behavior. In the long run, it will, not only save a significant amount of time, but also prevent many problems from coming up.

3. **Validate direct algorithm complexity.**

   Measuring direct algorithm complexity is relatively simple and, additionally, there are also many situations in which you can automate this effort through the use of

---

[1] For the purpose at hand, the fewer the better and, preferably, with default values whenever possible.
[2] Which handle a relatively high volume of data.
[3] In the case of an operator, think of an overloaded operator that is commonly used to index an array such as square brackets in some programming languages.
[4] In the case of a method, think of something like a *GetItem* method that receives a parameter indicating the position of the element to be accessed.
[5] Especially when no documentation is available to clarify this issue.

appropriate tools. Algorithm complexity can be measured through its Big-O level and, generally speaking, you should definitely look into any situations where you find a complexity level above linear level. Quadratic or cubic complexities are almost always guaranteed to deliver non-acceptable performance when operating on a set of data elements that goes beyond a few items. Plus, even constant complexity can be way too much for sets of elements that have a considerable number of items, especially if such an operation is either performed in time sensitive scenarios or often executed within the processing flow of the solution.

Therefore, you should not only analyze exactly which algorithms you are using and what kind of complexity they introduce but, whenever possible, also use tools to run a discovery analysis of the codebase so as to detect which situations may be problematic.

4. **Validate direct algorithm performance time.**

   Although complexity is, by itself, a great measure to determine the overall performance, there are situations where algorithm complexity is just not enough[1].

   As such, you should use profiling tools that instrument your application at runtime and, therefore, detect both slow performing routines and sections on your codebase that need refactoring. These profiling tools can quickly point out where you need to focus on and, usually, allow you to quickly deal with the most problematic parts of the code by reengineering them so as to bring about significant improvements to the overall solution's performance[2].

---

[1] Either because you simply cannot reduce its complexity by implementing a better algorithm or due to there being certain operations within the algorithm itself that are slow and, thus, time and resource consuming.

[2] As defined in item **31 Generate performance data and pave way for proactive alarms**.

Item recap:

This item's fundamental guidelines can be succinctly systematized as follows:

- ✓ Understand the data structures you choose to use as well as the complexity they impose on the algorithms that operate on them.
- ✓ Beware of the hidden algorithm complexity that may exist at the core of the APIs you use (even if it is abstracted).
- ✓ Include in your code analysis a mandatory validation of algorithm complexity, preferably by performing an automated analysis through existing tools.
- ✓ Validate algorithm complexity and use input from code profiling tools in order to discover areas of code that really need improvement.
- ✓ Analysis of theoretical algorithm complexity may not be enough. Complexity, such as linear complexity, may not be suited for large volumes of data. Inversely, non-critical situations that are sparsely executed and which handle low volumes of data, may deliver acceptable performance, even with algorithms that have a higher complexity level.

9. Maximizing efficiency

As a little recap, while also looking to catch our breath, let us now turn our attention to a few items that can be used to maximize the efficiency of your solution.

Though the following recommendations are well-known and proven techniques that, nowadays, are probably second nature to most architects and engineers, let us be thorough and review them.

1. **Cache as much as you can.**

    Caching data can vary from being a heavy duty venture to a simple task. Nevertheless, managing this task effectively really depends on one's architecture. More specifically, it depends on whether one requires a simple local cache or, instead, a distributed caching layer.

    Regardless of whichever scenario one is facing, caching does need to take an important position within the architecture as well as within one's preferred design patterns. Caching can really help boost the overall system performance and ensure that one does have enough to provide a good scalability model.

    Caching can be used at many different points, such as a temporary replacement for backend databases or file systems. Caching can also be used to avoid the execution of specific flows which will produce results that have been previously calculated, and which will not change with every single iteration. Caching results for some HTTP requests is a perfect example of this latter situation[1], where a significant majority of requests sent to web applications are actually producing the exact same content as previously resolved requests.

    Furthermore, caching can be used to avoid lengthy computations and even to avoid slow operations like those that involve network traffic or slow IO operations.

    Thus, the secret lies with analyzing every layer and flow of one's solution so as to see how one can make the most out of caching while never forgetting to determine exactly which caching infrastructure will better serve the impending requirements.

2. **Pool expensive resources.**

    Some resources are just too expensive to acquire and, in order to ensure better performance, one ends up having to rely on resourcing pooling. Through resource pooling one will be able to hold on to resources which are expensive to acquire or create, thus reusing them over and over again and, consequently, avoiding having to go through constant cycles of resource creation/acquisition and resource destruction/release.

---

[1] Usually known as output caching.

Database connections are, usually, the best known example of pooled resources. However, recently, other elements[1] have been also widely benefitting from this practice. Despite this, pooled resources do not need to be exclusively seen as low level objects. One can have application level objects that can be regarded as pooled resources in just the same sense. Consider runtime objects that manage a solution's configuration. Often, these objects will spent a significant amount of time reading information from configuration stores, only to serve this information to other classes in a sporadic way. Hence, conceptually, you could easily create a configuration component as a pooled resource which started off by reading information from the persistent store and, then, survived for a considerable amount of time while serving many different consumers of this information. Plus, should you introduce the ability of having a reduced number of these objects effectively serving a large number of clients over time, you will have successfully pooled your resources.

Therefore, resource pooling can be applied to a diversity of elements and, the most important part, is its foundational concept: should you have elements which are expensive to create/acquire but which can be used to serve different consumers over time, you ought to consider using a pooling pattern.

3. **Use generic asynchronous patterns.**

   Asynchronous operations can be used in two main and distinct situations:

   - The first one is to avoid locking up user interfaces. Nothing makes an end user more nervous than working on a GUI that freezes for "no apparent reason". Thus, every time you have a GUI and an operation that will take more than a few milliseconds, you really need to follow an asynchronous pattern, so as to allow the lengthy operation to run to completion while still having a responsive interface.

   - The second one is when you are faced with operations that can only be completed after an external service is, somehow, performed by an independent entity. Although this is too generic as a statement *per se*, it is, nonetheless, accurate. Consider an IO operation that is performed to read data from a file system or to make a network-based call. Some type of external entity[2] will need to perform a few tasks before control is returned to you. Therefore, should you go for a simple synchronous route, you will effectively be blocked from performing any useful operation for a given time period. Although I clearly do not expect you to be consuming CPU power throughout this time period, you will still

---

[1] Such as threads.
[2] External to your own code.

have a few resources allocated to your processing thread, namely memory. Plus (and possibly more detrimental), your processing flow will be effectively blocked! Therefore, in many situations, you can really use up this time to process other business flows within your solution[1].

Although these are basic generic situations where asynchronous patterns can help, the critical element is to carefully organize your system design and codebase so as to constantly keep in mind where you can and should take advantage of asynchronous patterns.

4. **Consider lazy-writers and read-ahead techniques.**

    Lazy-writers and read-ahead techniques have already been discussed in detail[2] but, for the sake of completeness, here goes a quick review.

    Often, you will be able to delay writing information to a persistent store, especially when there are no transactional semantic requirements involved. Within this pattern, you will essentially buffer the information that is to be written to a persistent store somewhere in memory. Taking into account that the writing operation to the persistent store is far slower than other computational tasks which involve nothing but CPU and memory[3], you merely delay it by effectively executing it at a later stage.

    Conversely, read-ahead patterns benefit from the fact that, sometimes, you can read data from slow performing persistent stores before it is actually needed. This early read information is then stored in some memory cache, waiting to be served without any delay[4] upon having such a request coming through. The main drawback is that you run a significant risk of reading information that ends up never being used and, in turn, waste resources[5]. However, should this read operation perform to a level that is not acceptable to a specific business flow, then this pattern can be extremely helpful, especially in tandem with the caching principle.

---

[1] Until either you run up to a synchronization point where you merely have to wait for the external call to complete or, alternatively, until the external operation is completed and you effectively interrupt the alternative flow you were processing, thereby allowing you to return to the processing point where you were before dispatching the external call.

[2] As defined in item **6 Minimize the impact of slow operations**.

[3] Though this image is perhaps a bit crude and over simplified, I feel that it effectively brings the point across.

[4] Caused by a slow operation like IO.

[5] Memory to hold the temporary buffer and computational resources to perform the read-ahead task.

5. **Use compression.**

Though using compression can really save you a lot, it may also end up costing quite a bit. Compression is great in order to reduce the size of any stream of information but, the down side, is that there is a computational cost, which also implies added time, to actually compress or decompress the streams. Despite this cost, compression can really be beneficial, especially in the following scenarios:

- Reducing the size of information sent through slow or costly channels.

   This item naturally includes compression of streams that are sent through network-based channels where performance, throughput or cost, can really make a huge difference. Operations that rely heavily on distributed components, which run on different machines, need to be especially careful about server to server hopping. Sometimes, by applying compression, you can save a tremendous amount of time in bare data transfer and, therefore, gain a lot in overall system performance. Consequently, in such cases, the cost and overhead of compressing and decompressing the streams is clearly out-weighted by what you gain.

- Reducing the size of information that is stored in persistence storage.

   Regardless of whether we are talking about a naked file system, a database or another persistent storage device, the overall cost of executing the IO operations[1], is usually high. Therefore, reducing the size of stored information through compression is, often, a great solution to save resources while, sometimes, gaining speed as well, given that the time implied in the compression/decompression stage can easily be less than the time saved by reducing the size of the information that is to be stored[2].

6. **Throttling and internal queuing.**

The time will come when you simply will not be able to create your solution by assuming that it will synchronously scale forever[3]. Sooner or later, you will need to design your solution so as to create an internal queuing system which allows you to receive a vast number of requests while guaranteeing that you will not attempt to use parallel processing on a quantity that exceeds the existing capacity.

This can be achieved by using any mechanism that provides internal queuing, thus, creating a system where incoming requests are put directly into an internal queue from which, asynchronously, other internal threads will pick up pending requests and, hence, proceed to their processing.

---

[1] As well as whichever other overhead that might exist.
[2] Which leads to a more compact IO operation.
[3] Thereby attempting to process every single incoming request immediately as it arrives.

43

This design will enable you to achieve two critical things:

- Limit the number of requests that are processed concurrently, thus ensuring that you will not exhaust resources to a point where the server becomes unable to effectively respond in an adequate fashion. This limitation is usually known as throttling, and you should allow the levels of throttling to be configured[1] according to the server's capacity and the solution's profile.
- Limit the number of requests that are actually queued, thus allowing, if appropriate, an immediate response[2] to be sent to the client without further delay.

7. Consider warm up strategies.

There are certain types of initial tasks, often imposed by technology or functional requirements, which can introduce a significant lag when processing an initial set of requests. There are many known examples of such pattern3 and, therefore, it is vital to consider the feasibility of using a warm up strategy whereby one is able to automate or simulate the initial set of requests, or anything that is functionally equivalent, to ensure that the imposed lag does not produce any visible impact on any requests that are later on submitted directly by end users. Such a warm up strategies allow us to start up any relevant components of the solution beforehand, therefore preventing subsequent end user requests from feeling any performance delay, as the initially expensive tasks have already been executed. Naturally, this assumes that we are facing scenarios where such delays in performance are only really felt on the initial set of requests, which are thereby compensated by the warm up strategy.

---

[1] As defined in item **29 Configuration is needed: minimize the options and use a centralized resource**.
[2] Which usually relays information about the server's inability to currently process the request.
[3] Such as frameworks and technologies that support Just-In-Compilation.

44

Item recap:

This item's fundamental guidelines can be succinctly systematized as follows:

- ✓ Cache as much data as you can, by considering local and distributed caching options. Consider caching static data, data that can be used even if it is stale (within reason), and other forms of specific data caching such as output caching.
- ✓ Pool expensive resources, including low-level system entities, like threads or database connections, or application level components which have a costly creation step and can be re-used so as to serve many consumers over time.
- ✓ Use asynchronous patterns to maintain a highly responsive GUI as well as to circumvent situations where you effectively need to wait for an external component or resource.
- ✓ Use lazy-writers to delay IO operations whenever there are no transactional semantics involved.
- ✓ Use read-ahead patterns to acquire data that can, later on, be served to consumers, therefore avoiding delays in the processing flow.
- ✓ Combine lazy-writers and read-ahead patterns with buffering and caching patterns.
- ✓ Use compression to reduce both slow IO operations and storage requirements.
- ✓ Use internal queuing and throttling to ensure that you do not exhaust resources by attempting to process too many requests concurrently.
- ✓ Consider using warm up strategies to overcome scenarios where there is a significant delay imposed on the initial set of requests.

10. Think globally from ground up

There are certain things that simply cannot be easily retrofitted into an existing solution, as the reengineering costs are just too high and, supporting localization and distinct cultures for today's global market, happens to be one of them.

If you want your solution to play in a global market[1] you need to architect your product from ground up in order to support localization.

Contrary to popular belief, localization effort is not just about translating a few strings here and there. To truly support localization you need to think about several distinct items, and here are a few guidelines that will help you with such task:

1. **Understand how the technologies you are using support localized content.**

   The first thing you really need to do is research and understand how the technologies you are using support localization. Many modern development environments and programming languages already provide a predefined way of supporting localized content, which is made up of clear recipes regarding the required steps to execute necessary tasks, such as isolating localized content in autonomous modules and merging it into the application at runtime.

   Therefore, your first concern should revolve around understanding how you can use these instruments and, more specifically, which elements they address. It is critically important that you meticulously cover this, as it is highly likely that you will benefit from understanding:

   - How the technologies you have chosen to use will impact your development process[2], such as how they will constrain both the way in which the content is created and how it needs to be packaged and deployed, so as to be used by your running solution.

   - Which elements are directly addressed by the technology and which ones are left behind, thus forcing you to either select new tools to help with filling up the gaps or, alternatively, developing some extra base components to render the same effect. Regardless of your choice, both imply additional work and more research, which will force you to include it as another item within your overall plan.

---

[1] And really, who doesn't want to strive to, at least, have such potential these days!

[2] As defined in item **25 Having a formally defined development process does not imply adopting a formal process**.

2. **Understand all aspects of localization.**

   Localization is not just about translating strings of text, albeit that is, by itself, a major element. Apart from string translation, you usually need to consider other aspects that clearly influence graphical user interface design, and which may or may not require a lot of extra effort from the development teams.

   You will need to include within these different elements of localization, at the very least, features such as:

   - Date formatting,
   - Numeric formatting,
   - Currency conversion and formatting,
   - Text orientation,
   - Resizing and reorganization of graphic elements,
   - Keyboard and hotkey adjustment.

   With all these different issues to look into, you will need to incorporate within your project plan the knowledge acquired from the research suggested in the previous item. This will ensure that you can really support all these elements, either directly by using your chosen technology or indirectly through some extra development on your part.

3. **Use the selected technologies to support localization.**

   Although the technologies you have selected may already support a lot of your localization efforts, they will only do so if properly used, which isn't necessarily what all engineers on your team will be prone to do. Therefore, you need to clearly state within your rules and guidance[1] all critical steps that all engineers in your team must adhere to so as to ensure that the product is effectively built using the required techniques that will support localized content[2].

   Given that these techniques will force all engineers to potentially change, at least, a few tricks of their trade, you need to ensure compliance from the very first day. This means having all components being built according to these rules, so as to avoid facing a massive, if not impossible, task of reengineering some parts of your codebase. Therefore, it is critical and, thus, not negotiable, that every team member is aware and ready to support localization within the constraints defined since the early design phase.

---

[1] As defined in item **3 Coding rules: are we back in elementary school?**

[2] Even if such content isn't truly available in early versions.

4. **Understand the impact on testing.**

The impact of localization on testing is not neutral, nor is it a low one. Localization introduces a vast set of features that will force you to execute similar tests on different content so as to ensure the product behaves correctly, regardless of the selected culture.

There are many ways in which localization can introduce subtle errors into a product. One such case is that of differences in the graphical user interface, which come about as a result of needing extra space either in order to accommodate translated content. Another example comes about due to usage of distinct input rules, which can convey different meanings to validation routines. Of these routines, date entry and numeric entry are probably the most well-known[1].

Overall, the main message to take home is that you need to strategically plan all the different paths that your testing routines need to follow. This implies adding additional time, both to design your tests and their inherent routines, as well as to execute them (even if they happen to be mostly automated).

5. **Don't go for the multiplicity path.**

In the past, a common way of dealing with different cultures was to create distinct builds for products that were especially created to support one or a few similar idioms/cultures. Over the years, this technique has been proven to be less than ideal[2]. Given this, you should, from the very first day, look to incorporate all localization elements into your design.

Additionally, you should do so while ensuring that you keep a single branch in your codebase without any duplication of your codebase or build process, as well as without generating distinct versions of your software product.

Keeping this cohesion is the best way to avoid creating a scenario where different versions of your product behave in distinct manner as a result of unwanted differences that somehow crept into some of the different branches[3] of your codebase.

Furthermore, it also promotes the distinction that is critical between code and localized content, thus ensuring that there is only one codebase which can manage a vast set of distinct localized contents on request.

Finally, this does not mean that you need to follow up by distributing all different localized versions of the content to all your clients. Instead, you can, of course, create

---

[1] Who hasn't fiddled with the differences in using a comma or a point to separate decimal parts of a number? Who hasn't used different date formats, from two to four digits for the year to its distinct ordering regarding year, month and date elements?

[2] As the overhead it implied was much higher. Just consider the significant added complexity in terms managing all the branching and merging in your codebase.

[3] This can easily happen if you branch your codebase to support different localization options.

different packaging solutions that only deliver a subset of the localized content, while knowing that the whole development process was kept unified, without any subversion being thrown about, as well as maintaining full consistency when bug fixes and upgrades come along (guaranteed by the sheer fact that no additional branching was performed to support localization).

Item recap:

This item's fundamental guidelines can be succinctly systematized as follows:

- ✓ Ensure that you understand how the technologies you are using support localized content and, additionally, identify both the constraints they impose on your development process as well as which procedures you must follow in order to extract the benefits they provide.
- ✓ Understand all aspects of localization, including translation, input validation routines, data formatting and GUI adjustment.
- ✓ Identify which gaps are not properly covered by the technologies you chose and define how you will address them, either by incorporating a few extra tools or by adding extra development effort.
- ✓ Understand the impact that localization has on testing and identify both which types of test cases need to be changed in order to cover all localization options, as well as the impact these items have on the execution of the testing procedures.
- ✓ Do not support localization either by branching your source code or by creating different versions of your core product. Doing so would constitute a managing nightmare and, additionally, it will not force you to have a clear separation between code and localizable content.
- ✓ Should you support several distinct cultures, you can create different distribution packages. Nevertheless, consider such course of action only when feeling that distributing the whole content to all customers is a problematic solution.

11. Be defensive: choose the safest techniques

Given that compilers are, without a doubt, one of development engineers' best friends, instead of relying heavily on runtime features, all possible forms of validation and error checking that can be done at compile-time should be privileged.

We have, within the field of compile-time safety, important features that can lead to a vast set of validation rules used to enforce general code correctness. There are, however, different types of programming languages, as well as many distinct programming paradigms. Thus, choosing wisely which languages to use must include a careful consideration of what compilers can and cannot enforce.

Beyond the lexical and syntactic rules that compilers check, there are, often enough, features within development languages that offer similar effects while involving completely different implementation strategies and inherent risks.

Therefore, here is a quick review of what you should contemplate when choosing which languages and environments will suit you best:

1. **Privilege type-safe languages.**
   Type-safety is one of the best features that languages and compilers can provide as well as enforce, given that it guarantees an extremely high level of lexical and syntactic correctness of the existing code. Languages which are not type-safe will be prone to a ton of runtime errors that are absent from type-safe languages. As such, type-safe languages will ensure both:
   - Higher code quality,
   - Fewer runtime errors that derive solely from badly articulated coding constructs[1].

2. **Privilege patterns that automate low-level memory management.**
   Memory management has always been a plague for development engineers. Mismanaging memory can have really nefarious effects which, in turn, may lead to:
   - Memory exhaustion,
   - Memory corruption,
   - Buffer overflow exploitations.
   As such, whenever possible, environments that instill the application of patterns that automate low-level memory management should be chosen. This can be accomplished

---

[1] Which include mismatching data types, incorrect calling conventions, incorrect parameter ordering, *etc.*.

by means of several different routes, from which the following three are the most commonly used strategies:

- Using garbage collection mechanisms that automate the steps of cleaning up memory items no longer in use, as well as compacting heaps as they become vastly fragmented so as to boost overall performance, while allocating memory blocks.

- Using managed environments that will ensure memory buffers are safely written to so that, for the most part, the occurrence of buffer overflows is prevented. This will deny access to memory positions that have not been properly allocated, making this feature a major step towards eliminating the ability of exploiting buffer overruns so as to execute rogue code.

- Using, within non-managed environments, programming patterns such as RAII[1]. Doing so, by using language features[2] to automate this process, will effectively replicate an important part of what garbage collected environments deliver in terms of automatically cleaning up memory.

3. **Avoid massive usage of dynamic features.**

   Dynamic features that allow for the definition of code paths at runtime[3] are not usually type-safe and, additionally, will introduce overhead. Languages that provide features such as reflection, late binding or, to a certain extent, even virtual calls, will, quite naturally, need to perform all the required code binding at runtime, thus adding considerable overhead and drastically reducing performance. Apart from performance related issues, these features will also introduce some of the pitfalls of non-type-safe languages. More specifically, some elements of lexical and syntactic correctness cannot be ensured at compile time, thus resulting in a higher rate of runtime problems and exceptions.

4. **Understand the tradeoffs that stem from genericity.**

   The wider availability of generic programming, which is made available by many programming languages' and environments' use of template-like features, can also result in a significant performance tradeoff. Some languages, where templates and genericity

---

[1] Resource Acquisition Is Initialization.
[2] Such as scope and deterministic destructors.
[3] Defining code paths at runtime refers, in this context, to the usage of features such as reflection or late binding, and not to standard coding practices such as internal code branching following evaluation of logical conditions.

are resolved dynamically at runtime[1], will, by their own intrinsic nature, have virtually the same effects as the dynamic features previously discussed.

Conversely, generic programming that is supported by templates which are resolved at compile time[2] will not suffer from these problems. In these scenarios, templates can be seen as little more than syntactic sugar to reduce coding, since, ultimately, they will produce all possible and required types at compile-time and, in turn, ensure complete type-safety and compile-time validation.

5. **Balance managed environments vs. performance and flexibility.**

   Managed environments deliver a higher abstraction than non-managed environments and, furthermore, we can safely say that they shield development engineers from many issues that continue to exist and haunt us within non-managed environments. Nevertheless, as is usually the case in life, everything comes at a price. Given this, it is important to really understand what the penalty is in terms of performance and flexibility when deciding which path to take.

   In the vast majority of situations, managed environments are a great choice as they:

   - Reduce the overall development time,
   - Reduce the number of potential problems that may occur with one's codebase,
   - Usually, though arguably strangely, have a broader and more extensive set of supporting libraries, often called base class libraries.

   However, despite all of this, there will be situations where performance is just too critical and, therefore, some parts of the codebase needs to be built on top of non-managed environments. Nevertheless, performance is not the only factor that needs to be considered. Many times, when needing either maximum portability to support different environments[3] or great flexibility to perform low-level tricks[4], managed environments will simply fall short of what is required in order to successfully satisfy existing requirements.

---

[1] Such as generics in .Net.
[2] Such as templates in C++.
[3] Such as distinct hardware.
[4] Such as direct control over external devices.

Item recap:

This item's fundamental guidelines can be succinctly systematized as follows:

- ✓ Privilege type safe languages so as to reduce runtime errors. This will simplify test rigs and will deliver both higher code quality and performance.
- ✓ Privilege patterns that automate memory management in order to avoid memory leaks, buffer overrun exploitations or memory corruption. This can be achieved with both managed and non-managed environments and it merely requires the application of the right coding patterns.
- ✓ Relying too much on dynamic features will severely undermine performance and it will reduce, in many cases, the benefits that are obtained when using type safe languages.
- ✓ Some types of features within the boundary of generic programming will also imply lower performance and, potentially, higher runtime errors due to lack of compile time type safety.
- ✓ Managed environments will, usually, deliver a safer environment for development engineers but, quite often, fall short when performance is critical or when maximum portability is a must-have.

12.   Linking code: the static vs. dynamic option

A modern enterprise capable software product is bound to be composed of many different components, invariably executing in different servers. Additionally, and in equally invariable fashion, there are many sections of code that end up being repetitively used in many of those components. It is the holy grail of modern software development: code re-usage! No other software practice can be as productive as reusing existing[1] source code. If you do not write source code or, at least, do not write new source code, you will not be making any mistakes[2].

Along with code re-usage comes a critical decision that all software designers inevitably face: should these common and reusable code sections be dynamically or statically linked? There are many pros and cons to each possibility, although there are more pros than cons to preferring dynamic linking. Choosing to use dynamic linking will lead to a scenario where common code is packaged in a unique binary file, which is then reused by all running components. Let us momentarily ignore the possibility of having multiple versions of this same binary[3] which, by itself, introduces another management nightmare[4]. Thus, using dynamic linking and creating uniquely shared components means that any change made to this singular and shared binary will, eventually after any existing caching features are refreshed, be reflected in all executing paths. As this is, usually, beneficial to the system as a whole, it is the main reason why dynamic linking is, on the vast majority of situations, the preferred route[5].

There is, however, a downside to dynamic linkage, which merely constitutes a different perspective on the same fact: in a few less common situations, it might just be beneficial to be capable of changing a given shared source code section by only having a limited number of components being affected[6]. Hence, this raises the question of whether, when faced with such scenario, the solution should use static linkage and, if so, if there is a feasible way of determining, during the design phase, which areas are prone to this type of requirement. Interestingly, the answer to these questions is actually rather simple, as it is not only impossible to determine, during the design phase, which areas are prone to such an unlikely scenario but, furthermore, should it in fact come up, it doesn't necessarily need to be solved using static linking.

---

[1] As in written and fully tested.

[2] Quite naturally, there are some exceptions to this rule but, for the present case, it is more relevant to analyze the overall rule of thumb.

[3] Usually scattered in different folders.

[4] Due to the need to determine which version is used in each executing context, depending on the search and load rules enforced by the specific operating system or framework under which the solution is built.

[5] Yes, we are ignoring other advantages such as reducing the required storage space, given that the code is not replicated in different binaries, and more importantly, reducing the solution's memory footprint, given that the same code is also not replicated in memory pages corresponding to different components.

[6] As opposed to the whole system which is usually the most common scenario.

It is important to note that it is within the second part of this answer that the juice really lies. Even when having dynamic linkage and needing to make a change on shared code that does not reflect immediately on the whole system, one can simply update the components that require changing (forgoing any dynamic linking in this specific fix) or, alternatively, one can add new entry points to the shared component[1] and proceed to re-wiring only those components that need to incorporate these changes and which should therefore bind to these new entry points. Both solutions are possible and both prevent any sort of initial dependency on static linkage.

Finally, and in order to wrap up this item, it is important to ask whether there are any additional considerations regarding dynamic linking and, for those who like to get hung up on byte-size issues, the answer is yes. There are many more technical details that can be considered when analyzing dynamic linking versus static linking, with performance being one of them. Dynamic linking is, obviously, bound to be slower than static linking, nevertheless, the art of great software design resides in optimizing that which can generate a significant profit, and it surely does not include saving a few CPU cycles by avoiding dynamic linkage.

Item recap:

This item's fundamental guidelines can be succinctly systematized as follows:

- ✓ Dynamic linking is the best choice to minimize repetitive code sections within distinct components. Having shared code in a unique and shared binary unit that benefits from dynamic linking is, usually, the best way to ensure that a fix is reflected on the entire system.
- ✓ When needing to implement a fix within a shared section while avoiding having it reflect on the whole system, it is possible to use either static linking for the specific components to be affected by the fix or, alternatively, dynamic linking by introducing new entry points to which only a few desired components will bind to.
- ✓ Although dynamic linking can be slightly slower in performance, it is hardly a showstopper and, overall, its advantages far outweigh any disadvantages.
- ✓ Using static linking in main libraries will increase memory footprint and storage size, thus making it a fairly deprecated practice that is, nowadays, rarely justifiable.

---

[1] Which reflect the new behavior.

13. Do's and don'ts of APIs

Some products include a set of access points, usually known as APIs, which are meant to ensure that product to product integration is possible. Although APIs are nothing new in the realm of software products, it is still a bit strange that many products showcase APIs that are just too complex to use. However, it should be noted that this does not necessarily mean that these APIs are performing extremely complex algorithms. Instead, it is more the case that those who need to consume them end up spending a disproportionate amount of time on them, due to many distinct issues.

Given this, APIs really need to follow a few guidelines in order to ensure that those who use them will not be led into an abyss. Therefore, here are a few pointers that should be carefully considered:

1. **APIs need to be very well documented.**
    Documentation on APIs needs to be clear, pristine and unspotted. Any developer who reads through such documentation needs to easily understand both what the API's purpose is and how it can be used. Achieving this usually requires a lot more than a simple line of text stating the purpose of the method call. Instead, it is fundamental to really invest in generating documentation that clearly explains all the different actions executed by each method call exposed within one's API. Furthermore, it is vital to ensure that the documentation explicitly states whether there is a precedence order in which different API methods need to be called. And on top of that, all input and output parameters need to be identified, including information about:
    *   Their types,
    *   Possible default values,
    *   How these parameters influence the method's behavior.
    Finally, one should preferably supply complete and detailed samples of all APIs' possible usage patterns, meaning that APIs need to be thoroughly documented so as to cover all aspects of their functionality.

2. **Document the complexity of the API.**
    An API provides a great abstraction layer to hide complexity. However, this apparent isolation needs to be well documented so as to ensure that those who are relying on it really understand the implied cost of consuming it[1]. You do not want other engineers using your APIs without knowing that specific methods implement algorithms of high complexity which will inevitably render poor performance results in certain specific

---
[1] As defined in item **8 Algorithm complexity and optimizations.**

scenarios. It is far better to clearly publicize that which occurs inside a method exposed by your product's API, since such action allows those consuming it to be adequately prepared and, therefore, prevent the typical negative consequences of being caught off guard.

3. **Errors and exceptions need to be handled correctly.**

    Handling errors and exceptions within an API needs to be a well thought out task. As such, a consistent policy that allows consumers to easily prepare for possible errors and exceptions must be established, while also ensuring that errors and exceptions can be easily understood[1]. Here are a few things you should bear in mind:

    - **Do not return a numeric error code that is ambiguous as a result of being used in different scenarios or due to lack of contextual information.**

      It really does not help much if you return an error code that informs developers that a supplied parameter is invalid, in case your API call accepts many parameters that have some sort of dependency between them. This is a perfect example of a situation where an error code simply requires extra contextual information so as to allow those consuming it to happily move along after quickly fixing whatever issues exist.

    - **Do not return different types of errors using the same type of generic exception.**

      Many APIs that use programming languages which support exception handling fall into the trap of relaying all errors as the same type of exception. This is of no help to those consuming APIs, as their code will need a generic exception handler, which is then polluted with differentiating branches that try to pursue different routes, after determining what type of error actually happened by analyzing extra information usually embedded in the thrown exception.

    - **Do not catch all platform exceptions within the supplied APIs.**

      Some exceptions cannot be handled by an API that simply does not know what the executing context is. As such, and if you are building an API that is leveraging both a language and the inherent execution environment where structural or platform exceptions can occur, it is usually an unwise policy to catch them within the API calls given that, quite often, it is even questionable whether they should be caught by the code consuming the API at all. However, doing it within the API will hide problematic situations that should not be hidden, since they could actually result in greater loss of data or processing correctness. Consequently,

---

[1] How many products have you used where API calls simply return obscure and unintelligible errors messages?

these types of errors and exceptions need to be bubbled up from the API towards its consumer.

4. **Do not make an API call order overly complex.**

Inevitably, we must confront the, sometimes inevitable and harsh reality, that many APIs have an intrinsic state machine within, causing precedence and dependency in call order. Nevertheless, we must, at the very least, strive to avoid turning this situation into a complex graph, which can only be fully understood after a deep intellectual exercise. Some patterns within API call order have become quite common and, therefore, have become almost second nature to software engineers[1]. Despite this, the existence of too many dependencies within the API call order ought to be minimized whenever possible, given that it is responsible for making it too complex and, usually, too prone to being misused.

5. **Create a verbose API usage option.**

Do create a verbose API usage option that generates detailed information[2] which clearly allows those consuming it to understand:
- Which actions are being executed by the API call,
- Which parameters are being consumed within each action,
- Why any specific action fails.

Ultimately, this feature will turn your API consumers into very faithful and happy clients, more specifically, the kind that will, not only re-use your API and others you might produce, but also pass around the kind of positive reviews that we all want to attain as great software engineers.

6. **Use the appropriate granularity level.**

One common problem with many APIs consists of having the exposed methods being defined at a very low level of granularity which, in turn, forces consumers to call many distinct methods in order to perform any given specific business action. Although defining API methods with low level of granularity benefits delivering complete control over the available services, it also needs to be considered whether a higher aggregation level can be defined in order to prevent successive calls that will hinder performance. Furthermore, in many circumstances, providing higher aggregation level introduces a more effective transactional context[3].

---

[1] Such as those that roam around initialization/constructor calls and finalization/destructor calls.
[2] Potentially to a log file of some sort.
[3] Which would need to span several calls, were this higher aggregation level to be unavailable.

Hence, in order to simplify the task of those consuming the API, as well as allow you to directly manage structural constraints (such as enabling transactional semantics), the guideline really should consist of providing the level of granularity that reflects exactly how consumers will need to use the API.

7. **Support diverse client technologies and go for standard protocols.**
It is fundamental to be aware of the type of potential consumers your API can have. Additionally, since it makes nothing but good business sense to strive towards supporting the largest possible client base, technologies that can, not only be consumed from different platforms, but also adhere to common transport and messaging formats, should be privileged. Technologies such as web services, which expose method calls through standard protocols[1], are growing in popularity[2]. Consequently, and unless one is dealing with very specific cases that dictate otherwise, APIs should be provided in a platform and language neutral technology, so as to support as many consumers as possible.

Item recap:

This item's fundamental guidelines can be succinctly systematized as follows:

- ✓ Ensure that APIs are well documented, including information about actions that are executed, input and output parameters, inherent complexity and dependency call order.
- ✓ Always supply as many samples as possible, so as to ease the task of consumers.
- ✓ Ensure that errors and exceptions are handled correctly in the API. Do not catch structural errors and exceptions that really need to be bubbled up. Provide enough contextual information about errors and exceptions in order to allow consumers to quickly identify what the root causes are.
- ✓ Do not bubble up all exceptions by merely using one exception type.
- ✓ Deliver an appropriate granularity level based on the expected API use cases.
- ✓ Support diverse client technologies by using platform independent and language independent protocols.
- ✓ Create a verbose API mode that logs every executed action, used parameter and occurring error, including detailed contextual information.

---

[1] Such as HTTP and XML.
[2] Regardless of the distinct nuances that exist around them.

14. Leverage the full power of the IDE and all related add-ins and tools

An awful lot has changed since the integrated development environment was made up of little more than a rudimentary text editor with the ability to invoke command-line compilers and linkers behind the scenes. Integrated development environments are, currently, full blown tools that really boost productivity and, additionally, can also drive quality forward. However, to extract the most out of them, one needs to fully understand some hidden features and a few of the more recent and, sometimes, less well-known options.

Modern integrated development environments have state of the art debugging features, as well as wide support for direct integration with other supportive tools[1]. Plus, many such environments can easily be expanded through the use of a set of add-ins that further enhances their ability to be truly powerful one-stop shops.

Integrated development environments[2] must be analyzed in order to fully understand where the biggest benefits can come from. Thus, here are a few pointers on features that really do deliver great added value and, therefore, are naturally worth investing in:

1. **Extending intellisense through code snippets.**

   Most integrated development environments come with some type of intellisense features that speed up the process of code writing through:
   - A powerful schema for fast completion of word typing,
   - Correct application of semantic and contextual rules.

   Although this feature is extremely powerful by itself, it usually has the granularity of a single word and doesn't bring any added value when dealing with slightly more complex constructs which span over multiple keywords. These constructs can either be referring to a specific language feature that requires a few more elements than a single word[3] or to a specific pattern that one wishes to adopt (perhaps, even being part of your code quality rules[4]).

   When faced with these scenarios, intellisense will not offer any specific help. Nevertheless, that does not mean that one will be unable to create a fast and efficient schema, helpful in completing word typing effort in a fraction of the time that would be needed in order to manually write every single character. Integrated development environments often come with support for expandable code snippets. These can help

---

[1] Such as source control management or project tracking.
[2] Going past the obvious features revolving around code editing, compiling and linking chores.
[3] Such as the definition of a cycle that encompasses a set of inner instructions.
[4] As defined in item **3 Coding rules: are we back in elementary school?**

developers to easily create small blocks of code that represent certain repetitive patterns. Furthermore, these extended features should be used, not only to boost productivity, but also to further standardize certain coding practices that are deemed mandatory. By configuring and expanding the development environment through the usage of code snippets, the power and quickness of the intellisense auto-completion can be brought to the next level, where a few lines of code can be easily generated without that much typing going on. However, the best thing about this isn't even the time being saved, though this alone might justify the effort by itself. Instead, the standardization that stems from this practice is far more valuable. By having these code snippets available for the whole development team, the cohesion of coding patterns will be taken to a higher level. Developers will, automatically, be driven towards adhering to certain patterns, thus ensuring that these specific constructs enforce the same overall logic and structure. With this new level of codebase conformance, benefits will include reducing bugs[1] by creating common ground that eases developers' understanding of the existing codebase and, in general, boost collective code ownership[2].

Consequently, it is beneficial to invest in using and expanding one's code snippets, as well as forgoing the need to write repetitive patterns whose creation can be fairly automated.

2. **Code coverage.**

    Code quality is absolutely crucial and one of its fundamental corner-stones is test driven development[3]. However, adopting the policy of using test driven development does not constitute a magic formula that solves all issues. Even those who consider alternative testing practices to be superior and, thus, look to make use of them, are faced with a specific limitation: despite having tests in place to verify one's codebase, it is impossible to really be sure of these tests' precision and depth when verifying each line of code that has been produced.

    One's chosen testing strategy needs to be complemented[4] with another element, in the form of an automated mechanism that will accurately pinpoint what is being tested. Thus, this is where code coverage tools enter the equation.

    Code coverage tools allow for the tracking of which parts of codebase are being hit by a specific execution flow and, when applied in conjunction with automated testing rigs, code coverage tools will diagnose which code paths are being hit by the test rigs and which ones are not.

---

[1] The assumption being that the generated code will be bug-free.
[2] As defined in item **22 Store and share know-how: create an internal global knowledge depot**.
[3] As defined in item **20 Nothing works better then test driven development**.
[4] Regardless of one's choice, though it should leverage test driven development.

Not surprisingly, this type of knowledge is crucial in determining which areas of the testing scripts need to be enhanced in order to ensure that, over time, one is able to close in on the elusive target of achieving a complete code coverage. Plus, through the analysis provided by the code coverage tool, one will also diagnose which are the important elements that can best direct the work of engineers responsible for creating tests. If, for example, during the execution of the code coverage tool in conjunction with a test rig, you find out that the exception paths are not being properly covered[1], you can provide them with that information and, thus, ensure there will be greater attention given to this type of issue during subsequent tests.

3. **Code profiling.**

Solid coding practices, great architectural skills and superior testing processes, will not guarantee an issue-free codebase. There are many things that are simply unpredictable and, therefore, can only be determined through careful profiling. Hence, adopting a good code profiling tool can really help in delivering a better product.

Code profiling features of integrated development environments[2] can provide useful automated analysis of what your code is doing as it is running. Through code profiling you can easily learn about:

- Which code paths are being executed more often,
- How long each element is taking to execute[3],
- How many times each element is being executed.

By using these indicators, together with the graphical output that most code profiling tools create, you can easily locate bottlenecks and other problematic code strips, thus, quickly identifying the locations where changes are needed, before things go out of control.

This complete analysis of the executing runtime context will allow you to save hundreds of hours on manual code instrumentation and log analysis, by promptly directing your efforts to the areas that desperately need changing.

As is the case amongst many other situations, here too the key issue lies with the greater difficulty in locating the problem and defining its boundaries effectively, when compared to fixing it after successfully performing the prior steps. Given this, code profiling tools will easily pay off their required investment in a matter of minutes.

---

[1] A common mistake performed by novice test engineers.

[2] Regardless of whether they are features that are either native ones or being supplied through a set of additional modules.

[3] The granularity of an element could vary but, for argument sake, let us imagine that we would be working at the level of functions or methods.

4. **Code analysis.**

Enforcing rules isn't always positively accepted by everyone. Despite this, rules do deliver quality when applied effectively and, this being so, code analysis tools can effectively ensure that, not only is a wide range of code patterns correctly applied, but also that incorrect practices are eliminated from your codebase.

Code analysis tools[1] create a great mix to drive quality upwards. However, given that code analysis has been widely covered in previous items[2], I will immediately move on without further ado.

5. **Tracing and debugging.**

Is there a developer in the world who does not know about tracing and debugging? Surely not, but, often enough, the answer is not this straight forward. There are many features revolving around debugging and tracing that go well beyond the basic tasks of:

- Single-stepping through code,
- Conditionally outputting a few lines of tracing information.

Debugging is actually an art in itself and, therefore, there are different aspects to it. While debugging code as you are developing it is one reality[3], debugging production issues[4] is a completely different game. Nevertheless, despite these differences, the harsh reality is that, although the basic steps may be well known to all engineers of your team, solving the really tricky stuff takes more than understanding the essentials. Debugging can be taken to the next level in order to deliver higher productivity[5] and, to do so, knowing the nuts and bolts of the trade is a must. Debugging while developing requires knowledge of some features, such as:

- Setting conditional breakpoints using logic conditions or hit counts,
- Setting breakpoints on either specific exceptions or specific conditions,
- Comparing data from previous debugging sessions.

Conversely, debugging production environments usually requires knowledge of other more advanced debugging tools[6] that allow you to:

- Attach to live processes,
- Dump information on running threads,

---

[1] Used in conjunction with code coverage and code profiling.
[2] Namely in item **3 Coding rules: are we back in elementary school?**
[3] Probably the most common one for software developers.
[4] Often by analyzing process dumps.
[5] Measured by reducing the time spent on debugging a given problem while delivering the topmost results by clearly identifying the root causes as well as laying the foundation for required fixes.
[6] Most often you will not be able to connect your development environment, either locally or remotely, to the production servers.

- Analyze call stacks,
- Set breakpoints on exceptions,
- Apply these same techniques to process dumps while linking to the appropriate symbols[1].

Consequently you need to invest in mastering debugging skills. Additionally, and regarding production debugging and dump analysis, do not forget that you really need to use the best available debugging extensions in order to simplify this complex task.

So the main message to take home is that, should you desire to have your development teams being really productive while debugging, you need to invest time so as to ensure acquisition of these skills.

Naturally, the very same scenario applies to tracing. Conceptually, tracing is extremely simple and can easily be defined as outputting some information to one or more targets, though, usually, in a conditional fashion. However, modern environments have whole sets of tracing features, many of which can be automatically activated by configuration and, additionally, even applied to running production code, if and when required. Consequently, it is wise to carefully consider setting some time aside so as to ensure that your engineers do learn the ins and outs of what the platform you are using delivers in terms of tracing. Ultimately, such course of action will enable you to extract the platform's full potential.

6. **Integration with source control, project tracking, issue management and build systems.**
   Finally, modern development environments are, quite often, today's engineers' main elected tool, as they spare them from having to move between different tools in order to work at all different levels required by their daily routine.

   Software engineers need to do a lot more than simply writing code. They need to:
   - Respond to and work with the project tracking tool that is used to assign tasks and manage development effort,
   - Interact with the issue tracking tool to participate in the workflows that drive the process of fixing up detected bugs,
   - Interact with whichever source control tools are in place and, potentially, with whichever building system is being used.

   Until a few years ago this entailed dealing with a myriad of distinct environments, which implied a lot of context switching, together with having to learn a rather diverse set of graphical user interfaces.

   Fortunately, this picture has changed a lot over the years and, currently[1], the most well-known development environments have direct support for many different tools, which

---

[1] As defined in item **36 Prepare for the unexpected: setup a proper symbol server.**

vary between natively integrated ones, to those available through specific add-in modules.

As such, you really need to ensure that you can make all these tools, as well as their integration features, work to your advantage, thus, ensuring that your team is well versed in their intrinsic features.

Knowing how to use all of these products, even if they are camouflaged behind the look and feel of an integrated development environment, usually means learning a few new tricks and concepts. Even if not all engineers need to be completely familiarized with either the details of the branching strategy you have chosen or the automated build rules that are attached to your environment, they will be far more productive should they grasp their essentials as they interact with these tools through the integrated development environment.

---

[1] Even if all these required features are not supported by a unique product, but rather through an integrated usage of several products, it is, nonetheless, a common scenario in many development teams.

Item recap:

This item's fundamental guidelines can be succinctly systematized as follows:

- ✓ Use extensibility features of the development environment in order to automate code snippets that reflect specific coding patterns you wish to enforce.
- ✓ Use code coverage tools to ensure that you know exactly which code paths are being hit by your test rigs as well as which ones are not and, consequently, improve the test rigs accordingly.
- ✓ Use code profiling tools to get an analysis of which code sections may present bottlenecks. Code profiling tools can instrument your execution environment and acquire metrics such as time spent on each code element or number of times each code element has been executed.
- ✓ Code analysis tools can check whether the stipulated coding patterns are being correctly applied and, additionally, whether the general coding rules are being followed.
- ✓ Ensure that your engineers know how to use the advanced features of debugging and tracing available on the platform you are using. Knowing the ins and outs of these features can help them boost their productivity within a development context and, likewise, within a production environment.
- ✓ Advanced skills, like analyzing process dumps or performing live debugging on production systems, can be extremely valuable to resolve critical issues. Given this, it is wise to carefully consider investing in this area.
- ✓ Ensure that you leverage the existing integration between your development environment and other supporting tools. Doing so provides easy access to fundamental services such as work item assignment, issue tracking, source control, automated builds and project management.

Section II – Development environment and technologies

Over this section I will present and discuss five key items that must be viewed as structural technological elements capable of delivering enormous value to the development effort. These items will be crucial in creating effective software products that, regardless of the load scenario, perform adequately within production environments.

15.   Use as many enterprise building blocks as possible and refresh common design patterns

Some things go without saying but, just for the sake of thoroughness, let us say it anyway: there is no point in reinventing the wheel! Although this is ancient universally accepted wisdom, there are still many software engineers so absorbed by their work[1] that, now and again, they fail to take advantage of already existing and duly tested tools, libraries and components. On top of this, there are also a myriad of new offers being created every single day[2], with many being either open source projects or, at least, royalty free components sponsored by key market players. However, though it is far from crucial to be constantly up to par with yesterday's cool new toolkit, it is nonetheless advisable to be aware of which tools are the top ones used as true enterprise building blocks[3] since these will be the ones that supply the required reliability and depth.

Furthermore, it must be emphasized that almost all structural requirements of new software solutions have already been met by many others in the past, whose experience, through trial and error, has, for the most part, unraveled the most balanced and acceptable solutions. For example, consider a structural requirement such as auditing and logging[4]: with this being an extremely common and indispensable feature, it will, undoubtedly, be easy to find some free library that suits one's needs without having to endure additional expenses in the form of royalties. Plus, such research will even reduce the overall development time, since the integration of such a specific library into the codebase will usually represent an effort inferior than creating a similar tool from ground up.

Nevertheless, this guideline should not to be misunderstood, as these building blocks are not items found at programming language level. Instead, these are always libraries and software development kits that create higher levels of abstraction on top of a given programming language, thus enabling their integration within one's project.

Additionally, and from an entrepreneurial perspective, the best ones will be those that are, not only, royalty free, but also provide source code access[5] on a programming language that you are

---

[1] Their deadlines and deliveries.

[2] Which makes it simply impossible to keep track of every new thing.

[3] Meaning, those which managed to amass a significant critical number of users and are highly regarded by top software makers and by the majority of the market.

[4] As defined in item **30 Strange unexplainable behaviors are inevitable: create a detailed and systematic tracing** feature.

[5] Given that these software components can be reused without entailing a direct financial cost, while retaining the ability to be independent from specific vendors, they provide a safeguard against being dependent on vendors who, for some unforeseen reason, may go out of business.

comfortable with[1]. Interestingly, the internet is, definitely, an invaluable resource to search for these enterprise building blocks, including access to massive volumes of input in the form of other people's experience about these products' strengths and weaknesses. However, and as most things in life, although it is wise to skim through others' views[2], one should remember never to adopt technology without thoroughly mastering it[3].

Therefore, building an effective prototype, which enables for the complexity of integrating a selected toolkit to be identified, is undoubtedly a worthwhile task. Doing so is the best route to understanding whether one can truly take advantage of its inner strengths and features[4]. Furthermore, only by prototyping critical use cases will one understand whether a specific toolkit responds adequately to the specific key requirements that characterize each scenario.

Plus, to truly use the best available option, it is quite common to end up selecting different toolkits, so as to take advantage of a small subset of features that each one provides. There is nothing wrong with such an approach, as long as the appropriate tests are run, with the ultimate goal of being assured of the effectiveness of such third party components.

Interestingly, such building blocks can be applied in many different layers of one's solution, from logging and auditing, to graphical user interface components. However, do not exclusively opt for the royalty free ones, given that there are some truly worthwhile building blocks that are not free and worth every single cent! Again, this decision process requires experience, in the form of a keen eye and a balanced approach that ensures one is selecting the best possible fit.

Additionally, adopting component sets just to follow trends should be avoided at all cost. Independently of an option's source and price, no effort should be spared in testing them, obtaining a trial pattern and, finally, evaluating the results of this sort of experimentation phase. Doing so will guarantee the adequate foundations for a properly informed choice of the selected building blocks.

So having discussed existing building blocks, let us turn our attention towards code one writes from scratch. Should one simply hammer the keyboard in order to create the needed solution without following any specific guidelines? Most definitely not! The more one adheres to proven and tested solutions, the safer it will be and, therefore, the more likely it will be that one will actually be creating successful and robust solutions. **Enter design patterns!**

---

[1] Though it does not necessarily mean that it must be the programming language being used as your core platform.

[2] Which, in the present case, can often allow for the quick diagnosis of some libraries as being no match for one's requirements.

[3] As defined in item **21 Observe the 10.000 hour principle: be a specialist in the technology you are using**.

[4] As well as in which specific situations.

Many years ago, there was a strong push to document and disseminate a set of well-known and widely used coding practices deemed as appropriate solutions to frequent problems to which developers answered by creating many different solutions[1]. Although we are not arguing that there will be a known and common solution to every problem, it is, nonetheless, likely that many of the coding challenges faced by developers have already been addressed by others in the past, and from experience and refinement some optimal solutions have been encountered.

Just consider a common challenge like resource management in an unmanaged framework. Is there a better solution than adopting some variation of the well-known RAII[2] pattern? For those who have not come across it or who are simply failing to identify this best practice by its name, let us start by clarifying this subject. RAII is a coding pattern that attaches a specific resource[3] to the intrinsic lifetime of a controlling object. This guarantees that, whenever the end of lifetime of the controlling object comes, the resource is released. And on top of it, the controlling object also guarantees that there is no way (regardless of how its own end of life comes about) to prevent the release of the controlled object from being executed.

Thus, by using common patterns that have been tested over the years, many pitfalls can be successfully avoided. Given this, it should be ensured that software engineers building software products are truly aware of:

- What the most common design patterns are,
- How they are relevant,
- How they are applied to the technology being used.

However, it should be noted that not all patterns will be equally relevant in all technologies nor will you apply them all in the same invariable manner[4].

Finally, avoid being fooled into thinking that you can master the main design patterns in two or three hours of internet scavenging, as it is impossible to become fluent in this lingo without proper practice. Plus, while some patterns are very straightforward and easy to comprehend, others are more obscure and require, not only a deeper analysis, but also a maturation phase. Over the course of such phase most software engineers will, little by little, understand the advantages and disadvantages that these patterns bring and, ultimately, use them when they can render the best possible results.

---

[1] Some of which invariably fell short of constituting a good response.
[2] Resource Acquisition Is Initialization.
[3] Which is, by virtue of its nature, finite and potentially scarce.
[4] Despite the fact that most patterns will be re-usable across many different technologies.

Item recap:

This item's fundamental guidelines can be succinctly systematized as follows:

- ✓ Search the market and use the best available enterprise building blocks. Avoid writing code to create components that are already available and which have a great track record.
- ✓ Ensure these building blocks have strong support from the industry or, alternatively, that you have source code access to them as a safeguard against potential future problems.
- ✓ Though there are many great royalty-free and, sometimes, open source toolkits, there are also paid ones that justify every single cent!
- ✓ Ensure you apply rigorous testing and quality assurance practices to whichever enterprise building blocks you select.
- ✓ Ensure your team is adequately skillful in the most common and proven design patterns, since they will usually provide the best solutions to well-known problems. Spending time learning them is a wise investment.

16. Use in-memory distributed caching systems to enhance performance and scalability

Performance matters, and there is absolutely no other way to look at it! Within modern enterprise capable solutions, where we must support huge loads and scalability is a commanding tenant, in-memory distributed caching solutions are probably one of the best options in order to create responsive and scalable systems.

By looking carefully at common architecture design and scalability issues, we can usually identify an architecture pattern whereby systems respond to an increase in requests[1] through IP-based load-balanced systems that use a set of front-end servers. These front-end servers which, invariably, host web servers that are used to process IP based requests, often in the form of HTTP traffic, will actually scale out horizontally by the addition of more servers[2]. These servers will be mostly used in a session-less context, where subsequent requests from the same client can be processed through different servers[3] .

Despite this effective strategy (which is all the more interesting in cloud-based services, where provisioning new machines can be achieved in virtually a few minutes[4]) the reality is that scaling out the front-end tier is just a part of what it takes to create completely scalable solutions. Apart from the front-end layer, we also need to ensure that both the backend system and its inherent persistent storage[5] can respond effectively to an increase in load.

The most common problem in terms of backend systems consists of having a database server that copes well with a few front-end servers, only to fail miserably when the number of front-end machines is increased. Given this, the issue is simple: either the database endpoint is so powerful that it can directly respond to the overwhelming amount of requests being sent by front-servers without dropping its performance, or the database system becomes the solution's bottleneck. Often, and regardless of how expertly database systems are fine-tuned[6], there is always a limit to what this component will be able to accomplish. Thus, to solve this problem, one usually needs to look into the patterns of data that are flowing in and out of the database system. Naturally, the sooner this is performed within the design phase, the easier it will be.

---

[1] And a corresponding increase in load.

[2] All of which will process a small subset of the total existing load.

[3] As long as the inherent solution does not impose some sort of machine affinity, by using local storage and other locally-dependent resources.

[4] As defined in item **19 Shoot for the sky: leverage cloud-based services to provision temporary environments**.

[5] And, eventually, an existing middle-tier that mostly serves as a business layer container.

[6] And manage to use all of their inherent power stemming from internal caching, internal load-distribution, internal threading, *etc.*.

In-memory distributed caching systems, which are widely available these days[1], are a great solution in order to ensure having a set of load-balanced front-end servers that use a middle-tier cache in a coherent and redundant way. In turn, this reduces the load on database systems (and other back-end systems), allowing them to respond effectively to operations requiring true transaction-persisted semantics.

Transaction-persisted semantics is, actually, nothing more than a fancy way of defining a set of operations that, according to their intrinsic features, must be handled by a solution within certain specific constraints. One such example is that of as a database system that guarantees features like atomicity, consistency, isolation and durability.

Interestingly, the operations that expose such requirements are usually a very small subset of the total work handled by database systems. As such, the bottom line is quite simple: most systems will only need that which is considered to be typical database transaction behavior when performing small subsets of operations that represent business actions responsible for changing a given part of the overall business state.

Assuming the context of an online store[2], operations that need the previously discussed transaction semantics are actions such as the addition of an item to a shopping cart or, alternatively, the submission of a purchase order, as we definitely do not want to risk losing any details of such operations[3]. From a business viewpoint, these actions are so critical that no side effects that can stem from non-transactional operations are tolerable.

However, these actions are just a small part of the system. There are many more operations that, in fact, constitute the majority of the requests being processed by the system, which can actually endure the environment provided by a non-transactional component. Every now and then, these non-transactional components may end up either presenting data that is not up to date or even lose a portion of data that reflects some sort of input to the system, though not critical to the system's overall behavior.

Within this same context of online shopping, consider actions such as retrieving data from the product catalog or registering user feedback on purchased products. These are perfect examples of actions where we can definitely live without transaction semantics. Although no online store would like to lose a piece of user feedback, its exceptional occurrence does not undermine the solution as a whole. Similarly, would it be problematic if, exceptionally, the store presented product catalog data missing some items? Although there are many scenarios where it would be

---

[1] From many vendors and using all types of technologies.
[2] Regardless of the products being sold.
[3] Nor do we want the user to be misinformed as to the outcome of these operations.

harmful to present wrong data[1], this is not what we are discussing. Instead, we are trying to focus on scenarios such as not returning all possible items in a product catalog search as a result of a stale cache[2].

Consequently, it all boils down to the existence of many scenarios where we can effectively use middle-tier caching without supporting transaction semantics[3] and here are a few guidelines that should be followed:

1. **Ensure you are adequately familiarized with the cache consistency policy and, thus, code accordingly.**

   Not all distributed in-memory caching systems work the same way. Some will guarantee hard consistency that assures clients being immediately presented with up-to-date views of changes whenever one alters the cached data. Alternatively, other cache systems are eventually consistent, meaning that there are cases[4] in which data in the cache is changed in some way, with some cache clients still being presented with the previous view, while others already have access to the more recent image. Usually, these situations occur in extremely reduced time gaps, which prevent them from being a common occurrence. Nevertheless, they still require being highly familiarized with the respective policy and, thus, code in accordance (which, depending on the specific situation one is handling, may eventually require a lot or not that much!).

2. **The cache cannot be a new bottleneck.**

   Going back to the online store scenario, loading a product catalog from a database server into the cache and having front-end servers consume data from the cache, is a perfect example of freeing up resources in the database system. As catalog data does not change that often, using a distributed cache would shift the load and data flow from front-end to database servers, to front-end to cache servers.

   However, after having moved the load from database servers to cache servers, one needs to ensure that an existing problem hasn't simply been replaced with a new one. In reality, unless one is placing the cache in the database servers[5], this could hardly happen. Naturally, setting up the cache in the database server is clearly a questionable option and, as such, the common trend usually comes down to two other scenarios: having

---

[1] Such as pricing.
[2] Though the ones presented are correct.
[3] As long as these in-memory distributed caching solutions are used within limits and to support certain crucial features.
[4] Depending on internal synchronization features.
[5] And, even then, it is quite variable, since processing cache requests may actually consume both less resources and, especially, less IO, than when using a pure database server.

cache servers either set up in front-end servers or installed on a complete distinct set of servers.

Having cache servers installed in the front-end servers might save money through server consolidation and, more importantly, might increase the speed of executing a single request when the data that needs to be extracted from the cache in order to process the request is accessible locally[1]. Despite this, placing the cache in the front-end servers raises a lot of other issues, such as:

- Securing data on front-end servers,
- Forcing an increase in the number of front-end servers, as each server will need to process fewer requests in order to maintain overall performance[2].

Furthermore, and for this strategy to be of any useful purpose, one actually needs to ensure that the entire cache is replicated in all front-end servers, given that the whole purpose of sharing a physical machine for these two roles is to ensure that no machine-to-machine calls are required so as to access the cache. This requirement alone generates two additional issues:

- There will be added load on the system, as all cache items must be replicated to all front-end servers,
- Each front-end server will, potentially, have a lot of data in cache that ends up never being used.

On top of this, not all distributed cache systems allow for the replication of all cached data throughout all cache servers.

Given this, it is fairly common to conclude that the best path is to have a set of autonomous cache servers, while ensuring that all items may have redundancy if so required[3] and, additionally, managing the optional implementation of a local cache copy on the front-end servers in order to speed up access to previously retrieved data.

Within this scenario, all front-end servers would request data from a set of dedicated cache servers and the cache system itself will manage which of the cache servers it will access. Given that the cache is totally in-memory storage, there is no IO from a persistent storage and the only real point of delay consists of the network traffic circulating requests and responses between front-end and cache servers. As long as these servers have a great connecting backbone between them[4], one is assured of being off to a good solution.

---

[1] Thus preventing network-based IO.
[2] As it needs to allocate adequate resources for the cache.
[3] More on this later.
[4] Which ensures that no unduly latency is added through network operations.

3. **The cache may need to be redundant.**

Most in-memory distributed cache systems allow for the optional activation of a redundancy feature that has the cache creating multiple or, at least, secondary copies of added items, in order to ensure that the system is still able to respond appropriately[1] when a cache server becomes unable to respond to search requests.

This redundant feature may or may not be critical, as it really depends on the operating context. On some systems, the price to pay for a cache miss[2] due to the temporary unavailability of a cache server is an affordable cost that, usually, simply results in a slightly lower performance in execution, due to the need to look up the required data in a persisted component, which, subsequently, will result in adding the newly retrieved item to the cache[3].

However, on some systems, this performance cost may be just too high. Hence, it starts being mandatory to have redundancy at the cache layer itself. In these scenarios, a common strategy consists of having either secondary copies or replicated copies. In distributed cache systems that implement a secondary copy strategy, the cache will be responsible for creating one redundant copy of each item while also being responsible for the redirection of requests whenever a primary lookup fails[4]. When a primary lookup fails, the distributed cache should, apart from fetching the item from an alternative server, also promote the secondary copy to primary status. Naturally, this task should be complemented with the creation of a new secondary item.

This specific context requires being aware of the coherency policy when either adding or updating secondary items. More specifically, one needs to know whether the distributed cache system will either create/update the secondary copy in a synchronous and coherent way or, alternatively, if it will choose to implement an asynchronous replication algorithm in order to reduce the execution time of each request that adds or updates data in the cache. Answering this question is yet just another circumstance where one needs to apply one's knowledge regarding code conformance with the cache coherence policy.

In an alternative architecture, some distributed cache systems will simply replicate all items to all cache servers. In this case, as long as one has more than one cache server up and running, redundancy will be attained. This kind of strategy is less common for the following reasons:

---

[1] Using the previously stored information by looking up the item on an alternative server.
[2] Which is merely an attempt to look up an item in cache which is not present within it.
[3] To serve future requests.
[4] In a transparent way for the client component.

- First of all, it will consume greater resources in both memory and replication operations[1],
- Secondly, it provides virtually no added value on top of what a primary/secondary strategy delivers[2] and quite honestly, such a scenario goes against a distributed cache model.

4. **Should we organize and partition the cache?**

Using the in-memory cache without a clear policy that defines how the items are divided is pretty much the same as using a database, with only one table, to host all data. Partitioning the cache will allow you to create autonomous sections which may be subjected to a series of distinct administrative features, like:

- Security,
- Server distribution,
- Redundancy policy.

Additionally, a good partitioning policy, which is matched by an equally good server to partition allocation, may promote better lookup performance when the cached data increases in volume. The rationale behind this is quite simple: by distributing the partitions that are created, one can distribute the load generated by lookup tasks, as long as a balanced way of distributing the partitions amongst the existing servers is created so as to reflect an evenly distributed search load. This is pretty much the same reasoning that you will find behind the distribution of data amongst different database servers so as to spread searches and search load amongst them.

Apart from performance, partitioning also allows for the management of security features at a higher level[3], which will simplify administrative tasks as well as reduce execution complexity[4]. Similarly to the structure of typical file system, this is exactly the same as specifying permissions at folder level, instead of doing it at file level.

However, the real question is this: **does partitioning hinder the cache in any way?** Should each partition be bound to a single cache server, then the answer will very likely be a positive one[5]. In such cases, partitioning goes against distribution and scalability. Consequently, it should be avoided, despite the benefits initially described.

---

[1] Which will be critical should the replication be executed synchronously with any add or update requests.
[2] As long as secondary copies are promoted to primary ones and new secondary copies are created once a primary lookup error occurs.
[3] Higher than using a cached item as the atomic element to which such features are applied.
[4] Which benefits performance.
[5] Like what occurs in some systems.

5. **Know how you search.**

   A distributed in-memory cache is a key component in order to ensure performance and scalability. However, it will only be as effective as the effectiveness of its intrinsic searching mechanisms. As such, it is imperative to be aware of all the different options one might have to search the cache during a lookup operation. Some systems will allow for the search to be made using single item keys, while others will also support the use of data tags that are attached to the items[1] and, ultimately, this can allow for the search to have a broader range, instead of merely relying on single item identifiers. Some systems will also allow one to, not only create a content-based index, but also query the cache using such pre-created index that speeds up the search operation[2].

   Regardless of which choices one is given by the distributed cache, it is crucial to be aware of them from an early design phase, since:

   - In cases where it happens to be possible to limit searches to specific partition boundaries, then partitions will need to be defined by considering the type of searches one will perform.

   - In cases where searches can be executed by using tags[3], the process of inserting or updating cache items (including the established tag values) is critical in order to ensure an effective search process[4].

   - In cases where searches can be optimized through usage of indexes, their definition must also match the search criteria used by the vast majority of the lookups[5].

   - In cases where searches can be limited to a partition or group of partitions[6], the partitioning criteria must also take into account the most prevalent type of searches within the system.

6. **Decide which servers will host the cache and how the replication is handled.**

   Defining the distributed cache architecture is as critical as defining a database architecture and, the most important decision is, by far, defining which servers will host the distributed cache[7].

---

[1] When they are stored within the cache.
[2] Just like indexes speed up search tasks in database solutions.
[3] Tags are nothing more than extra metadata items that are used to characterize an item stored within the cache.
[4] Tags must be broad enough to group together the items we, not only want, but also expect as a result of a specific search, though not so broad that a search will return far more data than what we need.
[5] Just as in a regular relational database.
[6] Avoiding a complete cache transversal.
[7] Or, in other words, which servers will be cache servers – also called cache nodes within some solutions.

As discussed earlier, one of the best strategies for enterprise capable systems is to have cache servers as true middle-tier machines. This means they will not be the front-end servers[1] neither the backend systems[2].

Also as previously discussed, in scenarios that require redundancy, this middle tier layer should, at the very least, have two servers to support replication or a secondary-copy strategy. Interestingly, when dealing with secondary-copy strategies, most solutions will promote the usage of a minimum of three servers, so as to enable an automatic and immediate promotion of secondary copies to primary ones, as well as the subsequent creation of new secondary copies whenever the server that hosts the primary copies fails.

7. **Know if you can use local cache.**

Using local cache at the front-end layer can speed up search times by forgoing the need to perform any sort of remote calls[3]. If, on one hand, very little doubts can be cast on the performance increase that results from executing a local search[4], maintaining a local copy also has some downsides, with one of them being the impact on cache coherence and replication. Again, if the cache system uses synchronous replication to update local copies[5], the overall performance of insert and update operations will be worse given the need to update a whole set of different servers. On the other hand, should replication be handled asynchronously, cache coherence problems may appear over the course of updating some views, while others are still waiting for this update. Thus, this will create the possibility of reading distinct values for the same item from different local copies on distinct servers.

Consequently, knowing both whether the system supports local cache as well as if it should be used, also constitutes a design decision that must be reached early on and this decision will be strongly dependent on:

- The data that is written to the cache,
- Its inherent tolerance for potential incoherencies,
- The ability to pay an extra cost in replication operations when inserting or updating items in the cache.

---

[1] Which are the endpoint to receive incoming requests.
[2] Which, typically, hosts the database system.
[3] In this case, between front-end servers and middle-tier servers that host the distributed cache.
[4] Versus a remote search.
[5] And there might be one local copy for each front-end server.

Item recap:

This item's fundamental guidelines can be succinctly systematized as follows:

- ✓ Ensure that your architecture is designed so as to deliver high performance while also being highly scalable. Using in-memory distributed cache is a great step towards such goals.
- ✓ Ensure that you know the cache coherence policy, given that you need to create your code accordingly.
- ✓ Ensure that your cache can deliver scalability while not being a bottleneck.
- ✓ In-memory distributed cache systems can also deliver redundancy by supporting secondary or multiple copies of cached items. In order to support this, understand how replication is performed, as it may impact coherence and performance.
- ✓ Consider the benefits of organizing and partitioning the cache, but do ensure that it will not hinder the distribution and scalability model.
- ✓ Understand how to search the cache and the impact it has on both the cache distribution and partitioning.
- ✓ Understand the benefits and drawbacks of having local copies of the cache.
- ✓ Though caching is great, beware of features that require persisted-transactional semantics. These key operations should not be supported by caching systems.

17. Achieving scalability: scale-out and reduce resource consumption

Delivering a truly scalable architecture is probably one of the most difficult and important items within the list of any software architecture team. If we truly want for software products to be capable of scaling to a virtual infinite point, which enables them to perform adequately regardless of the existing load[1], we need to create designs whereby we deliver two critical guarantees:

- The system has no single point of processing in any layer or component, which would effectively create a bottleneck that could render the remaining parts useless, despite their own scalability,
- Regardless of the implied load, all components can scale with virtually no upper-bound in a way that they maintain a constant performance, or close to that.

Unfortunately, this is easier said than done and, many systems that fire away the scalability banner, end up falling short of delivering it. Here are some of the reasons behind these failures as well as the most common pitfalls that should be avoided:

1. **Do not believe that a powerful monolithic resource will ever deliver true scalability.**
   One of the best examples of this principle is that of confining data to a solid and robust database server, even if it is one that allows for some vertical upgrading[2]. This is hardly a scenario that will break down with a few requests but, should a heavy load come through, one will eventually stop being able to further increase resources on this single server and, consequently, a decrease in request response time will start being noticeable. The interesting thing is that though one can:
   - Be very clever in designing a database and configuring the server,
   - Use distinct storage areas for distinct data sections[3], thereby supporting parallelization of IO on many different data access tasks,
   - Use multiple cache features and settings to minimize slow internal operations and, thus, rely on in-memory buffered data.

   In the end, one will only be delaying the inevitable, as the server's limit will be reached and one will stop being able to cope with the load. Does this mean that we should not take upon ourselves the noble task of optimizing database design and its intrinsic resource usage? No, far from it! This is exactly the kind of procedure that any great

---

[1] Which can be measured in many distinct ways – more on that later on.
[2] By vertical upgrade we mean adding more resources to the existing server, including more CPU power, more memory or even bigger and faster disks.
[3] Tables, indexes, *etc.*.

software product must adopt. However, a pre-defined design that allows one to scale out needs to be added[1], since it can be easily used and put in place should one ever hit the scalability limit imposed by the single server.

A word of caution though: it is crucial to be aware of what some redundant architectures/products deliver, as many will only guarantee what is implied by their name, which entails a redundant architecture guaranteeing that, upon a failure of one set of resources, one will be able to recover and continue executing on a different set of resources. Often, such products do not deliver the ability to compute in parallel on the same data, so as to balance requests and introduce the scale-out feature one is attempting to achieve[2].

A good example is that of database systems through which one can indeed achieve redundancy though not directly scalability. By using these products, one will not be able to perform simultaneous operations on a single database, using several distinct servers to compute queries in parallel. In this sense, clustering only brings about redundancy. This situation is different within other products and versions, where one can have more than a single cluster node executing operations on a single database.

Thus, in a scenario where the chosen technology is only delivering redundancy[3], one needs to support a design that allows for the distribution of data between different databases in a way that the data is partitioned so as to ensure that parallel operations can really be performed on these distributed databases, spread through different servers[4]. This distributed design might imply using different databases and supporting either partitioning schemas or other elements, however the main goal should be to ensure that one can balance simultaneous operations on different servers and, hence, truly achieve scalability.

2. **Do not balance a certain type of operations while failing to do the same for others.**

It is very common to create an architecture where one achieves scalability by virtue of using some sort of IP-based balancing scheme in which one routes incoming IP-based requests to different, though similar, servers and, consequently, effectively distributes the load in a theoretically unbound manner.

Despite this, one of the most common pitfalls is that, sometimes, the solution[5] forces one to use a constrained distribution algorithm that will, in fact, limit the ability to scale out. Here are some common cases:

---

[1] And, by scale out, we mean scale horizontally by adding more servers so as to truly distribute the load.
[2] Which is the true ability of computing queries in parallel.
[3] And not direct scalability on a single database.
[4] Even if one cannot perform all operations on all servers simultaneously.
[5] And its inherent architecture or implementation.

- Using server-dependent persisted information through common session-dependent resources, forces the distribution algorithm to route requests from the same session to the same server, thereby introducing a constraint on the distribution algorithm.

- Routing requests through some existing proxies, thereby creating a situation where many requests appear to have the same origin when, in fact, that is not the case. These situations, in conjunction with the previously referred item of using server-dependent persisted information, will create an exponentiation of the constrained distribution algorithm and its inherent session affinity problem.

Another common pitfall within this category is, apart from supporting a set of IP-based balanced operations, introducing into the system other sets of operations that, given their nature, cannot use the same balancing system. These include both batch-based operations and time-based ones that, for the most part, end up producing heavy, though not constant, load on the system, often executed from a single server without the ability to scale out.

Scaling out is a technique that is not exclusive of either operations that are driven by an end-user and a graphical user interface or of those that arrive through an IP-based request. This means that it should also be used to accommodate and drive any other type of operations executed by a software product.

As such, it must be assured that all operations that can be executed within the system can, in fact, be scaled-out and distributed among several servers. These requirements spur implications that must be carefully analyzed given that, apart from being voided of any server-dependent resource, operations executed by the server must be designed and implemented so as to support parallel execution of both similar tasks and different ones. Furthermore, no one can afford the luxury of assuming to have exclusive access to a resource throughout the whole execution time and, therefore, synchronization primitives that allow temporarily acquisition of that exclusive access must be used while blocking other executing threads, either on the same or on different servers.

Give that this kind of parallelism is both required and complex, and using a high level set of APIs that shields one from the intricacies of synchronizing code is a definitive must in building great software products[1].

---

[1] Many such primitives are, usually, made available by the operating system, although many system-independent libraries will wrap around these system-dependent primitives so as to deliver a platform independent infrastructure.

3. **Asynchronous patterns and data caching.**

   Using asynchronous patterns is a good practice to further promote scalability, since its inherent nature forces software engineers to forgo certain less-than commendable choices that are typical within a complete synchronous execution path[1].

   Certain patterns, like lazy-writing, read-ahead and data-caching, will contribute to a scalable system. Though this does not occur by directly enabling a scale-out strategy, it does so by reducing the resource consumption and incrementing throughput on a heavy loaded system.

   Lazy-writing[2] allows for the delegation of the execution of IO to a background thread, when eventual failures on this asynchronous completion are not deemed prohibitive. This allows the main execution thread to move along with its chores, eventually wrapping up the operation in hands and, consequently, allowing the slow IO part to be accomplished latter on, when resources allow.

   Read-ahead[3] allows one to benefit from the fact that, within an IO operation, the vast majority of its execution time is actually spent moving the reading device to its appropriate place, while the actual reading action represents a reduced percentage of the total time spent in completing the operation. By investing in a read-ahead technique[4], one will read more disk sectors than what is strictly required, thus caching the extra data that can be used at a later stage without the need for a second IO task[5]. Again, this can deliver a great reduction in resource consumption and, therefore, propel scalability.

   Data-caching allows one to store in memory all sorts of data, from static data that rarely changes, to pieces of information that result from the execution of a specific computing task. By leveraging such a cache, the resources consumed to perform many tasks can be reduced, namely by forgoing their execution and, thus, jumping directly to re-acquiring their result, which also propels scalability.

4. **Use the most efficient algorithms and frameworks on the most critical computing tasks.**

   Not all computing tasks are equally demanding, and not all place the same strain on systems' resources. To enable great scalability we need, not only to be able to distribute load through several distinct servers, but also to reduce any resource consumption to the absolute minimum.

---

[1] Such as long blocking operations, locking access to resources throughout a vast part of the execution path or failing to attempt to optimize tasks by executing in parallel that which can be done so.
[2] As defined in item **9 Maximizing efficiency**.
[3] As defined in item **9 Maximizing efficiency**.
[4] Sometimes this may actually be left entirely to the operating system.
[5] As defined in item **9 Maximizing efficiency**.

Though this does not imply that we should all go back to coding using low level languages, it does mean that one should identify which set of operations within one's software product will consume the greatest percentage of resources. As always, there will be some sort of analogy with Pareto's 80/20 principle, whereby 80 percent of the resources are actually consumed by 20 percent of the operations.

By identifying these 20 percent of critical operations[1] and optimizing them, initially by choosing the most optimized algorithm and, afterwards[2], by using a potentially different framework than the one originally selected, we can easily streamline our solution. Regardless of which exact actions are taken, reducing the resources required to execute these operations will promote scalability.

A classic example is that of using the fastest and less CPU-hungry algorithms in search operations[3]. Any algorithm that needs to identify a part of a collection of items to which a given operation is then applied can be regarded as a search operation and, sometimes, simple handwritten loops that transverse a collection of items so as to single out a subset that must be subjected to a certain procedure, are far from an optimal solution. Carefully crafted algorithms as well as properly tailored collections can spear great gains in performance and, thus, drastically reduce the consumption of existing resources.

Item recap:

This item's fundamental guidelines can be succinctly systematized as follows:

- ✓ To truly achieve scalability you need to be able to distribute load through servers at all layers, thus avoiding having parts of your architecture that simply cannot scale out.
- ✓ In many solutions, only a subset of the processing flows is actually balanced across servers. Analyze the impact of batch-based processes and other non IP-based requests so as to carefully consider how to effectively balance them.
- ✓ Apart from distributing load through servers, consider whether you need to distribute data as well, such as through distinct database instances and servers.
- ✓ Using asynchronous algorithms, session-less contexts and specialized patterns, such as lazy-writers, read-ahead and data caching, can be crucial to scalability.
- ✓ Review algorithms in order to ensure that the most critical areas of your codebase are truly implemented using the best and most optimized available options.

---

[1] Which are the ones that really put a dent into one's resources.
[2] Should the gains justify the added cost.
[3] With search operations being seen in a very broad sense.

18. Prototype everything

When setting out to create either new software products or new versions of existing products, it is important to carefully consider prototyping. Some might see prototyping as a waste of money, given that it is something which is usually built only to be thrown away without actually being used within a professional setting. Nevertheless, the reality is that the insight gained by developing a prototype, and particularly a prototype that spans over the whole breadth[1] of one's solution, is absolutely enormous.

Building a prototype allows for the foundation of the architecture being designed to be validated, as well as for the compatibility of the chosen technologies to be verified. Additionally, one will also get a first-hand view of the problems that lay ahead, including the areas needing re-thinking, given that the prototype may well uncover many such issues.

Furthermore, one may subject the prototype to some very early review and feedback, with the intent of acquiring a first round of criticism that can successfully fuel future development cycles.

Overall, this means that the real issue boils down to how the prototype should be built and what it should include and, therefore, here are some interesting guidelines regarding these subjects:

1. **Use the exact same technologies that you have chosen for the product's development.**
   The whole purpose of the prototype is to get a first view of how things will work in the future, so as to diagnose, at an extremely early stage[2], what exactly needs changing. Therefore, it is really important that the prototype is based on the exact same technologies that are to be used in the final product[3].

   Without this adherence to the exact same environment that one will be dealing with in the future, there is a high risk of failing to detect issues that only exist within specific technologies[4], which will bring about prototype related results that will be far from what is desirable.

   Following this policy also ensures that one's engineers have first contact with all the tools they will be using in the future, which is quite relevant in building their confidence and understanding of how everything works. This will be vital to ensure that best practices are adequately followed and understood, which, ultimately, may prove to be a vital step in guaranteeing their broad and successful adoption.

---

[1] Or, at least, a significant part of it.

[2] Where changes are possible at a reduced cost.

[3] And, preferably, at all levels, including: programming languages and integrated development environments, build technology, source control products, *etc.*

[4] Or specific versions of specific technologies.

2. **Be especially focused on new technologies and distinctive business features.**

   Beyond what was said in the previous item, it is critical to focus on specific technologies that are either new or in which one's team showcases a noticeable lack of expert knowledge[1]. Prototyping whichever components rely on these lesser known technologies is vital so as to ensure that one does not run towards an abyss when choosing to use certain technologies, given that, in the end, they may either not serve one's objectives or, alternatively, might even introduce such limitations and problems that one is better off just staying clear of them and adopting other solutions.

   There is no doubt that all software products will encompass some grey areas that will require practical testing, given that theoretical reasoning alone will not suffice. By prototyping the components where the underlying technology is not your *forte*, you will be almost guaranteed to intelligently uncover critical issues that need further clarification before getting too far into the development cycle.

   Plus, prototyping should be targeted at studying those few features that are so distinctive that they effectively tell a product apart from its competition. Despite the solid ideas behind them, one may occasionally need to actually study these innovations at work in order to fully comprehend their implications, how they are used and, thus, effectively assess the true business value they will render for clients. This type of empirical knowledge is critical in order to find the right course, which may lead one to either reinforce the initially defined path or adjust it through corrective strategies that successfully act on the negative aspects that were diagnosed.

3. **Implement as many support processes as possible.**

   Although the prototype will focus on creating a crude version of the product that is to be built, focusing a bit of one's available resources[2] on supporting processes, can also prove to be quite valuable. Support processes have enough complexity and importance so as to justify their inclusion in the prototype and, doing so, will bring about a complete overview of all the aspects concerning the development environment. Aspects such as the building process or the installation procedures need to be sketched out as soon as possible, so as to ensure they can be successfully integrated with all the remaining parts of this complex puzzle, while still delivering the added value that is expected of them.

   By investing in these early versions of the above mentioned support processes one will also allow the whole team to get a clear view of how they will be working in future. Consequently, this will enable them to discuss these issues based on first-hand practical experience and, therefore, generate better ideas regarding needed improvements.

---

[1] As defined in item **21 Observe the 10.000 hour principle: be a specialist in the technology you are using**.
[2] Time and manpower.

4. **Include all components in validating boundaries, defined interfaces and underlying communication strategies.**

   Moving deeper into lower level elements showcases that all layered or distributed architectures are dependent on:

   - Some underlying communication protocols,
   - Well defined interfaces that support integration of distinct components.

   Although many of these protocols are fairly mature and, currently, even straight forward to define, it is still quite useful to create mock up versions of every component present within one's architecture. Doing so will ensure that one can specifically test how well information will flow from one element to the next and, thus, diagnose any lingering negative impacts that might exist.

   Stress loading these communication routes is also quite important as, historically, they present potential bottlenecks that can lead to severe problems in production environments. Therefore, a lot can be gained from simulating complete data flows from end to end, even if little more is done other than flowing the stream from internal endpoint to the next one, until the whole circuit is complete. Although no real business logic is executed, the internal hops and routes[1] are still tested.

5. **Implement only a feature of each type.**

   Since it is unfeasible to implement, within a prototype, the whole set of features that comprises one's solution[2], the focus must be on identifying all the different types of features together with the traits that characterize each one. Once this short list of items has been created, one's efforts can be directed towards implementing each one by creating a representative sample of the full breadth of features that the product will encompass in the future.

   Once this is done, and as long as the initial analysis meant to produce the aggregated groups is solid and really conveys the proper sampling, one can be quite confident of having exposed any major issues that may derive from implementing all product features.

6. **Do not implement any optimization techniques that have been proven over time.**

   Prototyping time should not be invested in implementing optimization techniques that have been proven over the years. Things like caching or read-ahead algorithms have undisputed advantages that do not need to be tested. Therefore, one can simply assume

---

[1] Which, quite often, can hurt one's solution, despite any other problematic things that may stem from the business logic itself.

[2] And, even if it were feasible, it would be pretty useless.

that any experienced and competent team will be able to implement them by relying on past knowledge and experience.

Despite this, if one is going to implement either other innovative optimizations or untested variations of old and proven techniques, do include them within the prototype, given that any innovation needs thorough testing before being suitable and mature for a production environment. Therefore, a lot can be gained by testing them as early as possible through a prototype, especially considering that it will be quite inexpensive and non-disruptive to select an alternative path, should it be concluded that they are not delivering the exact added value that was to be expected.

7. **Review the prototype and determine where the main engineering problems are.**

   After implementing the prototype, it is crucial to have an open mind in order to analyze whichever results come about. Funny enough, I have witnessed more than a few examples where the rightful questioning of ideas and principles brought about by the prototype collided with the development team in such a way that a negative aura surged around the prototype itself. Hence, it is imperative to be sure that the team understands that they are far better off feeling the harsh bite of failure on a prototype than at a later stage upon presenting the public version of the product to the market.

   As it is commonly said, it is not about the number of times one falls but rather about how many times one gets back up. Therefore, the key resides in learning that it is from failure that triumph will come about, as one learns what not to do, where not to go and how not to implement! To **fail** simply means that one has gone through the first attempt in learning.

8. **Prototype all areas required to assess security boundaries and transitions.**

   When using multiple security contexts within the product's processing flows, namely due to shifting the execution context between different servers or different processes within these servers, one needs to:

   - Carefully prototype these flows,
   - Ensure that a flow which adequately replicates all processing points is simulated.

   This will validate that no security context transitions that occur impose any critical limitations on the system, thereby preventing their expected usage. Failure to observe these special conditions will, usually, drive one towards late adjustments within the security context, which invariably leads to either less restrictive policies or a more privileged account being used[1]. However, such last minute changes are, quite often, opposite to the careful and planned approach that is needed regarding security

---

[1] As quick fixes to eliminate any detected problems.

boundaries. Consequently, they are a source of vulnerabilities that can be exploited over time. Furthermore, almost all quick fixes end up being more than a mere transitory adjustment, in the sense that they seem to perpetuate over time and, thus, generating an attack surface that is out there just waiting to be taken.

9. **Prototype all areas that are key to simulate load testing.**

Some areas of the software product are crucial in order to achieve the desired performance level, while others will play a far less critical role. This latter circumstance mostly occurs because they either do not reflect a common operation[1] or reflect an operation that follows some sort of asynchronous pattern where a certain inefficacy can be tolerated.

Regardless of the scenario, all operations deemed to have a high susceptibility of displaying performance issues that may derive in a bottleneck should be prototyped. Admittedly, it is not easy to determine which operations will form such a group but, common examples include:

- Validation of security permissions[2],
- Intensive IO operations,
- Complex mathematical computations,
- Repetitive tasks that must always be performed within the processing flow[3].

10. **Prototype all areas that are public boundaries.**

The most critical area to prototype is very likely to be the public boundary that the product exposes, given that this frontier will determine how other systems interact with each specific solution, thus, ensuring a solid boundary that exposes all the essential and required features and nothing else. This means that throwing in more than what is strictly necessary should never be attempted, given that the pubic boundary will constitute a huge constraint that we will be imposing on ourselves. Plus, once it is published it will be almost impossible to change[4]. Additionally, should one decide that imposing some heavy changes will be absolutely required, it is very likely that you will then be burdened with[5] supporting more than one set of boundary features in order to deliver, at least, some level of backward compatibility. This will introduce very high costs

---

[1] Thereby being able to sustain less than optimal performing code.
[2] Especially if these permissions are configured at a low level of granularity.
[3] Regardless of the request being executed.
[4] Unless one desires to have a product which is labeled as one of those software solutions that breaks compatibility every time an upgrade is executed.
[5] At least for a significant period of time.

for both development and maintenance teams and, in the end, will be a difficult and costly problem to manage.

Therefore, the product's public frontier must be defined after careful thought and, preferably, after prototyping, so as to ensure having a real example of all the ramifications generated by the consumption of this public boundary.

11. **Incorporate any changes that stem from the usage of the prototype and adjust your development plan accordingly.**

Finally, and following suit with the previous items, once all issues detected in the prototype have been reviewed, one needs to carefully[1] decide about alternative routes.

As such, the main goal should consist of reengineering whatever needs changing and, if possible, cycling again through the prototype until attaining a final version, with which, one feels comfortable with the acquired results.

Considering that the number of cycles may not be limited to one or two iterations, one may consider moving in parallel with product development. Essentially, after a few rounds, one will have amassed enough knowledge to determine which product areas are less likely to require any change in the future and, therefore, it will be possible to move along with their development while rooting out any remaining issues using new prototype versions[2].

---

[1] Meaning, without jumping into quick and untested solutions.
[2] Whose changes are limited to the specific areas not yet included within the product development cycles.

Item recap:

This item's fundamental guidelines can be succinctly systematized as follows:

- ✓ Prototype as much as you can in order to test all chosen technologies.
- ✓ Include support processes within your prototype so as to ensure that the team becomes familiarized with the specific working protocols that are to be followed.
- ✓ Focus on new technologies or technologies that your team has less experience with.
- ✓ Include all components defined in the architecture, so as to ensure that complete processing flows as well as all underlying communication protocols are tested. Use mock versions of components that implement the established interfaces.
- ✓ Attempt to implement one feature of each type within the prototype. Group similar features before deciding what to include in the prototype.
- ✓ Do not spend time on already proven optimization techniques. Focus on testing new things, including new business features, in order to understand their real added value.
- ✓ Be very careful about prototyping the public boundary of your product given that, once it is published, it will be very difficult and costly to change.
- ✓ Prototype all elements required for a thorough performance evaluation.
- ✓ Prototype all elements required so as to ensure that you can evaluate all occurring security context transitions while business flows are being processed. This is vital in order to validate that you will not be forced to make late changes to your security policy which, were it to be the case, would usually lead to an increased exposure as well as a higher probability of attacks and exploitation.
- ✓ Evaluate the prototype. Review and accept the results and, additionally, implement all required changes. If possible, conduct another cycle so as to test the newest changes.

19. Shoot for the sky: leverage cloud-based services to provision temporary environments

How many times have you desperately needed more hardware to either run a batch of tests[1] or shelter other temporary environments, only to find out that there was no way of obtaining the required resources[2]?

I am willing to bet that almost all software development teams have suffered similar constraints, despite the fact that many such situations have, over the last few years, been mitigated by the massive evolution and natural adoption of virtualized environments. By using in-house virtualization, many teams have been able to quickly setup new temporary environments that enable them to gain rapid access to the required context.

These environments are, often, used to harbor testing scenarios that must use particular versions of either operating systems or other supporting software, not used on a daily basis, which leaves little justification to allocate dedicated physical machinery. However, in-house virtualization frequently fails to respond to existing needs, such as when the existing physical platform is unable to stretch beyond a required threshold, which commonly occurs when one needs to sporadically[3] use a massive amount of virtualized machines.

Such a huge requirement of capacity is a natural fit for load testing environments where it can happen that one's needs go well beyond the existing physical capacity. Unfortunately, I have seen too many occurrences where, when confronted with such a situation, development teams have been forced to run limited versions of their load tests by, usually, cutting down on the load itself and extrapolating expected performance[4] from the obtained results[5]. Furthermore, I have also witnessed situations where the scope of the test itself was cut back so as to be made to fit into small windows of opportunity where the physical layer could actually be used without significantly impacting other business areas.

The main problem with these types of solutions is that one doesn't really know whether the extrapolation will hold, meaning that one is limited in the ability to assert if the product will deliver a certain behavior upon a specific load[6] .

---

[1] Though not exclusively load tests.
[2] Mostly due to financial reasons although, occasionally, some operational hurdles also come along.
[3] Which may be a periodic or repetitive limited time frame but, in either case, viewed upon as short considering the broad picture of the overall project's timeframe.
[4] For heavier loads.
[5] For smaller loads.
[6] To which some people respond by doing it just the same, despite the absence of definitive proof.

However, load testing scenarios are not the only viable candidates for temporary environments. There are many situations where new environments must be used in order to test both new and old versions of operating systems, as well as other supportive software. In such cases, and because these needs do occur sparsely, one does not need to have resources permanently dedicated to them. Alternatively, in-house virtualization is usually able to deliver, unless one is dealing with so many simultaneously requests for these temporary environments, that building them would still overrun the existing capacity[1]. Though not that common anymore, certain situations may still occur where in-house virtualization is either simply not available or, at least, beyond one's control, which truly prevents the creation of these temporary environments.

Regardless of whichever scenario one is confronted with, cloud-based services are, undoubtedly, a great and cost-effective solution to harbor these temporary environments. Most cloud-based services offer a very effective financial model for temporary usage, given that, quite often, the costs are directly proportionate to the usage rate[2]. There may be an eventual setup fee but, overall, the financial model is quite good, very much resembling a pay-as-you-use system.

However, the best part is that these offerings are truly elastic and available at one's fingertips. They are elastic given that one can easily allocate between one to hundreds or thousands of machines[3]. Spawning off a new server[4] for which one already has an available image is really a matter of minutes[5], most often accomplished by using an available web portal where each one manages their own individual cloud-based subscription.

Additionally, they are also at the control of one's fingertips, given that one can perform it as previously stated, meaning through a management environment made available by the cloud services provider while not requiring any intervention from other specialized teams[6].

Despite this, the greatest thing consists of being able to use it without constantly going through whichever internal purchasing model one's company imposes, should one manage to get a certain budget allocated to the subscription. Ultimately, this boils down to streamlining one's procurement services.

Despite all these brilliant advantages, a few notes are in order for those who have not delved into the world of cloud-based services:

---

[1] Or, more likely, the existing capacity is simply already stretched to its limit and, therefore, is unable to accommodate any more virtual machines.
[2] Therefore, forgoing any costs whenever you are not using these environments.
[3] As long as it is affordable.
[4] Or a new set of servers.
[5] For some platforms as little as 5 minutes.
[6] Which would, inevitably, delay the process quite substantially.

1. **Understand the cost model.**

   One has to be careful about the concept of usage, given that many cloud-based services view usage as having the machines merely turned on, even if no real work is being executed on them. The reasoning for this model revolves around allocation of physical resources, meaning that, should one's virtual machine be up and running[1], the physical resources to support it have been allocated and, thus, one is charged for them per time unit. Hence, every minute that one's virtual machine is running, even if the logical CPU load is zero, one will be charged a certain fixed cost corresponding to that specific time unit. Thus, temporary environments enable one to save money by using one of two strategies:

   - Rebuilding the machine every time one needs it as well as tearing it apart once it is no longer necessary. This is actually, or was, the only viable option in offerings that did not support persistency of one's virtual disks, therefore forcing one to start up from scratch every time after rebooting the virtual machine.

     Although, at first, this may seem like a bad deal altogether, it is not necessarily so. There will be plenty of times where people need their virtual machines for a limited period of time, after which no relevant state is stored in local virtual machine storage. In turn, this enables one to easily destroy the virtual machine without further ado[2]. Furthermore, quite often[3], one actually wants to start each session from the ground up with a clean environment. In these situations, the prospect of booting a new machine from a predetermined clean image happens to be exactly what the scenario is demanding. These scenarios can be applicable both to a single or a set of machines, which will save no local persistent state and, thus, act just like a typical stateless load-balanced farm.

     Reinforcing the obvious, the key here consists of having to shut down one's virtual machines as soon as one no longer requires them and, therefore, needing to account for an initial lag time when bringing them back up[4].

   - When working with a cloud-based offering that supports persistency of one's virtual disks, it is possible to simply shut down one's virtual machines whenever they are not required and, additionally, bring them back on when they happen to be needed once again[5].

---

[1] Regardless of what processes it is executing and which load it is processing.
[2] By destroying I simply mean shutting it down without transferring any persisted local state to an alternative persistent storage, which might also be cloud-based.
[3] Especially when running automated tests.
[4] As the cloud-based infrastructure will be rebuilding them from your pre-defined image.
[5] Overall, it will be exactly like using a local server, where all persisted local state will be recovered once the virtual machine is back online.

2. **Cost is factored by many variables.**

   Do not assume that once the capacity of one's virtual machine is established[1] it will be possible to get a final pricing model. Most cloud-based services will, actually, take into account other variables, such as:
   - Upload and download traffic,
   - Available bandwidth,
   - External storage that might be accessible beyond the virtual machine's local storage.

   Given this, the total cost[2] of the virtual machines is frequently determined by a combination of factors, meaning that we need to proceed to their sum when putting together the financial analysis regarding the impact of using cloud-based services.

   Regardless of the exact variables impacting the final price, most cloud-based services have fairly accurate calculators that allow one to run several scenarios and, ultimately, project with great accuracy the final cost. In turn, this allows for comparisons between alternative solutions, such as in-house virtualization or other forms of hosting, which are not considered cloud-based.

3. **Some platforms limit the ability to deploy certain images.**

   Before delving into this item let us review the concepts associated with two industry acronyms: IaaS and PaaS.
   - IaaS, which means infrastructure as a service, is used to characterize a cloud-based offering where one is, essentially, paying for physical resources that are to be used as if they were one's own servers sitting within one's own local datacenter. This means that, once the physical resources are made available[3], the operating system has to be installed and the servers have to be patched up, so as to be used as each person sees fit.
   - PaaS, which means platform as a service, is used to characterize a cloud-based offering where one is, essentially, paying for servers that are configured so as to run a specific image[4] and, consequently, one is offered both the infrastructure[5] and the basic management layer and operating system[6].

---

[1] Usually defined in terms of virtual CPUs, memory and local storage.
[2] As low as it might be.
[3] In the cloud.
[4] Possibly selected from a list of available images.
[5] Which translates to the inherent physical resources along with the virtualization layer.
[6] Which justifies the usage of the term "platform".

From this initial introduction, and despite being somewhat of an oversimplification that mostly looks to convey the essential differences between these two types of offerings, we can now jump into the limitations that are imposed on both scenarios.

Just as everyone has their own limits, so do cloud-based services. Therefore, even when using an offering that is exclusively allocating physical resources to the user, there may be restrictions regarding the types of images that can be deployed. By mentioning images I am naturally referring to operating systems and other foundational software. Plus, beware that, within some offerings, where you are offered a platform instead of physical resources, you one may actually be very limited as to the available choices of images. Thus, in some scenarios, one may be either restricted to certain base images supplied by the cloud-service provider[1] or allowed to use one's own custom made image while perhaps being restricted to a predetermined list of supported operating systems.

4. **Some platforms may limit the control you have over these virtual machines as well as the visibility to and from the outside world.**

There are many scenarios where some limitations do exist regarding both the direct control over these virtual machines as well as the accessibility to and from the outside world. Most limitations that used to exist within these areas have been considerably reduced over the last few years but, still, it is fundamental to keep in mind that the openness one has to the outside world may actually be restricted. There will be situations where one may be unable to allow external access to one's own virtual server, exactly as it would occur in an in-house scenario. Thus, some applications as well as a few enterprise integrations may need tweaking in order to support a different, though probably more restricted, access model.

Carefully evaluate with the cloud-service provider which limitations actually do exist and, therefore, determine whether or not they affect the required context.

5. **Not all software is able to run on these environments[2].**

Some existing applications have not been built for the characteristics of the cloud-based offerings, especially if one is using a pure PaaS service without persistency of local virtual storage. In these scenarios, one needs to ensure that applications do not use local virtual storage, otherwise one risks losing the processed workloads once the virtual server is shutdown or rebooted. Furthermore[3], one needs to ensure that these same applications do, in fact, support a scenario based on a completely unattended installation procedure,

---

[1] On top of which one may then install further software in order to create one's own tailor-made environment.

[2] Much like in-house virtualization where some limitations do exist.

[3] When using pure PaaS services without persistency of local virtual storage.

given that the virtual servers need to be built from scratch using a base image[1], on top of which one's solution package is then automatically applied on start up.

For this type of deployment to work correctly, one needs to be capable of creating a complete unattended installation experience. Otherwise, one's virtual environment will not actually be useful until manual intervention is applied to it[2].

Although we are mainly concerned with provisioning temporary environments[3], we still want to ensure that tests do run without any sort of human intervention. This means that the environment on which they run must be built without any manual procedures.

Item recap:

This item's fundamental guidelines can be succinctly systematized as follows:

- ✓ Using cloud-based services can be a great way to leverage the need for temporary resources, such as when you do load-testing.
- ✓ Ensure you understand the cost model behind them, as well as all the variables that must be accounted for.
- ✓ Understand the differences between offerings. IaaS and PaaS are different and imply distinct limitations.
- ✓ Understand when you need your images to be persisted and maintain local state and, alternatively, when you can leverage a stateless, non-persisted local state solution.
- ✓ Understand which images can be deployed and how you need to deploy your solution packages. Beware of unattended installation procedure requirements, especially on PaaS offerings.

---

[1] That, usually, only supplies the operating system and a minimum management layer.
[2] Following any reboot or initial deployment.
[3] Such as for testing purposes.

Section III – Development process

This section will focus on presenting and discussing seven key principles and practices that are fundamental in maintaining a healthy and sustainable development environment. These key elements should help shape organizations, their processes, and how to prioritize certain vital elements.

20.   Nothing works better then test driven development

Thousands of books have been written on how to build and properly test software solutions so as to ensure great software quality as well as the fewest possible bugs. Trends have come and gone and software building processes have changed over the years. All software engineers are bound to have their own personal view on which practices are most effective when testing software solutions and, chances are, that no two engineers will recommend the exact same recipe.

Personally, I find that test driven development is my preferred option and I view it as the topmost measure available so as to craft great software. Plus, I find that the really beauty of it is that one doesn't really need significantly evolved frameworks neither highly complicated processes to abide by. In short, all one needs is to have more time, which, ultimately, means more money. However, let us first clarify what test driven development entails, and, subsequently, we will come to the financial aspects that surround it.

Should one decide to perform test driven development, it consists, essentially, of coding a test function that automatically verifies the contract that is implicitly accepted by another existing function. If one happens to be writing a specific function **F** that accepts a set of inputs and returns a set of outputs[1], the testing function **T** is nothing more than another function that verifies that the function **F** does work as implied by the contract it specifies. This means that, for each possible set of inputs, it produces the expected outputs. This system's beauty is that, in order to do this, one needs to clearly specify the contract implemented by function **F**[2]. This will, by its own, lead to better code quality, given that the developer clearly knows what needs to be implemented. Furthermore, this practice implies that careful thought has been put into the different executing paths and constraints that must bound function **F**.

Afterwards, creating the testing function **T** can, and actually should, be a task executed by a different developer, meaning that functions **F** and **T** will not suffer from any error propagation that stems from proximity, such as having the same developer implement function **F** and misinterpreting some part of the contract, thereby creating a scenario where function **F** is incorrectly implemented while function **T** is equally bound by the same error in a way that it actually fails to detect that function **F** fails to respect the defined contract. Or additionally and, quite frankly, even worse, the developer that wrote function **F** merely copies bits and pieces from it so as to implement function **T,** bringing into function **T** all sorts of errors and mistakes that may exist within function **F**. Thus, by clearly defining the contract for function **F**[3], one will have a

---

[1] Either directly or indirectly, by affecting some sort of existing context state.
[2] Thereby enhancing the specifications and ensuring one has a real deep understanding of what function **F** is as well as what it does.
[3] So that testing function **T** can be implemented.

detailed understanding of what function **F** must perform. Furthermore, by splitting the responsibility of implementing function **F** and function **T,** one will have a double assurance that errors will be flagged, given that it is not very likely that two different engineers working in separate environments will, actually, code the same mistakes in a way that both are wrong and yet the execution of function **T** to exercise function **F** fails to detect any inconsistencies[1].

Test driven development does not necessarily mean that one needs to code the testing function **T** prior to coding the base function **F**. That which must be ensured is having the contract for function **F** being defined before the creation of any of these functions, together with having them being implemented by different engineers. This policy and practice will spur the added benefit of enabling immediate knowledge redundancy by virtue of having two distinct software engineers being deeply familiarized with the contract of function **F**[2]. By itself, this will be a solid step towards solving the common software engineering issue of collective code ownership[3].

As documentation goes, test driven development will also be a step in the right direction. It will enforce the clear documentation of contracts so that functions **F** and **T** can be implemented by different software engineers, thus, generating the production of the detailed documentation that so often fails to exist. Such documentation is critical in order to, sometime in the future, when the software product moves from its initial development phase to its maintenance stage, ensure that one will be able to track root causes, architectural decisions and software dependencies.

A final word of warning on test driven development: testing the implied contract[4] through the negative form[5] must be mandatory. Since the development of function **T** is done without any knowledge of function **F**'s codebase, there really is no way of coding function **T** to hit all code paths within function **F**. Although it is expected that, by executing function **T** with all possible sets of inputs those paths will be hit, test driven development can be further enhanced by using code coverage tools that automatically indicate which code paths weren't hit upon running the test. Ultimately, this knowledge allows for one to proceed in enhancing function **T**'s testing abilities.

Therefore, regarding the financial aspect of the equation, the final conclusion is that test driven development works and, although one increments the time and money spent so as to implement

---

[1] Or, in reverse, executing function **F** by an erratic function **T** would produce results considered to be correct.
[2] And its implied testing function **T**.
[3] Or, at least, avoiding individual code ownership, which means preventing having organizations becoming dependent of certain individuals due to unshared and, usually, undocumented knowledge.
[4] Its inputs and outputs.
[5] Testing the contract by using all types of invalid inputs, given that doing so will force the internal execution of function **F** to go through its intrinsic exception paths.

function **F,** given that one also needs to implement function T^1, one will end up saving money by reducing the number of fixes that function **F** will, ultimately, be subjected to[2]. Even more importantly, one will save a lot in what is usually known as soft savings by delivering a better product and, thus, avoiding the cost that comes with an unhappy client who is constantly hit by a buggy system.

Additionally, we should question ourselves about the overall results upon comparing it with other software assurance techniques. Well, my experience is that no other practice is as effective as test driven development, given that no other practice is really extensively testing the existing software contracts. Most other practices test either the existing GUI or some limited patterns of usage that don't really reflect a vast set of scenarios that will occur in production. Therefore, they will be unable to catch such a high amount of faulty code during early development stages. Plus, test driven development will promote exactly that: immediate testing results as one's solution is being coded, therefore avoiding long return loops from testing phase to development phase while hitting, at a very low granularity, the bricks that actually do build the solution. It is a technique that, like no other, effectively reaches the code's core, which ensures that all atomic pieces are healthy. It is far easier to build a high quality solution if one uses healthy building blocks and, not surprisingly, it is far more difficult to be as successful under opposite conditions. Finally, it is far easier to certify a whole system once its building blocks are bullet proof, rather than trying to attest the quality of the whole system when one doesn't even know how good the underlying structure is.

However, test driven development generates yet another added trump when looking at it from a software assurance perspective: it creates a superb platform in order to establish baselines and, hence, execute regression tests as a product evolves over time. Maintaining high quality and impeccable retro-compatibility is a must-have for any successful product, though far from easy to achieve. Nevertheless, test driven development does create the base platform for it, as it delivers a set of automated tests that can run against the product's codebase so as to test its inherent features. By doing so, one is able to repeatedly execute these tests as new versions are built or fixes are added to existing ones. By executing all available tests pertaining to a specific build against the codebase of a subsequent build, one can indeed ensure that the new codebase is retro-compatible in all aspects covered by those tests. It does not guarantee 100% retro-compatibility because, as we know, the tests themselves will never cover the complete breadth of the product but, nonetheless, it does deliver a degree of assurance that, is not only good, but as high as the percentage of code coverage that is delivered by the tests.

---

[1] And despite having, previously, spent more time on specifying the implied contract for function **F.**
[2] Which is translated into direct or hard savings.

Therefore, the final question is whether test driven development can be applied to GUI-code[1]? The answer is not straight forward but, overall, it tends to lean more often than not to a negative outcome. Most of the times, test driven development is not applied to GUI code. Hence, the development of GUI does not usually follow this technique. Although there are great tools out there that can automate GUI testing by replicating and simulating human interaction with the GUI, this is not usable as a test driven development technique. There are, however, some technologies that have been crafted so as to effectively support as much test-driven development and automated codebase testing as possible and, many of these technologies, end up significantly reducing the size of the GUI layer by using architectural patterns[2]. Consequently, these enable one to use test driven development on a broader codebase while stopping right on the edge of the very reduced and streamlined GUI layer.

Thus, what really happens is that the GUI layer is much thinner than in other technologies or patterns, which allows one to rip the benefits of test driven development in a bigger percentage of the codebase, while still not applying it to the pure GUI code. To close down this gap, one would then use other testing techniques that will effectively handle GUI testing. However, the development of the GUI code would not follow a test-driven pattern where one would create, either before or in parallel[3], the testing rigs and the product code.

Item recap:

This item's fundamental guidelines can be succinctly systematized as follows:

- ✓ Use test driven development to force great specifications and clear definition of contracts.
- ✓ Use test driven development on your core business and structural code. Look for other techniques for GUI code.
- ✓ Privilege methodologies that deliver the thinnest possible GUI layer, so as to reduce the size of code not covered by test driven development.
- ✓ Use code coverage tools in order to determine which code paths are not being hit by test rigs. Look out for exception paths.
- ✓ Have different engineers write the testing code and the corresponding product code.
- ✓ Use test driven development to further enhance your ability to reach either 100% retro-compatibility or something along those lines.

---

[1] I'm assuming that no one is actually questioning whether we can apply it within the remaining codebase.
[2] Such as model, view and controller, or variations of it.
[3] And by using distinct software engineers.

21. Observe the 10.000 hour principle: be a specialist in the technology you are using

Here's a bit of trivia: can good testing procedures deliver, by themselves, a high quality product? Although we might, initially, be inclined to say yes, the reality is that testing alone will not guarantee a high quality software product. Testing can definitely improve the quality of the product by introducing systematic procedures that validate the correctness of known and predictable conditions. However, there will always be areas not covered by tests as well as conditions that are too complex and difficult to predict to be part of the testing platform[1].

Given this, how can high quality be attained? Some methodologies have gone as far as suggesting that high quality products will be achieved by a work pattern where code creation is a bug-free activity. These methodologies suggest that quality assurance procedures are the ones that verify and guarantee bug-free code, but, on the other hand, it is the action of crafting code directly in a bug-free manner that delivers such a result. Although this line of reasoning does seem to be located somewhere between utopia and delusion, it does raise an interesting issue. What factors can contribute to enabling software engineers to create great code[2] from start, without requiring massive amounts of testing so as to validate its correctness? These same methodologies[3] propose several techniques that can get software engineers a step closer to achieving these goals. Regardless of what is in fact defended and recommended by all these methodologies, the reality is that software engineers will only deliver top rate products, as in top rate architectures and a top rate codebase, if they truly master the technologies they are using.

To be a true master of anything in life everyone needs to satisfy at least one of two conditions:

- Being so naturally gifted and talented that, in a very short time, a deep understanding of a specific field is developed,
- Overcoming not being naturally talented, by spending many hours working, studying and learning a specific field of knowledge.

Thus, unless one is a rare natural talent within a specific field[4], one will need to work extremely hard to achieve great knowledge[5].

---

[1] Unless they are added to it after a faulty feature is detected and, consequently, after concluding its root cause analysis and, subsequently, spawning off a specific test harness.
[2] As bug-free as possible.
[3] Usually within the realm of agile development.
[4] Which virtually never happens!
[5] Which, ultimately, is the case for 99.99% of the people when executing 99.99% of all possible tasks.

Given this, the main message to take home is quite simply that, although practice does not assure perfection, it is definitely a step towards it. Consequently, it is crucial to ensure that the technologies being used are the ones one truly masters. The empiric rule of thumb related to this consists of seeing 10.000 hours of experience as the absolute minimum in order to become an expert at anything. However, the pace and rhythm at which technologies emerge and evolve highly limits this need for stability so as to achieve such an elite stage of specialization. By thinking about this carefully, we end up realizing that most software engineers actually:

- Use somewhere between ten to twenty different technologies during a week of work,
- Are slightly familiarized with them all, and very knowledgeable about two or three,
- In a best case scenario, truly master one!

Over the years I have been given the same advice on how to succeed in IT by many different people: know something about everything and everything about something! Although this may in fact be the safest way to secure one's place in the job market, given that it will promote high levels of adaptability, it will not allow one to deliver the highest possible professional expertise[1].

Furthermore, if we think about this for a minute, what makes more business sense than selecting the most skilled person to execute each task? Regardless of how much sense this seems to make, that which is most commonly seen is people being given chores they barely understand while also being required to use tools that they do not really command, which, unfortunately, also occurs within software engineering. How many times have you used a development language of which you only knew the very basic stuff, without having ever delved into its inner workings? I bet more often than you would have liked!

Therefore, the guideline, though difficult to implement, is actually quite simple: one must ensure that the technologies being used to build software products are truly those that the team's software engineers do master!

Unfortunately, for several reasons, this is easier said than done. Many times, one selects the technologies that are, in theory, the best available option in order to execute what is needed, only to realize that part of the software engineering team is already set in place and lacks both knowledge and experience in them[2]. Other times, one tends to adapt to the existing brain power by picking technologies that, despite being far from ideal, are, at least, better understood by the team members.

---

[1] Except in those few opportunities when one is actually working on whatever rates as one's "everything about something".

[2] Albeit, possibly, being superb in other areas.

Lastly, quite frequently, people are somehow led to believe that they can pick any given technology and then turn their existing team members into experts by sending them off to a week-long training in a fancy tech-course which, invariably, includes within its designation attractive marketing words like "bootcamp". Since no single week training program will convert anyone into a master of anything, people would be better off if they were to finally come to grip with the concept that one will only become a master of an art by continuous and relentless practicing over the course of many months, if not years, which is exactly what the 10.000-hour rule implies[1]. Just to ensure that the message does sink in, here is a quick mathematical exercise: even if we were to do the calculations by considering an 80-hour a week workaholic, it would still take 125 weeks[2] to reach the 10.000-hour target!

Thus, it is best to forget about quick training paths altogether! Should one choose a specific set of technologies, it is crucial to ensure that the majority of the software engineers that make up the team have the experience required to really be considered experts in it. Only experts will be able to perform a mostly error-free job and, in this case, create a mostly bug-free codebase.

Creating such an environment, while also using other techniques that further improve one's chances of delivering high quality software products, will generate the highest possible likelihood of building something solid that paves the way for a great software product.

Item recap:

This item's fundamental guidelines can be succinctly systematized as follows:

- ✓ Restrict your product's core technologies to the ones your engineers truly master.
- ✓ Mastering a technology requires many months, if not years, of practice. Ultimately, such skill level is impossible to achieve through mere week-long training programs.
- ✓ Crafting top rate code requires deep knowledge of the technologies being used.
- ✓ Ensure that all engineers use their unique and individual best skills in their daily chores.
- ✓ Beware of new and unproven technologies and do not try to follow every newest hype and fad that comes about.

---

[1] Before truly mastering a technology, or any other skill for that matter, one needs to amass at least 10.000-hours' worth of experience.
[2] Or almost two and a half years.

22. Store and share know-how: create an internal global knowledge depot

One of the worst situations a development team[1] can face consists of having knowledge concentrated on a few team members, as it brings about a dangerous internal imbalance of a professional ecosystem. Just as it is beneficial to have knowledge being spread to the four corners of the globe, professional know-how also needs to be disseminated horizontally across the whole development team. The risks or drawbacks of doing so are extremely low, upon comparison with that which stems from not managing professional teams using such a balanced approach!

There is little to no benefit in having a few selected team members amass a disproportionate amount of knowledge, given that this leaves the remaining majority with either limited access or a shallow understanding of the internal processes and know-how. Such an occurrence limits the ability to really function as team, which requires having a fairly homogeneous internal pace and productivity, thus avoiding having a completely dysfunctional and inefficient organization.

Therefore, we need to ask ourselves what are the exact benefits of spreading the knowledge evenly and which pieces of information are crucial to unveil to the whole team? Here are a few key pointers regarding these topics.

1. **Source code needs collective ownership.**

   At the heart of any development team lays the source code. Nothing is more valuable to software engineers and, therefore, it is obvious why every piece of energy needs to be invested in protecting this valuable asset. However, once we go beyond access permissions, we need to ensure that those who are rightfully authorized to access the source code do in fact understand it and, thus, are able to:
   - Read it,
   - Comprehend it,
   - Change it, should such a need arise.

   Having whole scores of code being the personal treasure of either one or a mere few software engineers is a recipe for a disaster and, furthermore, a huge one!

   What if these developers happen to move elsewhere? What if they are absent, even if only temporarily, and quick action on that specific source code set is needed?

   This is a manager's nightmare and, hence, simply cannot be deemed acceptable. Despite this, it is interesting to note that, though this scenario is becoming increasingly less common amongst big development teams, it seems to proliferate quite abundantly

---

[1] Or a company for that matter.

within small ones! Might this be an irony of fate, or simply bad management? A big team usually implies a wider corporation, greater resources and, therefore, the capacity to reassign both people and funds so as to respond to unexpected events, such as requiring some sort of swat team to go in and figure out the scores of source code needed for a quick emergency intervention. Quite naturally, given that small teams usually reflect smaller corporations in possession of far fewer resources, it is much more difficult and unlikely that such swat teams can be assembled within the required time frame! Hence, it is definitely quite puzzling that those who are subjected to higher risks are also the ones doing less to mitigate the situation!

I guess this also has to do with managerial foresight, given that there are still many industry professionals who, when faced with tight budgets, decide to forgo important activities which are crucial in propelling the widespread understanding of knowledge, including source code.

Such activities[1] may include tasks like code reviews[2], which force those involved to truly understand the code they are reviewing[3]. Should a code review be properly performed, the overall structure of the code will be analyzed, as will all internal algorithms and data structures. Plus, this should be done to a point where, those involved, will have commanding knowledge of both the big picture and the gritty details. This constitutes that which should be regarded as desirable and, hence, the time invested in these activities should never be seen as a cost that one can afford to ax when tightening up the budget!

Additionally, code reviews also propel the original code writers to clean up their act, should there be some less than optimal code paths.

Another very interesting practice that promotes collective code ownership is the simple rotation of engineers between existing modules or components. By letting developers move around the product, it is possible to ensure that they are not exclusively dedicated to a single element. Additionally, they should be allowed to write new pieces of software whenever possible, but while mixing it up with mandatory trips to the bug fixing list, so as to force them to "get their hands dirty with other people's code". This will also force a sequence of similar tasks like those promoted by code reviewing, meaning that engineers' knowledge will improve as a direct consequence of needing to acquire a clear understanding of the code they will be fixing. Ultimately, engineers will move on to a questioning mode that comes about as a direct result of needing to absorb knowledge from those who originally created the specific software component they are assigned to work on.

---

[1] Those that propel widespread knowledge of source code.
[2] As defined in item **3 Coding rules: are we back in elementary school?**
[3] To an extent that they will become as proficient in it as those who wrote it in the first place.

These types of rotations are great to get everyone leveled knowledge-wise regarding all the components of the product, while also avoiding all the drawbacks that stem from a more isolated and less flexible approach.

Finally, given that many different activities can effectively promote the spirit of collective code ownership, the most important thing is to keep this overall goal in mind and adapt one's strategy according to the specific constraints of each professional setting.

2. **Issue tracking tool is mandatory.**

A good issue tracking tool, integrated with a work item distribution module, is a must have for any serious development team. Using it allows team managers to easily allocate work, by assigning work items to team members while resting assured that everyone will be able to identify their pending tasks. Issue tracking is a vital piece of supportive software, almost as important as a compiler. Through issue tracking one can create effective workflows within the team, therefore, easily orchestrating the jobs of different roles such as developers and testers. On top of that, one will be given a suite of reports that instantaneously show:

- Exactly how the team is presently allocated,
- Which tasks are already finished,
- Which tasks are overdue.

Other common reports will provide great insight as to the team's historical behavior, namely by supplying information about:

- Trends and patterns in the appearance of issues[1],
- Time-related information about production of fixes,
- Reappearance of items previously thought to be solved.

These tools usually deliver far more reports than one will ever need to use and, by investing a bit of time analyzing the existing options, one will be able to select the few that deliver the key relevant indicators.

Apart from reporting, one should also use issue tracking tools as an internal knowledge base, making it easy to find information about issues that existed either at specific points in time or with specific builds. Within these tools one should be able to track or link:

- Which build fixed a specific issue,
- Whether any temporary workarounds existed,
- The issue with the corresponding source code change that fixed it.

Furthermore, because many of these tools are integrated with source control tools[2], one can use them in a truly correlated way[1].

---

[1] Ok, shall we just call them bugs?

[2] Many times being, in fact, either a single product or components of a larger suite of products.

Despite the fact that many of these tools do have components to integrate with modern integrated development environments, they always provide a portal-based solution that allows non-software engineers to easily browse and search for information.

Summing up, issue tracking is complex and requires a good tool to:

- Register problems,
- Distribute and control tasks,
- Allow one to review historical information.

Overall, it is a must-have tool that needs to be used transversally throughout the whole team, since it propels the spreading of knowledge!

3. **Requirements and features also need tooling and tracking.**

   For a software development team, new requirements are not all that different from bug fixing, in the sense that they need to be managed in similar way[2], though, quite often, with far less time pressure on them! Requirements should also be managed by a robust tool that allows one to control exactly the same key points that are relevant when managing bugs, meaning that one needs to be able to register requirements as well as assign corresponding tasks to the team members responsible for implementing them. One needs to have a supportive workflow so as to orchestrate both the different roles and steps involved, as well as powerful reports to track work and acquire key indicators that allow for better team management. One also needs to be able to link requirements with specific builds as well as with source code.

   From these main items we can easily conclude that requirements and bugs need very similar treatment and, usually, modern issue tracking tools have been broadened to support work items that are of diverse types and nature. As with bugs, one can also use this depot as a source of knowledge, since these tools will deliver a portal-based front-end that allows any team members to scavenge through information and acquire whichever knowledge is stored!

4. **Products need documentation and, preferably, by build level.**

   No product can be a good one if it lacks proper documentation. We have long moved past the time of having products coming along in a bunch of disks and a set of books that looked like a small encyclopedia. Nowadays, it usually boils down to performing an immediate download and accessing an online documentation portal. Clients will have a far better experience and the environment will be better off as well! However, to get to this level one needs to be sure of having a great documentation system that allows

---

[1] Often even from one's integrated development environment.
[2] Thus, also integrated with a work item distribution module.

everyone to easily search its content and quickly access the required information. Furthermore, one needs to make sure that the product has been thoroughly documented and that existing documentation is not only accurate[1] but also properly written, considering the target audience.

The same documentation cannot be used for all sorts of people and, thus, one needs to understand which target audience will end up using it. Documentation on APIs, used by developers, is necessarily different from marketing flyers. Hence, these variables need, unquestionably, to be added to the equation.

Unfortunately, the automatic documentation frenzy[2] that, a few years ago, was believed by some to be the holy grail of documentation[3], can only go so far in terms of the complete spectrum of documentation and, usually, it does not even go far enough in terms of documenting APIs. Therefore, the harsh reality is that technical writers have to be present within one's team, should one wish for the product to have proper documentation. It must be ensured that they are in the circuit orchestrated by one's issue/requirement tracking tool, given that implementing a new feature or fixing a bug are not merely about source code.

Should one adopt test driven development[4], the test harness must be created, together with the code that implements the new feature or fix for the detected bug. On top of this, one needs to run the new tests against the new codebase and, should the result be successful, the documentation needs to be updated[5]. After completing this step, one can then proceed with all other tasks required to wrap up the opened item.

Finally, do not forget that:

- As one links and relates both issues and requirements with source code and builds, documentation regarding building a level[6] must also be appropriately synchronized,
- One definitely needs to have a portal-based solution that allows everyone to easily search and access the information, thus ensuring that the knowledge is effectively spread.

---

[1] Yes, bad documentation is even worse than no documentation at all!
[2] Generation of documentation by running tools that gather pieces of information from source code.
[3] Thankfully, not by many!
[4] As defined in item **20 Nothing works better then test driven development**.
[5] And here is when one's technical writers need to be in the loop.
[6] Including the corresponding issues and requirements.

Item recap:

This item's fundamental guidelines can be succinctly systematized as follows:

- ✓ Ensure that you have a proper environment that propels knowledge sharing, so as to create a homogeneous team, knowledge wise.
- ✓ Instill practices that promote collective code ownership, such as code reviews.
- ✓ Use a great issue tracking tool to manage the workflow inherent to fixing any existing problem. Ensure that such a tool is integrated with a work distribution module.
- ✓ Treat new requirements or new features similarly by ensuring that you can register them, support the required workflow and integrate it with the work distribution module.
- ✓ Produce great product documentation using technical writers. Ensure that the documentation is suited for the target audience.
- ✓ Promote portal-based access to all these different tools and types of information.

23. Do not leave the build for last: invest in an automated build system from the very first day

Long gone are the days when building a product was a matter of opening a single and simple project by using one's favorite IDE and executing the build command. However, even more time has passed by since the days that saw us happily going about creating simple makefiles that compiled and merged a few source code files into a full blown application.

Nowadays, reality is nothing like this kind of medieval software building scenario I alluded to. Building software products has grown to be much more than just compiling a few source files. Currently, it is almost a science, and one that must take into account many distinct aspects, such as source code compilation, automated execution of testing procedures and preparation of the deployment installer.

The complexity and depth of what is accomplished through a building process is dependent on the scope of one's product. Nevertheless, here are a few guidelines that will be a good fit to almost every scenario:

1. **Define, implement and test the building process from day one.**
   Every time one starts building new software products, it is important to look at the building process as just another component, albeit one with the highest priority[1]. Do not relegate defining and implementing the build process to a low priority level, since this is probably the most important support process that one absolutely needs to have.
   The building process must be implemented from the very first day. Plus, the build process needs to ensure that one can accomplish a complete build without any sort of manual intervention. Quite frequently, this is not that easy to achieve, given that one needs to coordinate a complex process characterized by having a set of specific dependencies where a very specific building order needs to be followed. On top of it, it is very likely that, within an enterprise capable product, one will be building for different target environments and, therefore, commonly using distinct building tools[2].
   Such a complex workflow is, usually, interleaved with check points where one needs to validate specific intermediate results and, possibly, choose different alternate paths[3].
   Thus, one must resist the temptation to postpone this task. Instead, it is crucial to ensure having a build process that is used every day in building the most up-to-date source code, while remembering that the build process is also source code in its own right! This means that one needs to manage the different versions of the build process in the same way as

---

[1] Contrary to what used to be common practice many years ago.
[2] Different compilers, scripts and platforms.
[3] Depending on the active build settings.

managing source code since otherwise, it will be impossible to repeat builds that were executed either at an earlier date or at a specific point in the development timeline.

Using appropriate tools that hide most of the complexity and deliver many of these features from the very beginning is, probably, the best way to go. However, in most scenarios, one will be using a wide range of different tools which require a significant integration effort so as to create that magical fully automated build system that is highly needed.

Therefore, one must truly:

- Allocate resources from day one to this task,
- Ensure proper knowledge of the tools being used,
- Be prepared to perform regular updates to the build process over the course of adding more and more components to the product[1].

2. Build source code and run all available tests.

Compiling source code is, naturally, the most obvious task that will be given to a build process. However, the reality is that a build system is far more complex than just compiling source code. Furthermore, even within the compiling steps, there are a few pitfalls to consider. Let us think about compilation for a moment. Which are the issues that usually emerge? First and foremost, we have dependencies. When establishing dependencies between components that are building to the same platform, we are usually before a simple task of configuring a single compilation unit. But what happens when we need to interleave building tasks that are actually creating binaries for different platforms, using distinct building environments? Usually, this is where the headaches start and where the value of a controlling workflow environment, which can orchestrate the execution of isolated build steps in different build environments, shows its true value. Without it, it is almost impossible to coordinate these disparate compilation steps. Afterwards, we will come to the problem of automatically analyzing the outcome of the compilation steps. Each compiler will output different information that must be understood by the workflow orchestrator, and in some projects, one will need to adjust many compiler settings to build without errors and warnings[2]. Such as option may lead to relaxation of compilation rules, especially if building third party source code[3] which itself was not built under the same stringent requirements that one wishes to enforce.

---

[1] Which, ultimately, will require a more complex building system.
[2] Assuming one does desire a complete warning-free build.
[3] Which occasionally does happen.

Additionally, careful consideration must be given to how settings for different build configurations are to be differentiated, namely debug and release builds[1].

Subsequently, and after processing the compilation results and establishing a clean and successful build, one needs to run the set of automated tests that have been created.

Usually, within this step, one will run functional tests on all existing units, many of which representing regression tests that certify retro-compatibility. In some scenarios, one will run graphical user interface simulated tests and, eventually, a limited version of load and stress tests.

Again, running the tests is the easy part. The main difficulty will consist of having an adequate environment to run the tests against, meaning one that is always clean and fresh for each new build[2]. The best way to solve this is by automating the process of recreating all the dependencies that the different testing features require from scratch and, potentially, using virtualized environments for assistance[3].

Finally, one will also need to ensure that the controlling workflow system can also analyze the test results[4]. Interpreting tests results and deciding when to stop, as well as when to continue and whom to notify once those results start coming in, is all about the magic that the controlling workflow supports. Consequently, this is where one will see a significant part of its added value.

3. **Create the deployment installer and automate the drop off procedure.**

Having built the source code and, thus, having created all the binaries that will comprise the solution, together with running all the tests that certify its quality, one is left with a final step to tackle: the creation of the deployment process that will allow everyone to actually install the product. Often, this installer phase is a project on its own, given that additional source code is likely to be needed[5]. This new source code compiling phase will use a different set of compilers. These are specific to the task of propping either one or multiple installers, depending on the supported platforms and, once again, this will increase the complexity, since one will need to handle yet more distinct environments.

Plus, any source code brings about a set of tests. Thus, one will need to run specific tests to certify the installers, using fresh and clean testing environments[6] to avoid any sort of contamination from a previous run.

---

[1] Although, within many products, one will have to deal with many more flavors of build configurations without actually being restricted to the more academic debug and release scenario.

[2] Remember that, depending on one's policy, one may be running the build process either daily or even more regularly than that.

[3] More on this later.

[4] Even if they come from different platforms.

[5] Albeit, in a different programming language from those used to build the product.

[6] As stated earlier, this is clearly a situation where one should consider virtualization – more on this later.

Ultimately, the main goal will be achieved and the solution will be built without detection of any inconsistencies. Nevertheless, one's task is not yet finished as a build master. Often a few additional final steps are in order, namely managing the drop off procedure and, eventually, setting final touches within the source control system.

Managing the drop off procedure will ensure that all the built binaries are properly sent to whichever file system, web portal or alternative mechanism you have put in place to hold on to the binaries and installers, and to spread them around one's audience[1]. Within this task you will, usually, update the symbol server[2] automatically, so as to deliver a good and productive debugging experience to those faced with the task of either analyzing crash dumps or performing some live debugging when things go sour in production.

Finally, one may need to proceed with the integration with the source control system in order to wrap up any procedures that close off the build activity, namely setting labels or closing up pending work items[3].

4. **Use a clean build environment and consider leveraging virtualization.**

   Every time a build is executed it must be initiated from a clean and fresh environment that:

   - Could not have been corrupted by a previous build[4],
   - Could not have been jeopardized by the previous execution of any sets of tests,
   - Respects the defined baseline building environment, such as delivering the right operating system build and patch level, the correct compiler version, *etc.*.

   Achieving these stringent requirements on physical machines is both costly and time consuming. It is costly because one will need to commit resources to hardware that will not be used during a significant portion of the available time, while being unable to allocate its free quota to any other tasks, as the environment must be unchanged and available as needed. It is time consuming because one will spend more time rebuilding the physical machines after each build process[5].

   As such, one should consider virtualization as a feasible option to both reduce costs and buy time. Through virtualization, one can run several different platforms and environments, which might be required for a multi-platform build, on top of either a single or multiple physical servers. Additionally, one can easily start with a clean and fresh environment by using a saved virtual disk image or, alternatively, by using available

---

[1] Either public or private, depending on what type of build being run.
[2] As defined in item **36 Prepare for the unexpected: setup a proper symbol server**.
[3] To link either bug fixes to specific builds or new features to certain releases.
[4] Either a successful or unsuccessful one.
[5] Regardless of any optimized system that was chosen, including techniques that ghost hard drives.

snapshot technologies that all major virtualization platforms support. Thus, rebuilding the environment really becomes a non-issue[1].

By setting up all the required virtualized machines, one can have as many different build and test platforms as required, relying on very few physical resources, given that performance is not usually an issue. Plus, one can easily ensure having completely standardized and uncorrupted environments, so as to always run the process with little hassle. Finally, and to ensure that one has a repeatable build system[2], one can easily store the virtualized environments and recover them whenever needed[3].

5. **Use continuous integration or periodic builds.**

    Who broke the build? This is one of the most famous expressions hovering over development teams. No one really wants to be the culprit of breaking the build but, beyond this unofficial blame game that is responsible for keeping somewhat rogue software engineers on track[4], there are additional implications to consider.

    Firstly, it usually means that the build process is being managed independently of the development process and, furthermore, developers are not relying on their own private environments for routine builds. This implies that a build process is in place and running regardless of development engineers' actions. Most often, these builds run either based on predefined schedules[5] or, if the build times are short enough, by continuously picking up the latest source code changes[6]. Plus, some systems have fine-tuned these continuous builds so as to enforce a minimum delay between two consecutive builds[7], given that there is usually little to be gained by running builds too close together.

    In most large and complex software projects, where the full build cycle takes hours and not minutes, daily builds usually end up being the norm[8].

    Regardless of how these builds are triggered, the advice is simple: builds should be run often and within an automated and clean environment. It is unadvisable to wait for several weeks in order to pick up a massive amount of changes in source code, to produce a new major build. Running frequent builds, picking up whatever source code

---

[1] One will be discarding the environment that was, somehow, changed by the build process, and not really rebuilding the base one.

[2] So that one can always pick any version of one's source code and test set, and create the previously existing environment, thus delivering the exact same build output.

[3] Either through snapshotting the virtual disks or by using any other alternative that delivers the exact same result.

[4] Or, at least, close to it.

[5] Usually, running at night after most developers have left.

[6] In what is known as continuous integration.

[7] Some tools call it rolling builds.

[8] Given that, by lacking a window of opportunity, any other scenario would actually be impossible.

changes are available and running all existing tests[1], is a good way to ensure all-around quality, since each source code change must be buildable and, therefore, conformant with the existing tests. Even if one fails to test new features by using new tests[2], one will still benefit significantly from running all existing tests that certified the previous build. Any detected problems, which tell off the existence of retro-compatibility issues, can be sent immediately to development teams and, thus, the sooner they are aware of it, the sooner they will fix it. Consequently, the sooner this is accomplished, the cheaper it will be!

Beyond regular builds and automated build processes, one can also analyze ways of validating source code changes[3]. Most source control tools have ways of running either scripts or other procedures which execute specific tests on new source code, so as to ensure that it adheres to certain rules that all developers and source code alike must abide by.

These controlled check-ins[4] can be a significant step forward in avoiding the global build breakdown. Since a full build cycle breakdown can be very costly[5], one should invest in setting up whatever procedures are deemed adequate so as to submit the new code through this sort of triage. This early validation means that non-conformant code will not be accepted into the source control system nor considered usable for the next build[6].

Interestingly, this feature is quite well regarded by the development teams, which are usually quite keen to invest their own free time sprucing it up. Most engineers will rather fail silently without a wide impact, than out in the open, given that the latter tends to turn them into the chat of the day. Should such a situation happen, they would, ultimately, be frowned upon by all those co-workers who will happily inquire into the air[7] the infamous old adage: *who broke the build?*

---

[1] Especially regression tests.

[2] Which is something that would not occur had one chosen the route of test driven development, as defined in item **20 Nothing works better then test driven development**.

[3] Usually through controlled check-ins.

[4] Or gated check-ins, as some tools call them.

[5] Especially in large teams, where a failure in a daily build really puts the whole team off by another day.

[6] Therefore, preventing the breakdown.

[7] Though without being that much interested in either getting an answer or understanding whatever rationale the problem revolves around.

Item recap:

This item's fundamental guidelines can be succinctly systematized as follows:

- ✓ Create a fully automated build process from day one.
- ✓ Ensure the build process runs all compilation steps as well as all automated tests.
- ✓ Leverage orchestration tools that can help when building to multiple platforms, given that you will have different sets of compilers and testing environments.
- ✓ Use virtualization to ensure ease and effectiveness in having clean building and testing environments each time you run the build.
- ✓ Ensure that the build process includes creating the installer and, additionally, also handles all finalization tasks, such as dropping off binaries or setting up final labels in your source control depot.
- ✓ Use continuous integration policy and, if possible, invest in controlled check-ins in order to reduce the chances of having breakdowns in the build process.

24.   Time is precious: invest wisely in worthwhile features

When building software products, one of the biggest decisions all teams are faced with is determining which features the product should harbor. It is very difficult to decide exactly what needs to be placed into the product being built, especially because there is a vast number of different things that have to be taken into consideration.

Firstly, one has to ponder about innovation. Very seldom will the new product being built consist exclusively of features that already exist within other products. For the most part, software creations will be a mixture of features that already exist[1] and others which constitute innovative content that will tell it apart from the competition. The exact profile of such a mixture of features will be heavily dependent on the context of what is being built. However, in the vast majority of situations, the section representing the innovative group of features is, usually, smaller than its counterpart.

Since innovation is not something that most people can handle in large doses, the degree of innovation brought about[2] is often managed so as to be made up of small incremental steps. On top of it, creating an innovative feature that is of significant added value for users is, quite often, an activity that involves a high investment. Therefore, one must be very prudent when defining the software product's boundaries, while also ensuring that the following questions can be clearly answered upon commencing the product's design phase:

1. **What are the features that the software product must have in order to deliver a valuable user experience?**
    Within these features one must encompass all the features that will give users a complete experience. Be very detailed in defining all use-case scenarios, so as to ensure being fully aware of how the product will be used, namely, which precise operations users can execute, what are the dependencies between available operations, *etc.*.
    This kind of analysis will allow for great insight as to what is really being built, namely by promoting a broad and detailed view of what has to be included so as to claim property over a complete and usable product. You can be sure that there have been many products which have failed in the past because, despite having some truly innovative features, lacked others equally important and even indispensable.

---

[1] But which are, nonetheless, indispensable to make the new product function properly.
[2] Measured as a rupture with all past experiences.

2. **What are the product's innovative features that really tell it apart from others already available in the market?**

   Competition is everywhere these days and, to succeed in building software products, one needs to know precisely what the product will be doing better than the competition. As such, the product might be addressing:

   - A market gap,
   - Something that no one has ever tackled,
   - The refinement of the experience created by other existing solutions[1], while bringing in a fresh view that stems about a scent of innovation. This can be accomplished through either the creation of a new way of doing "an old thing" or by bringing together elements that were previously kept apart.

   Regardless of how innovation creeps into one's product, it must be ensured that it does bring about some new features that are really welcomed by users. Though one does not need many, it has to be assured that users will appreciate them. To do so, there is a mixture of two possible routes to choose from when deciding the path to take. Often, to really understand users' acceptance level, one will rely on market studies, evaluating user feedback, based on concepts, prototypes or early versions of the solution. Other times, one will simply rely on a gut feeling that tells you that this new idea you have is just what the market wants. Though, in this last scenario, people are highly likely to fail miserably, but those very few highly enlightened and lucky ones that do hit the sweet spot, will come to enjoy an extremely successful future, given that they have managed to successfully create an innovative product.

3. **What is the main problem one's product is solving for its users?**

   All software products must know what they are really good for and, quite naturally, they must be very good at something or, otherwise, they will not succeed.

   Knowing exactly what is already available in the area one is addressing, as well as what the pillars of one's software product are, is absolutely mandatory in order to guarantee being able to build a product that will be valued by users. Though this pertains to both marketing and basic common sense, it is, nevertheless, vital to keep in mind along with all the remaining technical elements.

4. **Should one invest in developing new technology?**

   This is one of the most difficult decisions to make when faced with the dilemma of deciding on investing or not in building some low level piece of technology that, somehow, surpasses what is already available. On one hand, doing so has the potential of

---

[1] Generating, for the most part, a better user experience and, hence, greater added value.

attaining some sort of competitive edge. Nevertheless, it can also lead to an unrewarding path, should other existing big players come to decide on building something that will surpass one's own creation.

Having a sense regarding where the market and its players are heading is key in determining where to invest. Doing good research so as to adequately profile roadmaps of big players is absolutely crucial, as is having a bit of an instinctive feel towards the available areas that can end up being a highly profitable investment[1].

Sometimes, one will even be forced to invest in creating low level technology that is destined to be replaced in the very near future[2] since, strict time constraints, may generate the need to have access to a specific set of features before they eventually become commercially available. Alternatively, the cost involved in using a commercial solution might be too high, thus making it justifiable to invest in generating one's own custom made tool.

Regardless of the reason, great care is required in building low level technology, given that it is a costly endeavor that, often, ends up providing very little return.

5. **Which features should be built now and which ones should be put off to a later date?**

   Sooner or later one will be forced to make a decision regarding which features will have to be cut off from one's release. Once this point is reached, one will have to balance whether to put off either features that are part of the technical infrastructure or those leaning more towards the functional side of the software product.

   It is not absolutely imperative that the items within the functional field are the ones to be always picked, nor is it the case that the technical infrastructure will always be the place to cut corners.

   Instead, this decision ought to effectively portray the features' intrinsic value. What exactly will users be missing should a certain feature be absent? Will user experience be really affected? Does the feature have a high usage frequency or, on the other hand, is it something that is touched upon only ever so often?

   Additionally, what is the technical debt one is incurring in by postponing a technical feature and, thus, relying on a not so good alternative? Will this hinder the product in a way that it simply jeopardizes its future evolution[3]?

   All these issues will, usually, be contradicting and, in most cases, the functional features will prevail. However, it is wise to be on the lookout for those few situations where the

---

[1] In producing some sort of low level technological piece that will bring about the competitive advantage everyone dreams about.

[2] As some big player is also moving in a similar direction.

[3] To a point that forces one to focus immediately on securing a proper path.

technical and infrastructural items are so critical that they must be equally leveled with the functional items and, hence, brought into the release.

Item recap:

This item's fundamental guidelines can be succinctly systematized as follows:

- ✓ Carefully decide which features need to be in your software product. Balance innovative features with the ones that already exist in the market (within other products) but which you simply cannot do without to have a complete product.
- ✓ Understand the added value that each feature brings to your clients.
- ✓ Beware of investing in low level technology. It is usually a very risky strategy.
- ✓ Carefully consider which features must be chopped off from the current release. Although, for the most part, technical and infrastructural elements are the ones not included, occasionally, the price to be paid in technical debt is just too high.

---

25. Having a formally defined development process does not imply adopting a formal process

There are several well-known and properly documented development processes, currently used within the software IT industry, that have been created over the years in an attempt to achieve higher productivity and a better quality of the development process. These processes usually embed distinct ideologies as well as methodologies and, quite often, are presented as a series of techniques, actions or routines that development teams need to embrace in order to improve and, thus, deliver better results.

As development teams embrace one of these formal processes, many actions and day-to-day activities are changed. Overall, such change should generate better results! Nevertheless, the challenge resides in the fact that no one recipe suits all scenarios and, while many development teams benefit from adopting certain practices, others will actually do worse[1]. Furthermore, not only will distinct results be achieved by the different teams adopting the same specific task or set of tasks, but it is also crucial to recognize that virtually no team will benefit from adopting all the different elements that constitute one of these formal processes.

At the very best, teams will be able to endure some change, should they manage to warm up to a few new techniques that, probably, stem from distinct[2] formal processes. Thus, while a complete process revamping is, almost always, doomed to be unsuccessful, selecting a few crucial steps from a whole set of different procedures can actually render very good results.

Over the years, I have actually been involved in many attempts to perform changes in the development process that specific teams followed[3]. From these attempts, and more importantly, from observing which ones led to positive results and which ones failed miserably, I have created the following list of guidelines that should help in successfully dealing with the task of implementing a formally defined development process:

1. **Having a formally defined process is better than ad-hoc behavior.**

   Have you ever worked in a company where no one knew exactly what triggered a specific action or, on the other hand, what the consequences of a specific decision were? I am sure most, if not all, of you have. The interesting thing is that these working environments have a kind of long standing embedded chain of behaviors that are uniquely known by those who work there. As a result, they often end up being passed

---

[1] In terms of overall results.

[2] Although, sometimes, related.

[3] Admittedly, in some cases, there wasn't even a formally defined process within the development team.

along to every new hire without anyone really questioning or understanding their relevance.

Furthermore, no one really knows how different teams interact, nor how people with different skills actually cooperate, by leveraging their own specific expertise, in order to deliver high quality products.

Interestingly, in environments where chaos rules[1] great products are sometimes created. This means that ingenious people and brilliant ideas do not really need nor should they be confined to more controlled approaches[2]. However, the challenge resides in being beneficial to have a mixture of creative liberty and an appropriate dose of formality[3].

Hence, by having some type of formally defined process, one will, at the very least, have some much needed overall standard guidance in the form of a path that pinpoints a few key milestones that have to exist. These milestones will ensure some basic, but required control. Doing so is effective in both letting people know and understand what is expected of them, as well as sorting through some very individual and erratic ways of thinking and working.

With this environment in place, the chances of building great software products are significantly heightened.

2. **Look at the main development processes currently in use by the industry, and pick those that are applicable to your own context.**

    Many trends in life are, objectively, short-lived. Plus, in many cases, it is wise to avoid following the crowd just for the sake of assuming that the majority is always right. Nonetheless, it is also true that, if something is used by many people and successfully sticks around for a while, some good must be coming out of it. With this in mind, one should approach the task of defining a formal development process for one's team by, first and foremost, examining the major choices that are being made by the competition. Knowing what others are doing brings about a better understanding of the existing options and, frequently enough, which results are being produced by such choices.

    Knowing which processes are, currently, being adopted by most development teams entails having a wealth of relevant information upon which subsequent decisions can be effectively based on. This wealth of information implies being able to:

    - Easily grasp what actions are portrayed by each process,
    - Which type of skills they require,

---

[1] Or where one simply plays the follow-the-flow game.
[2] If anything, it is mostly the other way around.
[3] Otherwise, one will, most likely, run the risk of failing by being too dependent of individual inspiration from a few engineers, together with some luck as well!

- Which environments they have been applied to[1].

Additionally, one will also be able to clearly identify both the frontiers that exist between them as well as their common ground. It is very important to understand which activities or traits are shared by different processes, as well as what elements can clearly single out each and every one of them.

Finally, understanding which type of teams opted for a specific process[2] will provide for a clearer picture of key variables that are more aligned with specific development processes, such as:

- Team size,
- Product type,
- Company culture.

Knowing whether such an alignment exists or not can be essential in determining if a certain process can or cannot be applied to one's own operating environment.

3. **From this set of processes, identify which are the key changes or activities they embrace.**

As previously stated, knowing which are the key activities and traits of each process is essential to understanding its true nature. Each formal development process will have a thorough protocol that is, essentially, made by:

- A large set of activities,
- Tasks,
- Documents,
- Roles that must be fulfilled at different stages of the development process.

However, as always in life, not every item has the same relevance, given that not every single item will influence the final results in the same way. Plus, often enough, a few items will be capable of providing both many benefits, as well as negative consequences, depending on the circumstances.

Identifying these tasks and traits, in the sense of diagnosing those that deliver real value, brings one a step closer to success. Keep in mind though that the game being played is capped: you cannot change everything or the whole world will fall into pieces. It is crucial to know which battles to pick and, furthermore, which will truly have an impact. Plus, it should not be overlooked that a specific adopted task may be very successful within a certain team and terribly unsuccessful within another. Thus, in order to bring about successful change, it is fundamental to have a keen perception of:

- What one's team will be able to do,

---

[1] Both with and without success.
[2] In detriment of others.

- What it will be able to absorb,
- How it will react to each change.

Furthermore, one cannot be afraid to pick and choose tasks and traits from different processes. From personal experience, I can tell you that a mixture of techniques from different formal processes is not unheard of, given that different items from distinct processes can, indeed, complement each other very well and, thus, deliver a great custom made, but formally defined, process.

In fact, in cases where either process proximity is close or, somehow, a specific process can be seen as an evolution or an off-shoot of another one, this mixture of elements is, usually, extremely sensible and easy to implement.

On the other hand, forgoing elements that either seem to be bad choices during an analysis stage or which have been proven to be a failure within a real implementation experience, is also a good practice. Overall, do not expect every change to be successful and, furthermore, do not be afraid to recognize that a certain change did not deliver its expected added value[1]. The great thing about attempting a change is that one can easily see whether such strategy was profitable or not and, thus, act accordingly. It is those who are afraid to test new strategies that will forever be uncertain as to whether the right path was taken as well as whether a more successful approach could have been encountered.

Pair programming is an example of a technique I have tried in different contexts without, however, seeing it succeed a single time. Consequently, I have decided not to proceed to its implementation and, thus, forgo its usage[2].

4. **Implementing a few of the changes and activities identified earlier, together with measuring their results.**

   Though change should be sought, it should rely on a method when being put to practice. Changing certain practices that rule how the development team works ought to be conducted in a mindful way that accomplishes two distinct goals.

   Firstly, it ensures that the team can embrace the change. This requires time along with the appropriate mindset. Given that no change can be consummated instantly, people need a reasonable amount of time in order to successfully adapt to a new or different context. Thus, it is perfectly normal to test out a new way of doing things for a few weeks by using a limited number of team members. Hence, this leads to repeatedly tweaking it[3]

---

[1] Meaning that it needs to be replaced by another option, which may, sometimes, include backtracking to a previously adopted practice.
[2] After a few unsuccessful and rather frustrating attempts, though I do not question that others have achieved great results with it, given that it is still standard practice amongst extreme programming.
[3] As well as refining the model as a whole along the way.

according to the feedback from those involved. Afterwards, as time moves on, one should push the change forward by making it broader and, thus, ensuring that it is adopted by more and more team members. This careful introduction of a new practice will be more prone to success than any alternative radical approach.

Secondly, one should limit the number of changes introduced at each stage, meaning that the introduction of several new practices should not overlap. Instead, during the time period allocated for introducing a new practice to the selected team members, one should not instill other parallel changes. Before moving on to other variables, it is crucial to ensure that the new way of doing things is firmly consolidated within the team's spirit[1]. Ultimately, people need to recognize the value of the change from their own experience, for only that will actually have the team truly embracing the change!

Apart from this paced rhythm of change, it must also be ensured that the results brought about by these changes are measurable, in the form of objective performance indicators, which quantify the team's pre and post change output. Additionally, it is also required to establish the time frame for the execution of such measurements, given that some elements of these processes cannot be measured immediately. Some need to be constantly measured over a given time period, while others can simply be measured at specific points in time. Thus, before making a change one needs to establish a baseline that allows for the precise evaluation of where one is at the start of this process, so as to acquire the information that will objectively allow for the characterization of the change's influence on performance[2].

5. **Retain the activities that resulted in a positive output and abandon others.**

As stated in the previous item, one should not be afraid to attempt changes nor of abandoning new practices that, contrary to one's best expectations[3], failed to deliver any added value[4]. Likewise, when abandoning a specific new practice, one can either replace it with a new one or simply go back to whichever method was previously in place, with both options being equally valid[5]. It is very important to avoid rushing the decision of adopting of a new practice, which usually comes about as a result of trying to be too fast in replacing an unsuccessful prior attempt. It is highly likely that such a rushed decision will result in an equally unsatisfactory outcome.

---

[1] To a point where it seems something natural and, thus, no longer a new imposed effort.

[2] Obviously, evaluation of changes should not be based on intuition. Instead, one should give it his/her best to be as objective (mathematical) as possible. Doing so ensures being able to truly evaluate the change and, more importantly, whether or not it really brought about the expected benefits.

[3] According to the results obtained within other environments.

[4] As measured by whichever indicators were defined, even before adopting it.

[5] In case one either happens to be unsure of an alternative path to take or when needing time so as to carefully study and define how a new practice will be implemented.

6. **Review the process, though not often.**

Besides conducting a careful evaluation of each new practice, one needs to establish a periodic time frame for a deeper analysis of the complete development process. This requires defining objective time periods that are sufficiently apart for it to constitute a productive exercise. Given the time one needs in order to perform a global assessment of a process, and considering the time one also needs so as to allow for each new practice to sink in, reviews of the process should only be performed after a full year.

This type of major revision needs to gather input from all team members, while also looking for new areas to improve in. Additionally, it is also quite frequent for one to have to scout for new practices being successfully used in the market. All these elements, given that they require time to perform, fully justify the infrequency of the procedure.

Apart from this, one should not consider that a major revision implies either a significant or a limited number of changes which would, nonetheless, impact core activities. A major revision ought to be viewed as something that will allow for a broad and in-depth analysis of the complete development process, though the consequences that derive from it[1] are often:

- Limited in number,
- Subsequently implemented carefully and without overlapping,
- Subjected to a careful analysis of the generated outcome.

Summing up, it should be kept in mind that this constitutes the ideal moment to get input from everyone on the team, since, the closer the team feels to the changes, the easiest it will be to have them successfully adopted.

7. **Some key activities for a great modern development process.**

Although no two teams are completely alike, here is a set of items that I have introduced and successfully used at different moments:

- Manage your time using short sprints[2].

    The best way to deliver a constant velocity[3] is to have a detailed plan of what everyone needs to do over the upcoming days. Doing so allows everyone to

---

[1] Meaning the changes that will stem from such an exercise.
[2] One or two week long sprints have been ideal.
[3] Meaning having one's development activities and their generated output play out at a constant rhythm.

clearly know which features will be touched in the forthcoming builds[1] and, thus, it ensures that engineers' minds do not drift into hyperspace[2].

Keeping these sprints short will guarantee a systematic control point that allows one to implement any required changes to the project's plan. The worst possible thing that can occur in a project consists of implementing control check points too far apart. Doing so makes it almost impossible to recover from[3], upon having issues detected at those points.

- Include any needed research activity in your sprint definition.

    Though coding is not an exact science, it will be all the more complicated if done over a glass roof. There should be no attempt to code production modules or features when there are any technological uncertainties within their reach. Thus, things such as using unknown APIs, unknown platforms or previously unused versions of compilers, can create chaos within the planned activities. Therefore, one needs to contemplate research activities, which will resolve these unknowns, just like any other activity within the plan. This is the real key! Once a production coding activity is planned, it must be ensured that all the unknowns have been dealt with, for without this pre-requisite, planning a production coding activity within a week-long sprint is nothing more than a random guessing effort. Contrary to this, by having the unknowns adequately taken care of beforehand, one will easily plan and deliver according to it. Hence, it is crucial to have any research activities that will help resolve these unknowns included in the sprints, just as any other regular activity!

    Final warning note: these research activities should have a reduced scope. I am not talking about full-blown R&D which is, naturally, a beast of its own and, often, guided by completely different rules.

- Finally, other practices that should be included and which are analyzed thoroughly in other items include:
    - Code reviews,
    - Test driven development,
    - Automated building system,
    - Global knowledge sharing.

---

[1] Assuming one has a proper building system, as defined in item **23 Do not leave the build for last: invest in an automated build system from the very first** day.

[2] Yes, should too much room be given to one's software engineers, most will wander off to uncharted territory, without much good coming out of it.

[3] At least within the initially defined timeline.

Item recap:

This item's fundamental guidelines can be succinctly systematized as follows:

- ✓ Ensure you have a formally defined process in your organization. Ad-hoc routines don't usually cut it for great software development.
- ✓ You do not need to adhere to a full single formal process that already exists in the industry. Instead, you can pick and choose key activities from different processes. Just ensure that you can make them work together within your own custom, but formally defined, process.
- ✓ Test new changes with care. Measure results against the results delivered by previous practices so as to objectively decide whether the new practice is really viable.
- ✓ Do not implement too many new things at once. Give people time to absorb changes and new procedures. Introduce new practices at a slow pace.
- ✓ Do not be afraid to scrap a change that fails to deliver the expected results.
- ✓ Use well-known practices within your development process, such as: short sprints, code reviews, test driven development, automated builds and global knowledge sharing.

26. Testing and quality assurance procedures

Although a lot was said about testing upon discussing test driven development[1], in general, testing goes well beyond that. As such I feel that it is important to focus a bit more on general testing procedures and quality assurance practices. These constitute a cornerstone of products' ultimate reliability, more specifically, their adherence to existing requirements.

Having a product as free of problems and bugs as possible is a key goal of software development, given that it is one of the key elements in ensuring users accept and enjoy using one's product. Therefore, testing and quality assurance is a noble activity which warrants being at the same level as development. Overall, testing should be thought of as a continuum parallel to development, meaning that it should not be looked at as a minor step to be performed only once the real important task of coding is completed.

Placing a great emphasis on testing is truly and absolutely required, so as to deliver quality. To do so the following guidelines should be taken into consideration:

1. **Have high caliber engineers as test experts.**

   I have worked in many different projects where testing engineers were, somehow, regarded as less important than product developers. Unfortunately, this type of reasoning is, not only old-fashioned, but also down right incorrect and counter-productive. Test engineers are just as important as software developers[2], given that it is impossible to deliver great products without a great testing team on board.

   As such, teams must include great testing engineers who are truly there to, not only break the system, but, ultimately, to be the ultimate barrier in rooting out all existing problems before the shipping phase.

   In order to fully understand products and their inherent use cases, test engineers need to have a very special mindset. Most notably, they need to:

   - Fully comprehend how the different processes flow and which components are affected by them,
   - Have a sixth sense that can really make them spot the specific situations that may break the system.

   As for development engineers, they need to be aware of what testing engineers do and, additionally, understand that test engineers are, in fact, protecting their own work. A great testing engineer is one who is able to catch existing problems that, if left unchanged, would be extremely harmful to end users. Through their work, in the form of their relentless effort to find problems in the existing codebase, they ensure that the

---

[1] As defined in item **20 Nothing works better then test driven development**.
[2] And as important as any other role.

work performed by development engineers will safely shine for a long time. If it weren't for the testing team, very few software developers would see their work succeeding in the marketplace.

This kind of belief system needs to be protected and stimulated within working teams so as to actually become their culture. Development and testing engineers should not be placed on different sides of the battle field. They need to be peers in technical skills and equals in both respect and responsibility for the product itself.

A final word on technical expertise: testing engineers need to understand the codebase and drive tests from it. Hence, they need to be as good as development engineers are, albeit with different personalities.

2. **Create robust unit tests.**

Having a robust suite of unit tests is absolutely vital to ensure quality. Unit testing is the first barrier against problems and, therefore, it needs to be ensured that every implied contract within the codebase is correctly implemented. Consequently, carefully crafting unit tests will guarantee that the codebase is fairly healthy and, furthermore, that individual elements have been proven to deliver exactly what the functional definition specifies, in the sense that, upon receiving a set of inputs, they will perform certain actions and, eventually, deliver some outputs.

However, one of the big problems with unit testing is that one needs to go beyond the lowest possible granularity level, since no codebase is truly stateless or composed of pure predicates[1].

Since a complex and broad codebase has loads of state scattered through a myriad of components and different lines of code, it is inevitable to climb up the granularity ladder and, ultimately, introduce certain unit tests that go well beyond atomic operations. By creating tests at this level, one will have a better chance of catching problems that stem from a specific computational sequence[2].

Therefore, very comprehensive unit tests are required. Such tests have to cover positive and negative outcomes[3] that run at distinct granularity levels, so as to test atomic and non-atomic operations[4].

---

[1] Functions that always return the same outputs, thus being completely stateless, if given the same inputs. Therefore they cause no other side effects and rely on no other external information or state.

[2] Usually influenced by the state that changes in each of its atomic constituents.

[3] Often, exception paths are missed – more on that later.

[4] Where existing state can make a difference.

3. **Rely on regression testing.**

    Guaranteeing backward compatibility is a must-do for any product that wishes to deliver an easy road to evolution and migration. If clients happen to feel any discomfort towards newer versions of a product, seeing them migrating and evolving together with the product, will be less likely. Plus, should clients fall behind, they will start complaining about features missing on older versions and, soon enough, they will quickly start thinking about alternative products. Thus, upgrading a system is a matter of huge importance and, to ease such task, one needs to make it an absolute priority to ensure an extremely high degree of backward compatibility.

    Doing so requires a strong use of regression tests which, often, can be executed by running unit tests from previous versions[1].

    Regression testing is not as much about creating new tests[2], as it is about leveraging whichever tests were available for previous versions and, subsequently, guaranteeing that they still run successfully on new builds.

4. **Automate all possible forms of testing.**

    In the dark ages of computer science, tests were executed manually by testing engineers who wrote down the test cases and, afterwards, executed them in repetitive fashion on new builds. Such setting almost seems to have taken place a million years ago, since, currently, there is a wide set of tools that can help automate testing[3]. In fact, one can leverage these tools so as to automatically run tests within one's build process and, if done so successfully, these tools can automate all types of tests, including things such as API testing or GUI testing.

    Given this, when building a software product, it is wise to automate as much as possible. Products are expected to have a long life, with multiple versions along the way. Furthermore, each distinct version is the result of many development cycles as well as many builds that need deep and broad testing. Therefore, automating tests will help save a significant amount of resources[4] in a very short time period, while also ensuring that there are few lags between executing a new build and receiving a comprehensive report on potential issues.

    This ability to quickly get quality assurance results on a specific build allows one to immediately feed that information into the next development cycle[5].

---

[1] Therefore, ascertaining which conditions and contracts upheld by previous versions are also maintained in the new builds.

[2] Although some specific situations may require it.

[3] Particularly the repetitive execution of tests on existing builds.

[4] Time and money.

[5] If you feel that the severity of the problems justify such a prompt response.

5. **Constantly enhance test cases through incident analysis.**

   Many test cases can be directly drawn from technical specifications, while others are crafted by experienced testing engineers. A few, but nonetheless critical ones, should derive from an analysis of all registered incidents within one's issue tracking tool. By including every relevant registered incident, one will be protecting against future backward compatibility problems[1], while, potentially, also applying learned lessons to new but similar situations that may exist within one's codebase, allowing one specific incident to stem off many analogous problems. This type of scaling can be successfully attained whenever using techniques such as:

   - Code templates,
   - Coding patterns,
   - Code generation tools that can contribute to systematic introduction of similar problems[2].

   Therefore, analyzing one's incident database must be done with great care, so as to ensure going beyond the obvious. This is not just about replicating a specific issue in a dedicated test case. Instead, it is, predominantly, about ensuring that any possible patterns and similar occurrences that can either stem from it or be caught through it are, indeed, effectively addressed.

6. **Create a specialized team that draws the tests for critical use cases.**

   Not all business flows supported by one's solution are equally important and, usually, one can easily identify a subset that stands out as absolutely critical. Considering that this will occur with the vast majority of, if not all, software products, these special business flows should be given heightened importance. Consequently, it is crucial to be even more careful in designing the specific test cases that will certify their functionality.

   Simply by identifying what these flows are, those working on them will be more alert and, usually, more eager to double their efforts in pursuing top quality. As such, it is a recommended practice to assign the design of test cases that surround these business flows to the more senior and experienced elements of the quality assurance team.

   The main objective, of course, is to really leverage the knowledge that these senior elements have amassed over the years, thus ensuring that it is applied to the most critical items of the solution's processing pipeline. Through this particular spotlight, one will diminish the risk of having major problems on critical flows and, quite naturally, all customers will appreciate these features' flawless behavior.

---

[1] Thus enhancing one's regression testing level.

[2] Should the issue lie on the best practice that they themselves are attempting to impose.

7. Review code coverage of existing tests.

Code coverage tools are a great way of monitoring and extracting automated reports concerning which exact code paths one is both hitting and missing when running unit tests.

By using code coverage tools one will know precisely what needs changing within existing unit tests, so as to ensure that one is effectively covering all areas[1] seen as important and worthy of being included in them[2].

When running unit tests and evaluating code coverage, one gains knowledge regarding which areas of code were executed and which ones weren't[3]. However, should one merely focus on this information in guiding the construction of a quality assurance engine, both problems that stem from specific patterns of execution and specific changes inherent to the intrinsic statefulness of the different software components will be missed. Ultimately, though unit tests are great[4], they will only take us so far. Therefore, one needs to ensure that one's testing platform includes other elements[5], so as to avoid situations where one fails to identify problems that result from a more complex usage pattern, which is not detected through unit tests.

8. Execute load testing.

Unfortunately I have seen way too many cases where load testing is either ignored altogether or only executed once specific problems are identified on a production platform. In this latter scenario, performance tests are often directed at discovering what is wrong with a specific situation requiring a quick response, yet they fail to present or conduct a systematic approach and analysis of overall performance issues.

Such approach is just plain wrong and, executing comprehensive performance tests, should really be on the top of one's testing agenda[6].

When a specific problem happens to be detected in performance testing, it is very likely that it can only be resolved through some heavy reengineering. Alas, very few performance problems can be solved by either merely tweaking one's code here and there or by making a small change within a specific function, procedure or component. Often, the case is actually the opposite and, thus, performance issues will force one to

---

[1] At the lowest level of granularity.
[2] Having 100% code coverage is extremely expensive, potentially unattainable, and, usually, not the chosen target when developing a software product.
[3] During the time the unit tests were running.
[4] And using code coverage tools is a clear must.
[5] As previously discussed.
[6] Preferably being initiated from the very early development stages.

rethink the design of some areas of the solution and, as such, they will lead to a substantial reengineering effort.

Plus, given that any substantial reengineering effort will force one to commit time and resources to it, the sooner the problem is uncovered, the easier it will be to fix it. Detecting issues early in the development effort brings two added advantages:

- One will still have loads of small development cycles, which can be used to, hopefully, accommodate the effort needed to remove whichever performance issues were detected.
- One will have fewer components already developed. Therefore the impact of any forced architectural and design changes are minimized[1], thus reducing the amount of wasted time and money.

Item recap:

This item's fundamental guidelines can be succinctly systematized as follows:

- ✓ Hire great engineers as test experts. Do not take testing activities as something of lower importance than architecture and design or coding.
- ✓ Ensure your product has robust unit tests but, at the same time, do not forget that unit tests are, usually, too fined grained and atomic to cover problems that come from a complex usage pattern[2].
- ✓ Use code coverage tools to identify code sections that are not hit by existing unit tests.
- ✓ Rely heavily on regression testing so as to achieve backwards compatibility. Always run unit tests from previous versions on new builds.
- ✓ Automate all types of testing so as to ensure quick feedback on new builds. Afterwards, immediately feed these results into the subsequent development cycles.
- ✓ Enhance your test base through lessons learned from past incidents. Be thorough in your analysis and try to identify error patterns that can stem from a single incident.
- ✓ Give special testing attention to use cases involving the most critical business flows.
- ✓ Do not leave load testing for last. Performance issues usually require broad reengineering and, the sooner you know about it, the better.

---

[1] Eventually, even minimizing the potential need to re-write some components from scratch.
[2] Where some statefulness is implied.

Section IV – Deployment and supportability

Over this section we will focus on presenting and discussing sixteen key elements that, if observed, will guarantee that one's software product is ready for an enterprise production environment, in the sense of delivering all the required features that ensure an effective deployment as well as a highly effective support.

27.   For a product to be used, installed it must be!

Any software product can only ever be used if consumers, whoever they are, are capable of performing its adequate deployment, which, in very simple terms, entails the existence and successful execution of an installation procedure.

That which constitutes a good installation procedure is, quite naturally, a matter for a lengthy discussion. Therefore, the systematization of all important elements that comprise this process[1] is a fundamental subject that needs covering, given that the successful completion of this first step has to be executed before any product is ever used.

Interestingly, building a good installation procedure is far from easy and, in many aspects, it is as difficult as building any other part of the system. Installation procedures are, often, materialized in the form of a setup program that performs some simple, and others not so simple, tasks, such as copying files or registering components. To create a complete and robust setup program one has to, at the very least, observe the following guidelines:

1.   **Define, code and build the setup program from day one.**

The setup procedure cannot be an aftermath side-product. Instead, it must be looked upon as any other component being built and, thus, must have its own design phase immediately start off along with the product's overall design. The setup program must take into consideration many aspects of how the product will function and, therefore, must be designed so as to support such architectural decisions. If one's product happens to support side-by-side execution, then one needs to ensure that the setup program is, not only aware of it, but also capable of coping with it. Should one's product need to be deployed to different environments, showcasing distinct requirements and differences[2], the setup program must be aligned accordingly. Should the product support alternate architectures, such as clustered or non-clustered, as well as load-balanced or non-load-balanced architectures, so must the setup program step up to the challenge and naturally adapt to these distinct behaviors.

Therefore, there is no doubt that the setup is tied very closely together with the product's DNA, in the form of being adapted to the features created within each of the product's releases and internal builds. Given this, one should start writing the setup program from the very first day. Initially, it might simply entail either deploying a single binary or attempting to setup a non-working, non-functional and incomplete system. However, as time goes by and more features are added into the source code, more

---

[1] One that works as expected and delivers exactly what clients need.
[2] Namely production, staging or testing environments.

binaries end up being generated by the build process, which, in turn, ignites the setup program's continuing growth[1]. In no time it will start including:

- Copying files,
- Registering components,
- Configuring third party products.

Though the sky will definitely be the limit, the main goal will always be to deliver a safe and user-friendly experience. No one really wants a product that has a crashing setup or that, somehow, is left in a non-working state after the setup program finishes running[2]. Thus, to achieve all of this, one needs to:

- Start building the setup program upon starting to build the project,
- Keep the setup program aligned with the product's ongoing development stages.

Thus, leaving it to a final phase will make it extremely difficult to create a robust component, given that it will not have evolved and matured over time like the remaining components. Instead, crafting it from day one will showcase its behavior from an early stage and, furthermore, enable its usage within one's own testing and development environments. Doing so will place time on the development team's side, in the form of allowing for more features to be progressively added as input is received from early users[3]. As shown by history, there isn't really that much time to build new pieces from the ground up during the final development stages and, furthermore, trying to do so is extremely risky, which has us coming full circle and arriving at our guideline of focusing on performing incremental enhancements throughout the whole development process, so as to ensure the setup's overall quality.

2. **Think about all its different traits: clean installation and updates.**

A setup program is a monster of many faces. The most visible one comprises all the actions needed in order to execute a clean installation at the first attempt. As difficult as this might sound, you can be sure that it is the easiest path you will need to cover. There are other far more complex routes that require special consideration, such as upgrade paths, which, usually, end up having a few distinct peculiarities.

Upgrade paths are used to change existing environments and, contrary to what occurs with a base installation, they do not entail the luxury of starting with a clean slate. As such, they need to take upon their shoulders the difficult chore of validating the precise starting point, so as to ensure that the potential changes they can instill on the system will render consistent results. When an upgrade is executed, it is crucial to be sure that a

---

[1] Which naturally includes progressively undertaking more tasks and of higher complexity.

[2] Supposedly, in a successful manner.

[3] Even if they belong to the development team.

layer is being added on top of a compatible foundation. However, this is only a small fraction of the story given that all details have to be managed with great precision.

Generically speaking, upgrades may follow several different strategies. Some products require a strict installation sequence that forces users to perform the install action by using a predetermined order, where every single upgrade moves from one build level to the immediately subsequent one. Alternatively, other products allow one to move from a build level to another (not immediately subsequent one) without executing every single upgrade in between[1]. Plus, some products even adopt a hybrid scenario, where some upgrades require the pre-determined sequence to be executed[2] while others are truly cumulative. The latter ones[3] allow one to leap-frog some build levels, while ensuring that a stable and predictable installation level will be accomplished.

Regardless of one's choice, it must be ensured that every installed item is traceable and detectable by forthcoming versions. Only by doing so will the setup program be capable of validating whether it is safe to install a specific upgrade or not. Moreover, whichever tracking system is created, it needs to be quite detailed and effective in supporting new upgrades that take the system to higher build levels. Furthermore, it is also vital to support uninstall procedures geared towards reverting to previous build levels[4], even when such an uninstall procedure is reversing the effects of an upgrade that ignited a jump between non-consecutive build levels.

Summing up, registering exactly what is currently installed, as well as which features correspond to each level is an art, and it is the only way to support all different traits that a setup program must contemplate.

3. **Manage its sources as any other versioned component.**

The setup program will, inevitably, be composed of different items that range from scripts (being executed by existing setup bootstrapping technology), to source code (that generates binaries that perform specific configuration tasks), or even sets of shell-interpreted commands (responsible for carrying out more mundane instructions such as file copying).

Regardless of the exact blend being dealt with, one needs to ensure that all these items are managed as any other software component. To do so, one needs to treat its source code as any other piece of source code, which entails ensuring proper source control, versioning, branching and labeling, as applied to any item used to build other system binaries. This tight control is absolutely vital in certifying that one is able to:

---

[1] Usually implying that upgrades are cumulative.
[2] Usually in fixes.
[3] Usually in service packs, which are, typically, a mixture of fixes and new features.
[4] While still maintaining a consistent platform.

- Track any potential problems within the installation procedure,
- Build the installation procedure automatically, just as the rest of the product,
- Create a repeatable process, based on this structured and controlled approach.

One of the main challenges within the installation procedure consists of having its source code, in this context, usually coming about in disguised fashion. Many setup procedures are based on either commercial products or operating system features that allow for the optimization of the installation procedure by using a set of consistent practices, supported by a common installation engine. Often, these installation engines deliver a set of graphical and non-graphical features, easily recognizable by users, and which add great value in terms of the process's overall behavior.

These features commonly include either standardized graphical dialogs so as to gather input, or, alternatively, more complex solutions to tricky problems, such as guaranteeing transactional semantics on typical operations like copying or replacing files. Regardless of the exact features being provided, the common point consists of one's interaction with these installation engines taking place through the production of specific modules that, once executed, are interpreted by these engines[1]. This apparent isolation is, by no means, a reason to overlook these items and, additionally, no reason not to consider them source code. In fact, in most situations, these installation engines do end up generating either text files or analogous persisted information that directly reflect whichever options and configurations were defined through their graphical user interface. Ultimately, this is part of the setup program's source code, regardless of its underlying format.

4. **Contemplate side-by-side execution strategy and how it influences the setup program.**
   Side-by-side execution is one of the most influencing factors regarding how the installation procedure shapes up. Installation procedures for products that support side-by-side execution are, typically, more complex[2]. Supporting side-by-side execution will steer how one defines the deployment structure, as it will determine, not only how to align product binaries in a file system, but also which resources a product may or may not use. When supporting side-by-side execution, a product will, usually, stay clear of any shared resources made available by either the operating system or any intermediate layer possibly being used. Quite naturally, this will also impact how the installation procedure functions as well as which actions it executes.

---

[1] Which, at least in most cases, are usually created by virtue of using a graphical interface that hides most of the complexity and structure behind it.
[2] Given that they need to cater for very specific needs and cannot be, either implicitly or explicitly, shielded from such complexity.

Furthermore, should one be, somehow, interacting with other systems[1], supporting side-by-side execution will require doing things differently. Dealing with potentially multiple installations within the same server[2] forces the creation of different versions of the same sets of elements, so as to guarantee that one is able to identify which version relates to which installation, while retaining the ability to influence or change each one of them individually.

Just consider the following examples:

- Leveraging a database system within a product entails having a setup program recognizing different database instances, with potentially different schemas. This happens to be especially true when looking into the upgrade trait of the installation procedure. On top of schemas, one may need to deal with different security options which, in itself, may entail either different login accounts or, perhaps, something even more complex than that.
- If leveraging a web server, one will need to manage either different web sites or distinct virtual directories within a web site. Plus, one may also need to deal with different rules, namely access control or distinct port assignment rules.

The specifics of the exact variables that must be taken into account can only be defined by analyzing each specific case. However, the main take home message is that, supporting side-by-side execution forces the installation procedure to, inherently, know how the product is able to have different versions executing in the same server context and, potentially, within the same integrated set of supporting systems. Furthermore, it also needs to be capable of clearly identifying the resources being assigned to each executing environment, together with how it will only influence the specific version it needs to configure/install.

5. **Beware of shared components.**

Shared components were truly one of those ground breaking creations that only showed their inherent dark side once it was just too late. In the beginning, shared components seemed to be a promising move forward, given that they allowed for space to be saved within the file system. On top of it, they could even save memory (if the operating system supported it) by having executing code pages being loaded only once, independently of the number of processes that might actually map them. Additionally, should one ever require an upgrade, it was guaranteed that every process would pick up the latest version simply by replacing a single, unique copy.

---

[1] Such as databases or web servers.
[2] On top of the same set of supporting products.

At first, it seemed to be a winning deal. Nevertheless, and unfortunately so, time ended up showing that this feature was also responsible for major headaches, as some of its virtues could easily be turned into a true sin. Just consider the common case whereby an upgrade in a shared component introduced either a subtle and unknown error or an equally subtle and unknown incompatible behavior. Suddenly, everything would come crashing down. Instead of affecting merely one solution, we could easily break many or all solutions that were actually installed in the system, with this being especially true when the problematic shared component was either an operating system piece or a structural runtime element.

However, this erratic behavior isn't exclusive of operating system components or of structural runtime elements for that matter. One's own set of binaries may be equally troublesome when a single version or single copy is shared by many parties. Thus, one's installation procedure needs to take into account what the policy is in terms of shared components and the best practice, in order to reduce the risk of these wild contaminations, consists of avoiding any sort of shared distribution. Doing so can take many forms and, thus, one should be aware of the following potential scenarios:

- Consideration should be given to re-distributing any runtime elements used, and which can be privately deployed, regardless of whether they already exist in the system as a shared version or not.
- Consideration should be given to re-distributing exact copies of the same binaries to private and distinct areas, should that guarantee that one will be able to create, in the future, distinct lines of upgrade and evolution.
- The usage of technologies that are system wide and provide no way of supporting multiple copies should be avoided, and even more so if one is supporting side-by-side execution.
- When producing different elements of a suite of products that has several autonomous sub-systems which can be deployed independently, the existence of shared items that would have been deployed by a different installation procedure should not be expected.

Despite this, shared components are not exclusive to binaries that either one builds or incorporates into the product. One also needs to pay special attention to any sort of shared components within the boundaries of other supporting systems that are integrated into the solution. Make sure you analyze exactly which resources from third party products are used, ranging from their own configuration elements, to APIs, *etc.*, and understand how they will influence your installation procedure.

6. **Make sure it implements transactional semantics.**

There is only one thing that is worse than a failing setup procedure, and that is a failing setup procedure that renders the prior existing environment useless! This type of experience is, not only awful for the user, but truly complicated within an enterprise production environment. Should a setup procedure fail for some reason, particularly when executing an upgrade, it should be ensured that everything that existed prior to the setup's execution remains untouched. These so-called transactional semantics are, not only a safe guard, but also a trait of any respectable installation procedure. Just imagine what would happen if a failure in an operating system patch would render the system useless[1]. You don't want your product to be that kind of product as it will really hurt your marketing hype and eventually your sales. Consequently, implementing transactional semantics is a true must-have.

Many commercial products that are designed and built to support the creation of installation programs, supply a set of features that help achieve these transactional semantics. Usually, they support:

- A set of event calls that drive the initial installation phase,
- Followed by a set of event calls that drive either a logical commit or rollback phase.

Despite this basic event driven support, in most cases, one will be responsible for actually implementing whichever strategies are required so as to ensure that a commit or rollback is an all or nothing task. For the most part, this is usually quite complex, should one be meddling with configuration steps that touch other products. The simplest cases are those involving either replacement of files or configurations stored on files. Committing these effects or rolling them back can be done safely by setting new directories on the side with all the newly required content, together with simply swapping directory names at the final stage.

Other actions, such as upgrading multiple database schemas, are rather more complex. Nevertheless, the real problem stems from the complexity that develops from needing to change settings in more than one supporting product, such as when needing to configure a web server and a database server. Can one truly make this work with real transactional semantics? As a rule of thumb, no! Most often, there is no way of creating distributed transactions between them. Thus, usually the best possible course of action entails executing the tasks one needs in all integrated products[2] on the side, most often by duplicating what one already has. This way, one's rolling back phase merely consists of cleaning up these "on the side" duplicated items. Hence, even if this rollback procedure

---

[1] Well, sometimes it does happen, but nowadays not too often!
[2] Along with intrinsic operating system resources, such as file systems.

happens to fail, no definite harm occurs, since these configurations made "on the side" weren't really active.

Additionally, and for supportability purposes, one should document how to manually clean up an aborted rollback procedure, even if the remains aren't expected to jeopardize the system.

Interestingly, the commit phase is, usually, more problematic. Once everything is prepared on the side, it must be performed, on each system, that final swapping action responsible for moving the new environment, configured on the side, into the position of the previously existing one. Doing so in a single system is, for the most part, bearable. However, quite often, this swapping operation, within these other systems, is neither atomic, nor guaranteed not to fail, which constitutes a problem. Therefore, there will be a few very rare occasions in which one successfully commits one system only to fail on a subsequent one. At this point, one can try to reverse the actions performed on the systems that were previously committed, which might be achievable by operating a new swap-like procedure in reverse direction.

Hence, all these scenarios are tricky and need to be carefully analyzed, and it must be ensured that one creates the installation procedure so as to implement this type of transactional semantics, while carefully documenting the type of manual recovery actions needed within every possible failure scenario.

7. **Reversing its effects is mandatory: consider rollback semantics within uninstall procedures.**

As already covered in the previous item, creating a transactional experience with the installation procedure is mandatory to ensure a resilient and effective product. However, transactional semantics are, indeed, hard to acquire, though the few strategies previously outlined can get one very close to achieving such a goal.

Hence, having analyzed much of the mine field that encompasses this requirement, let us move on to the details of a very specific area: rolling back an uninstallation procedure. Is such a goal possible to attain? If so, are there specific constraints where it may simply be unfeasible? Again, there is no simple answer and, much less, a universal one. On some scenarios it may be simple to implement a rollback feature within the context of an uninstall procedure. However, on many other scenarios, it might just be impossible.

Should we be performing an uninstall procedure within a self-contained product[1], it is relatively easy to get there, as it simply requires following the same reasoning adopted upon creating a transactional installation procedure.

---

[1] One that doesn't really perform configuration or installation actions on other third party products.

Assuming we are uninstalling an update, everything should be done on the side, meaning that a new executing environment needs to be configured on the side by creating one that:

- Effectively implements a version prior to the one being uninstalled,
- Is prepared to endure the execution of the final swapping action in the committing phase.

Once this baseline is established, the rollback procedure will, pretty much, be limited to cleaning up the new "on the side" environment, after the non-failing swap. However, should a processing error occur in the midst of the committing phase, the previous existing environment needs to be recovered by reversing the swap actions already taken[1].

On the other hand, when uninstalling a base installation, instead of an update, one can afford to be a lot more lenient, which can even include questioning whether a rollback procedure should exist. Should a processing error occur within the uninstall procedure of a base setup, no one really expects or wants the product to continue fully functional[2]. Therefore, one's energy ought to be concentrated in ensuring that the uninstall procedure can be run multiple times, regardless of the state that the installed product finds itself in. Plus, it should attempt to uninstall each piece of the product, despite needing to assume that some components could have been previously removed. This will allow system administrators to fully remove the product, even after processing errors within the uninstall procedure[3].

8. **Treat it as any fallible component, by making sure you generate detailed logging.**

   As already covered within the items about the procedure's transactional semantics, errors will occur and, consequently, having a detailed logging system that allows system administrators to precisely identify what went wrong[4] is absolutely crucial. As stated, this is critical in ensuring that system administrators can proceed to fixing whichever problems prevented the successful completion of the procedure. However, should the need arise, this also makes it possible to detect, with great precision, both which steps were automatically executed and which ones failed. Profiling the system's state of affairs may allow for system administrators to manually complete some required tasks when

---

[1] Again, these procedures should be well document, so as to ensure that they can be manually executed by a system administrator, if so required.
[2] Were that to be the case, they simply would not have executed the uninstall procedure.
[3] As long as they fix whichever condition prevented the procedure from running to its end and, afterwards, follow it with a new run of the uninstall steps.
[4] As well as where, within the process, were things stalled.

having to either reverse or complete the effects of a partially completed commit or rollback phase[1].

Now, considering that the execution of the procedure is a rare event, we do not usually need to be as flexible as when dealing with other software components. Typically, we can be far less demanding in terms of how flexible we are when faced with the configuration of these logging features. There really is little to be gained from either setting different levels of detail or creating the ability to define, to a certain extent, what is logged and what is not. In fact, how such a configuration would be executed would be a challenge in its own and, therefore, for the sake of simplicity and in line with the inherent context, the logging system should always be on and, additionally, having its detail level as high as possible. It really makes little difference whether such a logging feature will cost a bit more[2] or require some extra storage space[3]. Given that this is something that is done quite infrequently, it should be possible to allocate these resources which are, anyway, merely temporary. What must be ensured is that they are either released automatically[4] or, at least, that what needs to be manually removed[5] is properly documented.

9. **Validate pre-requisites thoroughly.**

Considering all traits already discussed thus far, it is clear that one needs a lot in order to create a great installation experience. In fact, many big products are handling this as a sub-product in its own right. However, before actually performing a single deployment action, one needs to validate whether all the required pre-requisites are present and functional.

Validating these pre-requisites is not always easy, especially if one needs parts of certain third party products whose main installation is easy to detect[6] but, on the other hand, which lack the ability to easily detect whether a specific and, eventually, optional feature or component, is deployed. Such an issue can also be relevant in detecting the presence of either a certain operating system feature or of a specific version of a specific component, with the latter being more problematic.

Regardless of what the scenario is, all pre-requisites should be listed in great detail as well as duly validated before actually firing along any setup actions. If a specific component either does not provide a documented way of detecting its presence or whether it is configured in a certain required way, one may need to resort to the extreme

---

[1] Regardless of whether we were executing an install or uninstall procedure.
[2] Performance wise.
[3] For persistency sake.
[4] Eventually, at the end of a successful completion and by confirmation of a system administrator.
[5] As it is temporary data.
[6] And, thus, whose presence is easy to validate.

case of actually performing certain actions on such components[1] so as to actually know whether it is possible to proceed. Great care must be invested in planning this phase of the install procedure so as to avoid subsequent errors and, additionally minimize the probability of having to cancel the installation half-way through.

A final word of caution: even when uninstalling a product one should validate requirements. Why is this? Well, simply put, because the pre-requisites of the version that is to be configured by the uninstall procedure[2] may require different pre-requisites than those currently on the system. It is very likely that, though they were available at one point in time, they too might have been upgraded or, alternatively, even uninstalled, should they have been deemed as no longer required.

10. **Support an unattended installation scenario.**

In many production environments one will need to replicate install procedures throughout many servers. In other situations, install procedures cannot be executed interactively and, therefore, must be completely autonomous[3].

To support such environments, one will need to ensure that the installation procedures are built on technologies that support a completely unattended install scenario, where one can script that which would be manually entered inputs into a prepared and persisted stream, which, in turn, is supplied to the install procedure and used to, subsequently, supply the required inputs and, thus, execute the installation tasks Most technologies used to build setup programs come with specific ways of creating these scripted versions, thus allowing operation teams to create an automated way to bypass the existing constraints limiting their ability to run the install routines in an interactive manner.

Despite, currently, being a relatively standard feature, one should still ensure that the platform of choice supports such a schema, meaning that one needs to consider this to be a particular use case scenario, in the sense that it requires, as any other, detailed analysis and testing. Additionally, proper documentation of how to create the required unattended scripts must be assured, so that operation teams are able to effectively use the install procedure without needing to delve into avoidable nightmares so as to merely implement a completely human input-free install experience. Finally, it should kept in mind that this must be achievable both for the install[4] and the uninstall stages[5].

---

[1] That should be neutral from an impact perspective.
[2] Yes, I am referring to the uninstall of an update.
[3] Without requiring any human input.
[4] Regardless of whether one will be running a base install or an update.
[5] Again, regardless of whether one will be running the uninstall of an update or of a base setup.

Item recap:

This item's fundamental guidelines can be succinctly systematized as follows:

- ✓ Start working on your setup from day one. Design and code it from the project's starting date. Allow it to mature along with the product's development cycle.
- ✓ Think about all the different traits of the setup routine. Consider base installation, installation of fixes and patches as well as uninstall procedures. Define whether fixes and patches are cumulative or whether you need to go through every single update. Consider how you will handle uninstallation of these fixes and patches.
- ✓ Manage setup sources as any other part of your codebase.
- ✓ The setup needs to reflect the side-by-side strategy, should you adopt it for your product.
- ✓ Be very careful with shared components. If possible, choose only private deployment and avoid shared components. It will simplify your install and uninstall routines.
- ✓ Make sure you have transactional semantics in your install and uninstall routines. Given that real distributed transactions are not available, especially when configuring third party products, try to follow the "install and configure on the side" recipe in order to ensure that your logical commit can be something close to a non-failing swap and, furthermore, your logical rollback can be just a cleanup of these "on the side" elements, which shouldn't produce any really effect even if they weren't completely removed.
- ✓ Consider how you reverse the effects of an uninstall process, should it fail half-way through. Going for the "install and configure on the side" recipe, even within the uninstall procedure, is probably your best bet.
- ✓ Create detailed logging of your setup routines and include as much detail as possible.
- ✓ Ensure that you start your install and uninstall routines by validating the existence of any required pre-requisites. For uninstall routines, especially when uninstalling an update, you need to ensure that the system has whichever pre-requisites are required by the version which will be operational once the uninstall routine is completed.
- ✓ Support an unattended installation scenario.

28. Upgrades will happen: ensure you have an effective upgrade strategy

All things considered, installing a brand new system is always a walk in the park when compared to upgrading an existing production deployment. There are many reasons explaining such difference in complexity[1] but, overall, it basically boils down to one fact: installing a brand new system does not entail changing something that is already running and executing business processes.

Clearly, upon deciding that upgrading an existing solution is needed, there are a myriad of items to be pondered so as to avoid imposing any system downtime altogether or, at the very least, keeping it to an acceptable minimum. Quite naturally, doing so is highly dependent on what the system is doing, such as whether:

- One is facing a mission-critical system that needs to provide an uninterruptable and continuous service,
- Though dealing with a mission-critical system, it might provide some windows of expected inactivity which can, therefore, be used to accommodate any required downtime forced by the upgrade.

Unfortunately, each system's flexibility to deal with downtimes isn't the only major headache when performing an upgrade. There is another compelling reason dictating that an upgrade is always an uphill struggle which, quite simply, is the need to test or rehearse the whole upgrade path in a quality environment together with the inevitable task of preparing a rollback plan[2]. As such, it is imperative to have both a very carefully crafted strategy in order to perform the upgrade itself as well as an equally good plan to revert the process, should a real upgrade disaster occur.

To achieve this, we need to contemplate the technology being used and, right from the early design phase, comprehend what the requirements for upgrading a system will be. This constitutes a key area that cannot easily be retrofitted to a poorly designed architecture[3], and, this being so, the following elements should be used in putting together an effective strategy:

1. **Determine early on the system's acceptable downtime window.**
   Any ancient warrior knew that, in a battle, there were two commandments that ought to be followed to acquire any chance of winning:

---

[1] As defined in item **27 For a product to be used, installed it must be!**

[2] In case a catastrophic and unexpected situation stems from upgrade, rendering the upgraded system unusable and, hence, forcing the drastic recovery measure of backtracking to the previous status quo.

[3] In the sense that it failed to address the upgrade requirement as any other mandatory and critical tenant.

- Knowing the opponent,
- Knowing the battleground.

Although this might seem to be a far stretch for today's datacenters, it does, nonetheless, bear some relevance for plotting one's strategy so as to create a viable upgrade path.

Knowing exactly how the system will be used, as well as the environment on which it will operate, are key in determining how to perform a glitch-free upgrade.

Patterns of system usage are a key component, for they will determine whether we are facing either a system that must perform uninterruptable work 24x7 or one that, perhaps, has a schedule that includes some foreseeable inactive time slot[1].

Quite naturally, it will be much easier to design an upgrade process should a downtime window be provided. In such cases, it needs to be ensured that, within that window of opportunity, we are able to execute all the procedures entailed within the upgrading task, which include starting with any relevant initial backup operations and, subsequently, moving along to the true upgrading tasks. Finally, we should also ensure enough leeway in order to perform a system rollback, in case insurmountable problems do emerge after the upgrade[2].

It goes without saying that, the ability to accomplish all of this, vastly depends on several factors, such as the:

- Window's own size,
- Number of servers and components involved,
- Implied system data and any inherent manipulation possibly required.

As a final note we should discuss the bolts and nuts of scenarios where downtime windows are either inexistent or too narrow[3]. Although these scenarios are common and, therefore, as important as those where usable downtime windows do exist, this discussion will be deferred to a subsequent item (within this chapter) where side-by-side execution of different releases is contemplated.

2. **A detailed plan is always vital.**

Despite all the different variables presented thus far, one truth remains untouched: it is possible to perform virtually any upgrade task given that it is properly planned and performed by using the adequate tools and procedures. Such tools and procedures may

---

[1] Occurring either recurrently, with a certain pattern, non-recurrently, though in a predictable way. Although many mission-critical systems do need to run 24x7, many still provide daily or weekly windows of expected inactivity.

[2] Essentially, we should be able to backtrack to the previous existing environment within that same downtime window.

[3] Making it impossible to create an inactivity-based upgrade policy.

range from automated processes, based on software specifically built for aiding in the upgrade process, to either good old fashioned administration scripts or a set of manually executed commands (carefully assembled and previously tested). Overall, it really does not matter which avenue is taken, as long as it is in line with existing requirements.

However, one recurring problem that does show its unappealing face is that of not having had upgrading processes defined during the design phase, neither planned for, nor validated or sanctioned by, the team which built the solution. Ultimately, such an occurrence is, quite obviously, a dire mistake. One simply cannot expect operation teams to sketch out proper upgrade plans by themselves, given that they do not have a detailed overall view of all the intertwined dependencies present amongst all system components.

Furthermore, knowing whether the physical or logical servers hosting the solution are either dedicated to this specific system or, being shared by several systems, is also key to determining how to setup the upgrade route.

As such, the hosting context supporting the solution is also critical in defining how to prepare the upgrading tasks. It is necessary to bear in mind that, in many situations, no real access to the servers exists and, thus, a fully automated procedure needs to be created. In other situations, one may be allowed to have some manually executed tools and, sometimes, even be given the benefit of interactively performing tasks and checks along the way.

Regardless of the scenario being faced, two things need to be remembered and incorporated into one's plan:

- Definition of the hosting context,
- Characterization of how it will influence the necessary tools and tasks.

3. **Evaluate whether side-by-side existence of different releases needs to be supported.**
   Side-by-side execution of different releases is, probably, one of the most difficult things to achieve within any software product. Thus, when achieved, it is implicitly a hymn to great software design. Invariably, systems simply do not support side-by-side execution of different releases, with this being so for two main reasons:

   - Some product components take exclusive ownership of a system resource; in turn, this prevents any sort of version-capable usage, which makes it impossible to have several different versions executing in parallel,
   - Other product components rely on external elements being shared by either different products or different versions of the same product, which, somehow, renders them unusable in a version-capable way.

   Given this, let us clarify these two main conditions.

154

First of all, situations in which a certain software component takes exclusive ownership of a system resource are extremely abundant. Take, for example, the case of internal system files, queues, events or semaphores being acquired with an exclusive access, which makes it impossible to have different versions working side-by-side. Additionally, even if these resources do not need to be exclusive, just think about how:

- Few systems use some sort of internal versioning schema that allows one to use distinct instances of these resources,
- Configuration resources[1] are used or created in a way completely unfriendly towards side-by-side execution of different product releases.

Secondly, think about all those products which, once a new version is installed, end up replacing some elements and maintaining others untouched, creating a scenario where two versions cannot be made to coexist. Who hasn't seen a software product that updates a database by changing its schema, or even master data? Such a procedure makes it almost impossible to run different versions of the product, since the internal database itself wasn't designed to support a versioning schema.

Interestingly, supporting side-by-side execution can be a way of resolving the issue of an upgrade without any downtime. This can be accomplished by, essentially, creating a new instance of the solution which, eventually, leads to having previous versions/instances being, eventually, subsequently removed. By installing a new side-by-side instance one may be capable of routing new requests to this new version, while allowing requests that were already in-flight to simply finish their execution within the previously existing version. In the end, this plays out by having an upgrade being performed without downtime, courtesy of side-by-side execution!

4. **Make the testing environment a critical and non-negotiable part of the product/solution.**

Every now and then[2], a business opportunity comes along where a software product needs to be either developed or acquired so as to solve a specific business need which is, somehow, constrained by a budget[3]. This is, quite definitely, not an uncommon situation, given that it crops up more often than what any IT professional wishes for. Invariably, it increases, not only the risk, but also the stakes and, ultimately, the strain on the day-to-day lives of those involved in bringing the beast to life. When such a scenario comes up, it is very common for some people to react by trying to trim costs, so as to stay within a given financial target. In turn, this generates less than sound technical paths which,

---

[1] Intrinsic to either the software product or the operating system.
[2] Though, unfortunately, more often than one might either expect, advise or even conceive as probable.
[3] Either to reduce investment as an absolute value or to increase the theoretical/projected return on investment concerning said project.

often, leads to either forgoing the existence of a testing environment or creating a crippled one[1]. Funny enough and, perhaps, as an irony of fate, the latter situation is, occasionally, even worse than not having one at all, given that, when no environment exists, no assumptions nor risks will be undertaken as a direct consequence of a false reliance on its existence. However, when a crippled environment is made available, often enough, there is a tendency to ignore the fact that the environment is only a partial replica of the production set. Hence, people fail to see the inherent risk and, even worse, assume that any existing risk can be mitigated[2].

Despite this, the fact remains unchanged, in that we simply cannot run a simulated upgrade[3] if lacking a testing environment that is an exact replica of what exists in production. Furthermore, should one deviate by simply changing a few variables, the outcome may turn out to be extremely hazardous. As an example, merely replacing physical servers with virtualized environments can be dangerous, should people fail to see that they are not getting the exact same deal[4].

Regardless of the reasons that influence anyone into believing they can live without a true testing environment, it is always wise to invest time and energy in trying to bring them back to the side of reason. Ultimately, there is simply no way to effectively and comprehensively test a solution upgrade without running it on an exact copy of the real production environment. A mere similar environment will always bring out some false premises and assumptions.

5. **Determine how multiple server architecture impacts the upgrade path.**

One should never make the mistake of thinking that, if a solution runs perfectly on a single server, it will be equally as impressive on multiple servers. Such assumption is the same as thinking that, should some code run correctly on a single core system, it is sure to also run properly in a multi-core one. These situations are simply not that simple, and software developers have learned this over the years[5].

Similarly, multi-server architectures introduce odd peculiarities regarding system upgrades that require careful analysis and consideration during an early design phase.

---

[1] With the latter one being more likely.

[2] Since they believe that the partial environment is a sound enough test bed to support one's work, and specifically testing an upgrade path.

[3] And other types of tests for that matter.

[4] By no means do I look upon virtualization, *per se*, as detrimental. Instead, I am just attempting to point out that a physical environment is not the same as a virtualized one and, having a production environment sitting on a physical set and, on the other hand, a testing environment on a virtualized one, can induce certain changes which, now and then, prove to be quite decisive in the way the solution works.

[5] Though some had to do it the hard way.

6. **Handle upgrades with transactional semantics.**

    Database transactional semantics are just great, aren't they? Software engineers can just pound away, in the form of hitting the database within the context of a transaction, only to simply revert everything without any additional headaches[1]. Given its simplicity, shouldn't it be normal for this to be regarded as a model to emulate in a system upgrade? In fact it should, and for the following reasons:

    - Firstly, because we could easily rollback, should the upgrade process fail half-way through[2],
    - Secondly, because we could use this feature as an easy way to run as many test cycles as so wished within the testing environment and, furthermore, without any major headaches associated with restoring the existing environment prior to the start of the upgrade process,
    - Thirdly, because, though a transactional upgrade process is a truly difficult thing to implement, it is something that we need and would like to have for free!

    Thus, despite all surrounding difficulties, one really needs to implement upgrades using transactional semantics and, as far as install procedures go, one should refer to that which was discussed in the previous item[3].

7. **Consider operating system and base components upgrade policy.**

    Apart from the software product itself, operation teams must take special care of the base infrastructure that is used to run the solution on. Within this realm, we usually account for the operating system as well as any other mandatory elements[4] installed into the production servers. Although one will not be worried about how these items should be upgraded *per se*, it is, nevertheless, important to consider at least two things:

    - Will any of the used products, somehow, prevent the implementation of whatever strategy deemed ideal for the product being designed? Will, for instance, any of the base products prevent the implementation of side-by-side execution support? If so, do these limitations occur in few and contained places, or is it a more widespread problem? Whatever the answer is to these questions, one should bear in mind that the defined strategy must be aligned with them.
    - Given that many base products support regular and, possibly, automatic updates, should those be enabled? On the side of prudency the answer is no, since

---

[1] Just for the sake of this discussion, let us ignore issues such as concurrency and isolation levels.
[2] And believe me, it will happen occasionally, especially if one doesn't do a proper dry run in an adequate testing environment
[3] As defined in item **27 For a product to be used, installed it must be!**
[4] Of the defined architecture.

software engineers producing such base products are as human as the next person, and, therefore, mistakes will, invariably, crop up now and then. From a practical standpoint, and as a simple historical perspective, several systems have reportedly been involuntarily broken by simply allowing servers to execute automatic updates of infrastructural components.

Item recap:

This item's fundamental guidelines can be succinctly systematized as follows:

- ✓ Determine, from the first days of architecture design, whether the system will have a downtime window so as to perform system upgrades.
- ✓ Evaluate whether you need to support side-by-side execution of different versions. This will impact your design, given it may, in fact, determine the upgrade strategy. Take note that this is especially so if you cannot have a reasonable downtime window to perform system upgrades.
- ✓ Ensure you have a testing environment which is an exact replica of the production environment. This will allow you to test all your upgrade paths extensively.
- ✓ Determine how you will conduct your system upgrade when facing a multi-server architecture.
- ✓ Handle upgrades with transactional semantics. Drive your design in a direction that ensures having all upgrade operations being executed on the side, followed by a few final steps that perform low-risk, and easy to reverse, swap operations (preferably non-failing swap operations).
- ✓ Consider how side-by-side execution may help in implementing upgrades when no usable downtime window exists.
- ✓ Consider how operating systems and base component upgrade policies can impact your solution. Beware of automatic update features.

29. Configuration is needed: minimize the options and use a centralized resource

No real enterprise capable system will exist without a set of options that allows for operation teams to tweak its behavior according to the desired conformance level. Configuration options will range from simple security-related access settings to, sometimes, complex performance inherent choices or even conflicting feature selection.

As time goes by and new software releases are made available, configuration options also tend to blossom like unwanted garden weeds. Despite this, it is quite common to create configuration options that enable both the activation and deactivation of features, especially as a means to both ensure distinct *modus operandi* between releases and allow a configurable level of selective retro-compatibility. Configuration settings are also pervasively used to define thresholds for diverse options that, together, produce a complex intertwined set of possibilities. Surely enough, this ends up creating a monster that is, often, difficult to tame.

Consider the vast array of items that can be configured either in a modern operating system or a modern database system. The options are so abundant, and end up creating so many overlapping or touching points, that it is almost impossible to thoroughly understand or foresee the consequences of changes in either some or many of them.

Furthermore, many systems tend to be component-based and, too often, end up creating local configuration resources that affect one or more components, therefore forcing operation teams to delve into distinct assets in order to configure the system as a whole. Some solutions go even further regarding configurability, creating these distinct assets in different technologies and, thus, adding even more complexity. Finally, at the end of this apparent chaos lay the systems that create hierarchies of configuration assets. These overlap each other, further aggravating the task of troubleshooting production environments when specific behaviors need to be tracked down within the currently active configuration set.

Simply put, configuration options need:

- To be clear as to their purpose,
- Have an iron-clad boundary, so as to avoid side effects from other seemingly unrelated options,
- To be managed from a centralized configuration resource.

Thus, to prevent chaos and confusion within the configuration realm, it is quite useful to follow these guidelines:

1. **Ensure that you minimize configuration options to the absolute minimum required.**

    When building a software product, one expects a certain degree in flexibility in order to adjust its features to fit both different production scenarios and different commercially available licensing options. Nevertheless, it is relevant to keep in mind that, when the number of options increases, so will one's headaches. People will, usually, have unwarm feelings towards too many alternatives and, often enough, have trouble deciding between a couple of alternative paths, let alone ten times that number of options. As such, one should strive to keep the available options to an absolute minimum. Whenever possible one should make the system adjust itself by detecting both the existing environmental conditions and the executing context. Additionally, this should be accomplished while also avoiding requiring users to configure items that, somehow, purport to the existing context and which can be detected by using some set of existing calls[1].

    Having too many options can also be symptomatic of failing to determine early on precisely what the product should do, which can only come about by defining what it should be good at. Though there is no magical ideal number of options to go by, one should definitely avoid having hundreds or even thousands of options[2] in products that merely took between a few months and a couple of years to build. Finally, do avoid running off with comparisons with options that exist at either the operating system level or enterprise database systems level. Bear in mind that these products took many years to build and have millions of accumulated man/hours invested in them.

2. **Ensure that all options are persisted in a single centralized asset.**

    Too many systems have adhered to the trend of scattering configuration options through many different resources, from multiple files with varying formats, to operating-system provided mechanisms. This lack of centralization does not help operation teams, given that they need to master available configuration options without the added hurdle of also having to search through various assets. Furthermore, one does not want to have a single software component reading configuration options from different places. Were that to occur, it could, in the end, lead to scenarios where IT professionals merely manage part of the configuration set, while thinking that there were no additional options to meddle with.

---

[1] Most often, either the operating system or base product calls.

[2] Very rarely is that sort of complexity required and beneficial to whoever adopts the product.

3. **Ensure that complex storage formats are manipulated through appropriate tools, enabling proper configuration validation.**

    Since operation teams will strive for simplicity and effectiveness, the last thing they wish for is to be forced to deal with software products that use complex storage formats for persisting configuration data, while also failing to provide the appropriate management tools.

    Relying on free tools available on the internet should be avoided, as these tools will, almost always, fall short of what is required. They will not be implementing any validation rules on the content itself and, frequently, will even fail to provide support for proper syntax checking[1].

    Going back to the content itself, a proper tool will ensure, not only that invalid options cannot be set for existing configuration options, but also the correct enforcement of the dependencies between configuration options[2].

    Operation teams will not be happy about having to deal with scenarios where one can simply create invalid configurations that end up breaking the system. Furthermore, this is especially so if the system breaks sometime during production, potentially in a timeframe that is quite distant from the configuration change itself, since it makes it that much difficult to track down the root cause.

    When possible, provide the proper tools[3] and enforce rule validation, so as to ensure that no incorrect configurations can be persisted[4].

4. **Ensure that no items overlap and there are no side effects.**

    Should one create a pattern of simple configuration items, where each entry targets an isolated and concrete feature of the application, a gigantic step towards a stable configuration mechanism will have been attained. Nothing will make operation teams scream louder than realizing that, when they change a setting that is supposed to be related to a specific feature, they end up twisting a completely different and totally unrelated part of the system.

    Configuration settings need to be simple and clear as to their purpose as well as their effect, and, quite naturally, thorough documentation is a must-have for any enterprise capable software product. However, minimizing the risk by ensuring that, whenever possible, there isn't any overlapping or side effects between different options, is a definite sound approach to allowing the system to be:

---

[1] How many times have we seen IT professionals editing XML-based configuration files using the simplest and plainest of all text editors, meaning those that won't event validate an XML-schema?
[2] Should they exist – more on this later.
[3] Even for plain text-based configuration files.
[4] Failing fast is always better!

- Effectively managed,
- Resistant to the test of time.

5. **Hide magic values and privilege descriptive options.**

   How many configuration files have you seen that, apart from having a bunch of configuration options with designations that convey little to no information as to their purpose, also end up having a limited set of possible values, which, despite representing distinct solution behaviors, are translated to magical numbers that really provide little semantic context? Or, how many times have you seen products being configured using numeric values so as to represent a set of finite system states? Wouldn't it be much safer, as well as less error prone, to simply provide text alternatives to these odd looking and seemingly meaningless set of numbers?

   Hence, the bottom line really consists of avoiding requiring operation teams to use these magic numbers[1], thus preventing most people's standard instinct of memorizing information over time only to, unsuspectingly, end up misusing the supposedly memorized data.

6. **Ensure that all items have default values, while looking to have them being explicit and defined, instead of implicit and undefined.**

   A system that is optimally configured by default is a wonderful thing, although an unlikely achievement, considering the complexity and breadth of modern enterprise capable software products. However, even if some configuration items can be safely configured to their default values[2], it should still be ensured that the configuration set is explicit and defined, whereby these options and defaults values are, indeed, part of the configuration data, instead of simply inferred by the system as a result of their explicit absence.

   Implicit and undefined configuration values tend to obscure the task of those managing production systems, since many options simply seem to fall out of site[3]. Consequently, people will simply be more prone to forgetting what they do not see, even if, somewhere in the past, they were well aware of them. Overall, it is no different from the Hollywood syndrome, in the sense that if one is not seen, one will end up being forgotten.

7. **Always default so as to maintain maximum retro-compatibility between releases.**

   It is a common scenario to have features changing between different releases of a software product. Many times, in order to maintain maximum retro-compatibility,

---

[1] Again, proper tools to manage configuration can hide all this complexity.
[2] With little probability of requiring any change.
[3] Particularly when troubleshooting problems related to them.

configuration settings are used so as to allow IT professionals to choose which type of behavior the system should showcase:

- The newly created one, made available through a new release,
- The long-standing one that has been the product's trademark over the years.

To have a high likelihood of satisfying of the entire client base, it is usually a good call to allow the product to adjust its behavior to any of the many possible flavors. However, in doing so, it is important to be certain that the out-of-the-box configuration has the system behaving according to what the market is used to from prior releases. This ensures that no special action is needed so as to support an upgrade[1], thus improving the overall sense of stability towards the product.

Although I have sided with using default configuration values, this does not mean that they should be implicit. Instead, products should still make them explicit and defined.

8. **When appropriate, refresh configuration options without any downtime.**

    Configuration options exist to support specific changes in the system's behavior and, while many will spur the need to perform comprehensive testing prior to performing a production change, others[2] can usually be safely tweaked in most production systems without undergoing massive testing[3].

    When in a situation where, either a setting change can occur without massive testing or it has been concluded[4] that the change can, indeed, be executed, one still needs to think carefully about how this change will be picked up by all software components composing the solution.

    One also needs to plan how to perform such refreshment without any sort of downtime, including process recycling. For that to be accomplished the following few things should be considered and, usually, they need to be accounted for early in one's system design phase[5]:

    - It should be attempted to have all software components picking up the configuration change simultaneously, since the last thing one needs is to have a few components behaving in the opposite direction of the remaining ones. This usually requires software components to perform some sort of

---

[1] In the context of this specific feature.
[2] Such as defining logging levels.
[3] Quite naturally, this depends on what the system does and in which context it operates.
[4] From the performance of massive testing.
[5] Or else, a lot of reengineering may end up being required.

wait/synchronization step, so as to ensure that, not only is everyone aware of the new configuration, but also that the new behavior can in fact take over[1].

- An event-based mechanism should be used in order to notify all components of the new configuration change. One doesn't want to be forced to perform a sort of repetitive check so as to detect whether there are new values in place, given that this would hinder performance[2].

As such, ensuring that configuration changes are appropriately refreshed without any downtime is no easy task and, additionally, needs to be embedded into the system design from the very beginning.

9. **Ensure that configuration options can be managed using an authentication bound method and, additionally, consider requiring different credentials for critical options.**

The software world is not a place where democracy shines, meaning that security protocols and restrictions to access both content and functionality are the bread and butter of an experienced engineer's daily routine. Nevertheless, I have seen very few systems where configuration items are properly protected, and even fewer that differentiate access control between distinct configuration options[3].

Most often, both configuration options and their inherent security tend to be trusted to the operating system, whereby operation teams should, after installing the product, configure whichever mechanism the operating system provides in order to limit access to configuration stores. In most situations, this is never actually performed and, therefore, rarely will this enable one to differentiate access to distinct options based on supplied credentials.

Overcoming this limitation requires careful consideration as to the need for access control within the configuration options[4], while ensuring that the options themselves cannot be changed through an unsupported route[5]. Ensuring this is just another scenario of data protection, for which proven techniques like encryption and hashing can be used.

---

[1] The way this is implemented is highly dependent of the context of the solution. Usually, one needs to address both code synchronization sections and some potential data manipulation in order to realign information with the new configuration.

[2] Also, and quite likely, a spot needs to be placed on one's pristine software designing skills.

[3] According to criteria such as criticality or purpose.

[4] Again, using appropriate tools to manipulate configuration settings will also enable this feature to be built.

[5] Namely, by using free available tools.

10. **Think about centralization, or, at least, replication, so as to ensure that multiple-server systems are consistent and coherent.**

Multi-server architectures have become the common thing in modern enterprise solutions, either to support load-balanced scenarios or to merely create redundancy. Regardless of whatever reasons spurred the creation of a multi-server architecture, one always needs to evaluate how configuration settings will be kept available and synchronized for all servers.

There are many options available, ranging from a centralized location, which has all servers gathering the required configuration information from a unique place, to solutions where one has multiple replicas of configuration settings. The latter one allows for servers to look up data from different places, though with the added complexity of needing to ensure replication in a synchronized way.

Let us look at both scenarios in order to identify their respective pitfalls:

- A centralized configuration system will, automatically, guarantee that all look ups are performed with the most up to date data. However, it will be effectively doomed should it create a single point of failure. Consider the following potential scenarios as a result of having such a single point of failure coming about:

   What if one cannot access the configuration storage when starting up a server? Should the server simply assume default values? Surely not, given that other servers may have accessed the configuration storage correctly at a prior date and, thus, having already started processing according to totally different settings. Should the server simply abort its startup routine? Doing so would definitely be the safest route. But what if one is merely refreshing the configuration, having received a notification event regarding a configuration change? Should one shut down, given that other systems might have previously refreshed their configuration properly? Alternatively, considering that a synchronization feature that ensures that all servers refresh their configuration data has been implemented, should one simply ignore the refresh notification and continue processing according to the prior configuration?

- On the other hand, a non-centralized scenario calls for the implementation of some sort of distributed synchronization mechanism, so as to ensure that all servers refresh their configuration and start processing with the new values simultaneously. Additionally, it also requires the notification system[1] to be integrated with whichever replication technique one has selected in order to distribute the new configuration values through all existing servers. Hence, how about the replication itself? Is there a master server, as in the only one from

---

[1] That will inform all software components of there being a new configuration available.

which the configuration can be updated and from which the replication process both starts and spreads the data to other servers or, alternatively, are all servers equal, in the sense of displaying the possibility of having configuration changes being operated from any server? If so, how does one handle potential conflicts when changes are made simultaneously from different servers?

All things considered, there are no easy solutions! Nevertheless, the route that is, usually, less troublesome, is that of a centralized path. In this case, one's main concerns boil down to what takes place when one fails to read the configuration and, thus, how to react should this occur when either starting up the system or refreshing the configuration after receiving the corresponding notification event.

11. Ensure that you automate a historic record of past configurations.

Have you ever browsed through file system directories in production systems, only to find innumerous copies of the same file, usually, with the name suffixed with a date? Who hasn't used this remarkably simply, yet totally inadequate and completely unreliable method of versioning configuration files[1]?

Many operation teams follow this arcane pattern of backing up files by suffixing their names with a date. However, they do so while also failing to add any additional piece of information that will positively aid in the task of precisely understanding both what changed was and, far more importantly, the reasons behind it.

Again, this spurs the need to support proper tooling, as well as a historic record of past configurations with appropriate information to identify what was changed and why it was so. Assuring this level of information will give everyone a safer platform to work with and, hence, a far better system in ensuring the existence of a functional process of managing configuration changes over time.

---

[1] Or other files for that case.

Item recap:

This item's fundamental guidelines can be succinctly systematized as follows:

- ✓ Minimize the number of configuration options to the bare minimum. Too many options will create the perfect breeding ground for mistakes.
- ✓ Ensure that options are centralized in a single place. Having configuration options scattered around in different assets is confusing and, furthermore, leads to having some options being, occasionally, overlooked.
- ✓ Ensure that complex storage formats are manipulated through proper tools. Do not rely on free-existing tools that may, eventually, handle the format, while failing to understand the implied semantics[1].
- ✓ Ensure that items are tightly bound, in the sense that changing one option's value does not generate a side effect on a distinct part of the product that should be managed by a different configuration item.
- ✓ Do not use magic values. Hide them through proper tooling.
- ✓ Ensure that items have default values and, additionally, make them explicit within the configuration. Implicitly defined items, and their values, will simply magnify problems when attempting to understand/change the configuration.
- ✓ Always default to maintain retro-compatibility between releases by setting options that may change the product's expected behavior to the specific value that upholds the previously existing scenario.
- ✓ Always ensure that you can refresh the configuration without causing system downtime.
- ✓ Analyze whether you should supply an authentication-bound mechanism in order to control configuration changes.
- ✓ Centralized configuration is, usually, the best option in a multi-server environment, while preferably ensuring that it embeds no single point of failure.
- ✓ Ensure that you automate the maintenance of a historic record of past configurations.

---

[1] Such as each configuration item's allowed values.

30. Strange unexplainable behaviors are inevitable: create a detailed and systematic tracing feature

Probably, there isn't a single software engineer alive who hasn't heard tales of applications performing mysterious and inexplicable feats that defy logical reasoning, and for which there is simply no theoretical justification or even a valid conceivable execution path. Unfortunately, most of these casuistic events lead many IT pros into wild goose chases that consume a ton of resources[1] and, for the most part, end up concluding that either many facts about the event itself had simply been misstated, misinterpreted or misunderstood, or that, eventually, in what usually constitutes a less comfortable outcome, we are indeed in the realm of the unknown and further analysis requires gathering more information[2].

This constitutes one of the most problematic issues that we, as software engineers responsible for building successful products, must handle: how do we get more tracing data from a system that is in production and which must undergo serious and rigorous testing for any change to occur?

The painful, though truthful answer is that, in the vast majority of cases, one simply cannot choose such a strategy when dealing with an enterprise critical system. Therefore, it is adamant that detailed tracing features have long been put in place, including the added ability of being switched on or off as operation teams see fit.

This is a trend followed by many products and even operating systems, whereby one is given administrative power to turn on or off specific detailed tracing features which, when active, register huge amounts of information within a certain persistent storage[3], thus allowing one to almost replay all instructions executed so as to process a specific set of inputs.

Such a detailed analysis will, quite naturally, spur the creation of huge amounts of tracing data with interleaved information that purports to the execution of different requests running through the system in parallel. Furthermore, when dealing with distributed systems and architectures, where processing a request from start to finish will span through several distinct sets of servers and, possibly, distinct system components, it is even more difficult to process the scattered data and the seemingly unrelated wealth of information.

Therefore, there are a few guidelines that should be observed when implementing this kind of instrumentation, namely:

---

[1] In the form of energy and time.
[2] Dependent on having a similar event occur in the future.
[3] Usually, a logging file.

1. **Minimize hindering performance and take advantage of asynchronous patterns.**

   The information registered through this feature is, by no means, classified as critical business data and, therefore, does not require transactional semantics. This means that one can safely afford the risk of losing a few entries here and there[1], especially considering that:

   - The chances of these exceptions or errors actually occurring are, in fact, very slim,
   - Should they occur when trying to collect tracing data, no important business flow is actually compromised by its loss.

   Considering that the level of tracing data usually needed to be registered is overwhelming[2], it must be ensured that the impact of activating the tracing system on overall performance is minimized.

   Taking into account that we can indulge the luxury of losing some tracing records, we should definitely use an asynchronous pattern, whereby each piece of information that needs to be registered is passed into the tracing system by virtue of some in-memory registering schema[3] that does not have any attached persistency and, hence, introduces virtually no latency[4]. Once the entry is received[5] by the tracing system, the standard business flow can, then, move along as expected and, in parallel[6], the tracing system can asynchronously perform:

   - A batched-based registration of the received entries,
   - The slow IO tasks without hindering the performance of business flows,
   - The minimization of its own consumption of resources by writing a batch of entries, instead of processing each item autonomously.

   This reasoning ends up creating a lazy-writer approach that impeccably suits the requirements and constraints of the tracing component, while allowing the system to perform almost as efficiently as when the tracing mechanism is simply switched off.

2. **Consider filtering when both capturing and analyzing data.**

   Taking into account the vast amount of data that is usually collected in a detailed trace, carefully consider supporting filtering masks[7] in order to restrict the data that is to be

---

[1] Should an exceptional or erratic behavior occur within the tracing system.
[2] Since, when building the tracing system, we do not actually know what we will need, it is preferable to err in excess by throwing everything but the kitchen sink into the trace.
[3] Or a memory based inter-process communication feature.
[4] By forgoing using any IO-based mechanism.
[5] In-memory.
[6] Though with a lower priority.
[7] As configuration settings.

registered. Filtering upon capturing information will easily trim the persisted trace into a manageable set of data. Additionally, it will also ease the tasks of analyzing and saving the data itself.

The most difficult task about enabling a filtering process while performing the capture consists of ensuring that operation teams are capable of, easily and correctly, setting up the required configuration settings. Special care and effort must be invested in defining the capture filters, so as to allow them to powerfully reflect semantic constraints applicable to the solution's execution context.

The common trend within many enterprise capable systems has been comprised of adhering to some sort of regular expression based pattern, applicable to specific variables, which reflect the elements that make up the traced data.

Although this kind of configuration is both fairly easy to manipulate and, currently, considered "plain vanilla", it is yet another compelling reason that supports the need to have adequate tooling for configuration settings.

3. **Create adequate tools to explore trace data.**

    The sheer size of the recorded tracing data is reason enough to ensure that power tools exist so as to, properly and efficiently, search and analyze the existing information. However, carefully consider incorporating the following features into the analysis tools, so as to have a top notch product:

    -   The ability to group items that pertain to the same event, therefore, allowing users to easily step through the executed flow[1], while also ensuring the availability of drill down options[2]. Users tend to value an initial overall view, so as to more easily diagnose which specific steps appear suspicious and, therefore, elicit a more detailed analysis.

    -   The ability to perform some sort of automated first step analysis so as to quickly catch common and obvious problematic situations. Depending on the system, this can entail requests:

        o   Which were not properly completed, thus generating specific errors,

        o   Whose execution time surpassed certain defined thresholds,

        o   Which satisfy some specific given criteria[3].

---

[1] Almost, as if live debugging was being performed.

[2] Meant to expand or collapse all contextual information according to the specific step currently being analyzed.

[3] A good example of having filters to analyze data.

4. **In a distributed system, use correlation identifiers and ensure that tooling can process data from several servers so as to analyze the complete processing pipeline.**

    Most modern enterprise capable systems are, almost always, truly distributed systems where the execution of a specific business flow spans over several servers that harbor different components.

    As such, and in order to analyze the execution of the business flow, it is imperative that correlation identifiers exist, so as to allow for a complete and thorough analysis. Such process ensures the effective cross-reference of the tracing data registered in multiple files, despite having been created in different servers as a result of having had the flow moving through its inherent processing stages.

    This type of feature may also be required should we need to analyze several different processing flows which represent a logical business process, despite being spread over distinct servers.

    Now, considering that we need to correlate different trace data, it must be ensured that unique correlation identifiers are created within what is logically considered to be the system's entry point[1]. Furthermore, these unique correlation identifiers must be passed along the system's composing components, since the flow itself hops binary boundaries[2]. Additionally, this feature[3] must be accounted for during early system design phase, given that it directly affects either the different application binary interfaces that are defined or, at the very least, the data payload that is passed along in each binary hop.

    Thus, summing up, and given the sheer nature of the distributed system, the provided tools must ensure that we are easily able to process the complete breadth of tracing files being produced, as well as quickly and easily aggregating related entries while effectively drilling-down on each step of the overall process.

5. **Configure trace levels.**

    As defined for error and exception logging, trace data must also have a degree of configuration that enables operation teams to define, to a detailed level, what exactly gets registered. As a quick recap of what was defined for error and exception handling[4], consider embedding the following features within the tracing system:

    *   Ensuring consistency when registering trace items,
    *   Ensuring that the registered information is understandable by IT professionals and, actually, useful when performing analysis,

---

[1] The component that actually spawns the internal sequence of processing instructions which, in the end, complete the execution of the business process.
[2] Either within the same physical server or spanning several physical servers.
[3] Propagating correlation identifiers.
[4] As defined in item **1 An unavoidable reality: errors and exceptions will** happen.

- Being aware of the intrinsic risks of registering security sensitive information,
- Contemplating wrapping third party components, so as to ensure consistency,
- Ensuring that tracing levels can be changed dynamically, while also considering[1] a configuration level that creates no trace data whatsoever,
- Providing adequate tooling for configuration of trace levels.

Item recap:

This item's fundamental guidelines can be succinctly systematized as follows:

- ✓ Minimize hindering performance by ensuring that persistence features of tracing are delegated to asynchronous patterns, so as to ensure that slow IO operations do not influence the main business flow.
- ✓ Ensure that you support filtering of data when both capturing and analyzing data.
- ✓ Filtering when capturing is essential in order to limit the amount of registered data and it requires support at the configuration level of the tracing system.
- ✓ Filtering when analyzing must be implemented by the tools you deliver in order to support trace analysis.
- ✓ Create proper tools to analyze trace data, ensuring that it is easy to correlate entries as well as follow a complete business flow, while being able to drill-down on each piece of registered data.
- ✓ Be very aware of the need to propagate correlation identifiers within distributed systems.
- ✓ Support configuration levels for the tracing system.
- ✓ Beware of registering security sensitive information.
- ✓ Consider wrapping third party components so as to attain consistency.
- ✓ Ensure tracing levels can be changed dynamically without downtime and, additionally, support a level that creates no trace data.

---

[1] Contrary to what was suggested for error and exception handling.

31. Generate performance data and pave way for proactive alarms

Every now and then all products and platforms are plagued by some sluggish behavior and, although quite often there are external factors to blame, we must also recognize that our architectural efforts and coding sprees aren't always perfect. Though the art of assigning blame is older than the art of coding itself, attributing it shouldn't top anyone's priority list. Instead, it is far more important to focus all available resources in creating whichever features are necessary in order to allow system administrators to track down that which is truly happening with the system[1], and, preferably, deliver some level of proactive approach, so as to timely notify interested parties of the possibility that something might be off.

Generating performance data is, nowadays, a mandatory feature for any enterprise capable solution and, within this context, there are a few conditions that must be observed. Firstly, performance data must only be generated on request, meaning that it is not expected to have products constantly outputting performance data[2]. Performance data is only really interesting if there is a counterpart that is:

- Receiving it,
- Processing it, in whatever way is adequate for the context,
- Conducting some sort of analysis that can lead to the detection of both existing problems and their potential root causes.

Therefore, publishing live performance data usually follows a publisher-subscriber model where two decoupled systems actually communicate through a well-defined interface. The data consumer application acts as the subscriber and informs the publisher that is wants to start receiving performance data. From then on, the solution, acting as the data source, starts publishing it without any further constraints on the runtime.

The absence of any constraints on the runtime means that there will be no requirements for system initialization, creation of new processes or even tearing down of either any existing computational sessions or in-flight data flows. The solution is, therefore, expected to simply start pouring down data indicators without further ado and, furthermore, while showcasing no visible impact on whichever tasks are already being executed by the system. On top of this, everyone expects that outputting such performance data will not hinder overall system performance! Publishing performance data must be an extremely lightweight operation that imposes virtually no overhead on the system.

---

[1] In the form of its roots causes.
[2] Even if no active consumer is available.

However, publishing without overhead is merely one part of it and, given that, in most scenarios, one will be publishing the data into a set of interfaces that are defined by a specific platform gathering technology[1], it is usually the easiest one. Consequently, these interfaces will have been defined by other base products[2] and will have been streamlined over many years of usage. Quite often, these interfaces will also encapsulate any need to stream the data outside the physical machine's boundaries where they are, in fact, collected. Such streaming is mostly done asynchronously, without any sort of interference with the data collecting stage. Furthermore, this streaming is totally independent of the data gathering layer and, hence, one can pretty much forget about it altogether!

However, and contrary to publishing the data itself, one will be somewhat haunted by the task of actually gathering the data from the inner workings of the solution. Overall, this task is comprised, of at least, two very difficult elements:

- On one hand one needs to carefully identify which elements need collecting, since they will be the most likely pieces of information to be of help in analyzing and solving future problems,
- On the other hand, one will need to define how the internal process of acquiring the data, as well as bubbling it upwards towards the publishing layer, will actually work.

Defining which elements are to be collected is an art in itself. Essentially, one will be predicting which areas might be problematic together with which scenarios may turn out to be critical, so as to, hopefully, successfully diagnose which indicators will actually be useful. Admittedly, this will be far from easy and, although there is no full-proof recipe, here are a few guidelines:

1. **Identify any type of internal buffers or queues.**

   By reviewing the architecture and implementation plan, one will be able to identify any internal buffers or queues that might be used to hold temporary packets of data needing processing[3].

   These internal data structures, together with the level of data they are holding, will be great indicators of how the system is handling throughput and reacting to different patterns of load. Often, the higher the volume of packets on these temporary data structures, the higher the delay will be in processing pending requests. Should these data structures exist, the ideal scenario would consist of having them always virtually empty, given that the system would be able to outpace the rhythm at which these packets would

---

[1] To which many different solutions will end up publishing performance data.
[2] In some cases, at the operating system level itself.
[3] Usually, though not necessarily, in an asynchronous fashion.

be generated. Inversely, having requests wait for a certain time period in a dormant state within these queues or buffers usually implies an extra delay in processing.

Upon having these structures identified, the data indicators that should be published ought to identify exactly which data structure they relate to[1]. Afterwards, one should search as to which types of different operations are actually performed on these data structures, as well as whether they hold a single type of data packets or different types.

This implies publishing information that allows one to identify how different operations are executed on the data structures, namely operations that:

- Add items to them,
- Remove items from them,
- Perform any controlling tasks without actually affecting the volume of stored packets.

Furthermore, it also implies analyzing different types of packets, should they exist. In such case, publishing aggregated information about these types[2], would be great insight into what is happening in this part of the system.

2. Identify repeatable actions.

Another area that needs looking into consists of identifying any pattern of repeatable actions. All systems have, at one level or another, a set of actions being repeatedly executed in response to a given set of internal or external conditions. By measuring execution times of these repetitive actions one can allow administrators to perform two distinct, yet complementary, tasks:

- Set a performance baseline when the system is responding as expected,
- Afterwards, identify and quantify a specific level of degradation in a subset of these operations.

By establishing these initial baselines and comparing them with current processing patterns, system administrators will be able to supply detailed information about which areas of the product are not performing as expected. Plus, they will also supply specific values that will precisely showcase the level of degradation being experienced[3].

3. Identify different processing flows.

Each system exists so as to process a specific and pre-determined set of request types concerning what the product is meant to do. By precisely identifying these processing

---

[1] Especially if one has multiple similar structures within the system.

[2] Such as either the total count by type or the average, maximum and minimum time delay that the packets are exposed to by being stored temporarily in these queues or buffers.

[3] As opposed to merely relaying qualitative considerations about overall performance, which tend to be both inexact and pretty much useless in terms of effectively aiding in the diagnosis of potential problems.

flows and publishing performance data on each of them[1], one can allow system administrators to easily identify whether the system is behaving equally or unequally well on either all of them or only on a particular subset.

This type of differentiation is critical in understanding which parts of the system may be affected by some sort of unexpected condition causing the system not to deliver what is expected of it. By carefully outputting performance data reflecting the number of requests being processed at each time, their overall processing time and, probably more importantly, intermediate processing times of specific actions executed within the processing pipeline, one will allow system administrators to drill down on very specific parts of the system which have greater impact on overall performance.

Once again, aggregated information is, as a rule of thumb, a good starting point to reflect the overall trend. Publishing average, maximum and minimum processing times[2] is key in exposing a true picture of the inner workings of the system.

Finally, it is equally important to publish the total count of processed requests, namely to ensure that system administrators get a good picture of both what the system is actually performing and the kind of theoretical load being imposed on it.

4. **Identify key resources.**

Each system will rely on specific resources provided by the operating system, by the runtime environment or by third party supporting products. The key elements responsible for revealing what kind of impact the system has over its enclosing ecosystem need to be precisely identified, and these entail:

- Defining these types of resources,
- Characterizing how they are consumed,
- Diagnosing in which areas of the system they are used.

As always, should the environment be mistreated, one will suffer down the road. Therefore, publishing information on how one is consuming these limited resources constitutes the perfect strategy in determining what areas are being burdened beyond the acceptable level.

Some of these resources are clear cut, like memory, CPU or bandwidth, and most often one will have other routes to monitor their usage[3]. However there are two things to consider:

- By providing information on these resources from within the solution, one will be able to deliver insight at a level of granularity that is not supplied by other

---

[1] In an individual manner.
[2] Global and intermediate by request type.
[3] Using tools provided by the operating system, and not directly from one's performance data.

means. Specifically, one will be able to illustrate how memory or CPU is used by distinct elements within the same physical operating system process used by the product. This kind of detailed view is only possible with data collected from within the product and, furthermore, it will supply detailed information as to which components are responsible for whatever resource shortages do occur.

- Other resources, especially those not controlled or owned by an entity standing in a layer lower than one's product[1], usually do not have the same level of treatment. Therefore, they usually do not exhibit the same level of detailed performance data. Even when dealing with operating system-controlled resources, it is frequent to lack detailed information on consumption. As an example, just think about either synchronization primitives or particular API calls. In many cases, one will not find much about usage patterns nor about resource pressure on these elements[2]. Therefore, by collecting data on these elements from within the solution one can, once again, gain great insight as to what is happening as well as what may need further tuning or improvement.

Hence, after covering the basics on performance data, it is time to turn our attention towards proactive alarms and notifications. Creating a detailed logging system[3] is a great tool so as to perform an "after the fact" analysis. Usually, doing so takes a reasonable amount of time and, thus, cannot be seen as an effective and quick response strategy for when things go sour.

Achieving this proactivity requires establishing the basis that will allow key players[4] to be automatically notified when certain events occur. Consequently, this allows them to respond at once and, in many situations, to act as soon as a particular threshold is surpassed, without, however, reaching a subsequent critical level. Often, this type of notification system does not need to be built from the ground up, given that both operating systems and other supportive tools will allow one to generate specific events that they consume and, subsequently, execute the notification process. Moreover, many of these supportive tools can, and do, integrate with performance data. This means that one can hook them up together and, thus, ensure that these proactive alarms and notifications are automatically sent[5].

---

[1] Such as the operating system.
[2] As they are too fine-grained to be measured by whatever external performance data is available.
[3] As defined in item **30 Strange unexplainable behaviors are inevitable: create a detailed and systematic tracing** feature.
[4] Namely system administrators.
[5] Once certain indicators reach specific pre-defined levels.

Despite this, one needs to take into account the variety of environments where the product will run. This means ensuring the production of enough information so as to allow this level of control to be correctly and efficiently established.

In some situations one must output information to supportive systems while ensuring that it complies with pre-defined patterns. However, in other situations, one may need to create specific components that take care of monitoring certain indicators and, quite naturally, their inherent runtime values, on top of which one must also handle the notification process itself. It really depends on what one wants to precisely monitor, together with the granularity of information being used.

Most situations, where the standard integration with existing products will not be enough, correspond to occasions when one actually wishes to monitor specific conditions that implement complex business rules. Should one's warning levels[1] be defined through complex analysis of internal runtime conditions[2], building this ad-hoc warning component may be required.

Hooking directly into performance data is adequate when monitoring distinct and simple variables. When wishing to monitor complex conditions that integrate multiple variables, one will usually need to build, at the very least, components that evaluate these conditions and which, afterwards, are responsible for emitting the necessary packages of information[3], so that the existing support tools can process them and take care of the notification layer itself.

The key feature resides with the ability to evaluate conditions on the go, given that we are not looking into any sort of "after the fact" analysis. Instead, we need immediate data regarding the evaluation of specific conditions that can be tailored to fit the production environment. By planning this from the very beginning, one will attain a system that system administrators will love, for it will notify them of potential problematic situations. Furthermore, they will not need to spend considerable time reviewing loads of logging data so as to learn of problems that others have already experienced and suffered from!

---

[1] Those that trigger these alarms and notifications.
[2] Possibly complemented with data gathered from some other integrated systems.
[3] Using whichever standardized format is required.

Item recap:

This item's fundamental guidelines can be succinctly systematized as follows:

- ✓ Generate live performance data to be consumed by standard operating system or third party tools.
- ✓ Ensure that publishing these indicators has minimum impact on the overall system's performance.
- ✓ Rely as much as possible on the existing infrastructure so as to leverage notifications, which are often based on thresholds for performance indicators.
- ✓ Publish indicators that purport to internal queues or buffers, repeatable patterns of actions and distinct processing flows. Allow administrators to drill down on information in order to identify differences in performance delivered by distinct processing components.
- ✓ Do not rely exclusively on data supplied by the operating system so as to provide information on either memory, CPU usage or other indicators. Attempt to supply this information at a lower granularity level so as to enrich the troubleshooting sessions.

32.   Security is everything: make sure you know what privileges and accounts are used

Thousands of books have been written entirely dedicated to the issue of security and, if there is one common trait among them, it is that security can never be an afterthought, in the form of a late night addition or some sort of last minute enhancement. To put it bluntly, one either designs systems with security in mind from day one or the product being built will not be a secure one. To make matters even more challenging, security-awareness is, usually, quite poor within development teams, which invariably leads to a scenario where engineers code, build and test using administrator-level security contexts[1].

The main issue with this approach consists of, quite often, having software developers being unaware of the exact privileges they are imposing on the product, since the credentials they are using have virtually full access to, not only, the entire operating system but any existing resources. Furthermore, software engineers are often oblivious to the exact security context under which the software components they are building are executed. This creates a difficult hurdle when, later on, they happen to need to realign the components they created with security-imposed restrictions[2].

To create an effectively secure product, all product executing contexts need to be identified in the early design phase. Additionally, the exact privileges required in each case must also be determined, documented and passed along to development teams[3]. In the end, this is no different and no less important than any other business use case imposed by the stakeholders. Furthermore, the flow of security contexts through the product's own processing pipeline must also be clearly identified. Most products will satisfy different requests by using distinct approaches to security contexts:

- Sometimes going for impersonation, in the sense that they will maintain the clients' identity when processing a request on the server side,
- Other times they will settle on using the context of a specific service account, so as to execute the request on behalf of whichever client initiated the executing task,
- On yet other occasions, we will even have hybrid scenarios; within these cases, a client issues a certain request and, part of it, will be executed with a set of credentials while, other specific sections, will see a temporary impersonation that generates an execution under a different set of credentials.

---

[1] Yes, we just love to be in full control of our machines, especially if we are writing code!
[2] Either from architecture design/changes or production constraints.
[3] This should be looked upon as a hard requirement.

Truthfully, one can build equally secure products regardless of the strategy being used[1], however, one must be conscious of:

- What is being performed,
- The context under which one is operating,
- How one needs to perform different tasks, so as to ensure a globally secure product.

To achieve this, one needs to be constantly and fully in sync with the credential set being used as well as the tasks being performed[2] .

Nevertheless, security is not just about credentials and proper access to resources and, quite honestly, there are a lot more variables at stake. Although security could require a book on its own, here is a very short list of some critical aspects that need to be accounted for.

1. **Decide under which credentials you execute as well as which privileges must be acquired.**

   Certain architectures, as well as certain types of software products, will usually force one into a restricted set of options. However, the reality is that those are, in fact, the easy scenarios. For starters, consider a public internet facing architecture where there is the need to uniquely identify end users. In such a scenario, and regardless of whichever approach is taken in order to identify each end user, one will not be executing under a set of unique credentials specific to each user, as one will not be creating a one to one mapping between public application users and domain registered accounts . Consequently, one will be operating a web server that will accept some authentication process and, afterwards, will be executing the incoming requests under some specific service account. Additionally, there is a good probability that certain tasks[3] will need to, temporarily, execute under a different set of credentials, so as to properly access a more restricted resource. The latter stage can pertain to accessing either file system data or even an external product such as a database solution. It really depends on what the product needs to perform but, overall, the bottom line is that:

   - Despite the need to use a service account to execute incoming requests, one should setup a service account with reduced privileges[4] so as to execute the bulk of the processing logic,
   - When, within the processing logic, one is required to perform more security sensitive operations[1], a change of security context is in order; this means

---

[1] And, as with most things in life, there is not one single and universal correct path.
[2] And the resources that are, implicitly, being accessed.
[3] Due to their inherent needs.
[4] As reduced as possible.

temporarily executing under a different credential set while keeping that elevated execution environment during the absolute minimum required timeframe[2].

Consequently, the problem with managing this type of change in credential sets involves finding a way to, somehow, store within the architecture-bound resources sufficient information so as to execute the required impersonation and, thus, dynamically change the execution context. Given this, the most difficult question to answer really is how to store the credentials we want to use in a way that allows us to shift between distinct executing contexts without putting anything else at risk[3]? The solution to this problem usually resides in one of the two following alternatives:

- The operating system[4] being dealt with provides the means to, somehow, swap executing contexts without explicitly submitting passwords or similar tokens,
- Should there be the need to supply passwords or similar tokens, they should be stored in a protected resource.

In case this protected resource needs to exist, it must be ensured that either the operating system's internal features will prevent unwanted access to its content or, alternatively, that we can encrypt the sensitive part[5]. However, encryption raises the problem of having to be reversible. Thus, in the end, we will also need to have whichever encryption keys are used, protected from unwanted access.

Within other distinct scenarios the breadth of choices is quite larger. Let us imagine building a solution exclusively used within a corporate network. In such a scenario, we could easily adopt a strategy whereby we would execute incoming requests by using the credential set of the submitting end user. Doing so would easily prevent us from having to manage service accounts while also avoiding swapping execution context as the request is processed. However, the downside entails having to ensure that end user credentials were given access to all required resources[6]. This scenario usually comes along with the following issues:

- One needs to spend a greater effort in managing access policies to every resource as well as ensuring that end users are appropriately given access to them[7],

---

[1] Like accessing a file system, regardless of dealing with either a local or remote file system, or connecting to a database.
[2] Immediately receding to the lower level credential set initially used.
[3] Like storing these credentials in accessible resources.
[4] Or whichever external products.
[5] With this latter one being, sometimes, included in addition to the first.
[6] To all resources required to execute the received request.
[7] Depending on which roles they personify within the software product itself.

- By allowing users[1] to access a given resource required for a specific application, it will, usually, allow them to still access the resource in the context of a completely different application[2].

2. Beware of request manipulation and man-in-the-middle attacks.

Regardless of the technologies being used, most modern enterprise capable products will be distributed, meaning that the execution of a specific request will span through either different servers or, at least, different processes within the same server. Additionally, with all that "hopping going around"[3], there is definitely the chance and opportunity for the ill-intended to manipulate in-flight packages. The problem with this situation is that there is a wide variety of attacks that can be executed, either by changing data within the package or, alternatively, by acquiring information stored in the package and using it to perform some unauthorized action[4]. Many refinements and variations regarding this type of issues can be found within security literature. Nevertheless, the overall take home message is quite simple, in that, when transmitting data, it must be ensured that it either cannot be changed in-flight by an external party or, at least, that changes will be detected, therefore, preventing the execution of corrupted packages. Additionally, when transmitting sensitive data, one must ensure that those in-flight packages cannot be opened by unauthorized entities. The solution to these problems usually comes in two distinct forms:

- Encrypt data before passing it between components[5], so as to prevent unauthorized entities from accessing privileged content,
- Use security mechanisms[6] to control unwanted changes in in-flight packages, to which encryption can also be added[7].

The problem with such strategies lies in determining what constitutes a truly secure boundary and what does not. For example, consider the case of either user data or user input submission. In reality, any scenario where one is dealing with either user data or user input is problematic and, thus, prone to exploitation. However, some of the most common situations included in this field are those where deliberately malformed input can be used to explore a number of typical security issues, including:

---

[1] Even through properly organized groups.

[2] Yes, very few systems will allow one to grant specific user access to a resource while restricting it to only one specific channel/application.

[3] As information flows from one processing point to another.

[4] These two scenarios are what can be referred to as request manipulation and man-in-the-middle attacks.

[5] Unless one is within what is considered to be a safe boundary within the context of the supporting architecture.

[6] Such as digital signing and/or hashing.

[7] Again, which may not be needed, should one be within what is considered a safe boundary.

- Taking advantage of buffer overruns by submitting data that is executed as rogue code due to said overrun,
- Submitting form data that ends up being used in unprotected and, usually, dynamically constructed SQL statements, leaving the product wide open to injection attacks,
- URL tampering, where one bypasses security by chaining URL requests, sometimes, even after executing certain security authentication and authorization steps.

Regardless of the situation, the reality is that, from the early design phase, one needs to plan how to protect the solution from these situations. Often, one can rely on either existing frameworks or best practices in order to avert most dangers, however, this requires being aware of them, so as to choose a path that mitigates inherent risks.

3. **Ensure that existing logging is not the backdoor to break your system.**

How many times have you seen complex and well-engineered products encompass a few critical sections that, ultimately, bring down the whole effort put into building the system? Unfortunately, being 99% secure is just not enough, given that even the tiniest chink in one's armor can render all other efforts useless. Metaphorically, it is pretty useless to have the ultimate security and alarm systems installed in a house if a window is left open when going on vacation. It so happens that the rationale is in no way different with software products. Overall, the problem is that, usually, it is easy to identify and, therefore, protect those considered to be the "doors to the house", meaning that the main entry points are clearly identifiable as attack surfaces needing to be properly protected. Tried and tested solutions for these obvious entry points can, for the most part, be easily found. However, it is much harder to diagnose the not so obvious areas that can also be exploited and, which, therefore, require an equal level of protection.

These not so obvious areas of exploitation include all data that is logged, included either in an error and exception handling system or in a detailed tracing feature. More specifically, it must be ensured that information registered within such logs does not contain protected content that can, either directly or indirectly, be used to jeopardize the system's security. Doing so entails accounting for, not only the more obvious elements such as registering passwords, but also the less common pieces of information that can also be considered security-sensitive, such as:

- Session tokens along with data that forms a complete request[1],

---

[1] Thus enabling an easy way to execute many types of replay attacks.

- Temporary keys that are used as challenge-response mechanisms for extra security on risky operations[1].

Overall, the main guideline boils down to considering the review of all logged data and its conscientious analysis according to security issues. It is a task that must be performed within the development cycle. It is crucial to put forth the best possible effort towards identifying:

- Whether the availability of this information may compromise the system,
- Which actions need to be taken to prevent it,
- Which actions may come in the form of either encrypted content or operating system based features so as to protect access to this content.

Within the latter situation, it is important to carefully review whether this content can, somehow, be extracted from its original registration storage mechanism as well as copied to an alternative area[2] which, afterwards, might be sent around to unauthorized users.

Item recap:

This item's fundamental guidelines can be succinctly systematized as follows:

✓ Decide early on which credentials the solution will execute under. Identify all transitions between different credential sets and look to understand both how this context switch is made as well as whether it requires storing additional credentials, tokens or passwords in other resources.

✓ Always aim to use the lowest possible privilege level. Do not allow developers to generate and test their code on high privileged accounts, given that they need to mirror, as closely as possible, the real production security scenario.

✓ Beware of request manipulation, especially in distributed architectures. Ensure you have appropriate package validation so as to detect tampering. Additionally, also ensure that you have proper cryptography to prevent unwanted access to in-flight information hopping between servers.

✓ Ensure that you are effectively protected against known attack methods, such as buffer overrun exploits or injection attacks.

✓ Ensure that logging[1] does not constitute a backdoor to the system, namely by exposing security-sensitive information without any sort of protection.

---

[1] Which can also be used either for replay attacks or for creating distinct requests that use these valid temporary keys.

[2] Usually, copying data from a protected log file to an unprotected one.

33.   Know thyself: reduce the attack surface

Knowing precisely one's product, together with what it aspires to be, is crucial for success. Apart from all marketing related issues that deal with product, promotion and price[2], it is crucial to be fully aware of:

- The components that will constitute each product,
- Which business processes each product supports and implements,
- Which data flows occur as each product interacts with its context-specific environment.

This knowledge and the complete awareness that comes with it, generates many positive forces when building software products, including a clear view of what the potential attack surface on the product will be.

Knowing exactly how data flows between components enables the definition of which policies need to be followed so as to ensure that no harm can be brought about as a result of their manipulation. Furthermore, knowing the existing and supported processes generates a greater insight as to what types of computational operations are executed by each component, therefore reducing the probability of having a rogue operation of some sort compromising the system.

However, all these ideas are really no more than generic guidelines that ought to be followed. The real critical question that needs answering pertains to figuring out the exact measures that allow the reduction of the attack surface together with the creation of a more robust and safer product. Here is a list of must-do actions regarding it:

1. **Treat all data input as potentially malicious information.**

    Every time data is consumed, regardless of its origin, one is feeding the system with information coming from uncontrolled sources. This means that, in reality, one cannot have any legitimate expectations as to what its content or format will be. Although, in many scenarios, this data will have to be constrained[3] for it to be of any real useful value, there really isn't any strong assurance that one will only receive such compliant data.

    Consequently, processing this data should be a task executed under the most rigorous computational conditions, where one assumes that any atomic item can be wrong regarding both content and format.

    Relaying the processing of all inputs to specialized modules is fundamental in centralizing the code that handles these tasks. Doing so will enable the creation of an accurately

---

[1] Related to either errors and exceptions or a tracing system.
[2] As well as place, for those who want to correctly follow marketing literature.
[3] As to its content and format.

limited area where this raw information is both processed and converted into internal data structures that can be fully trustworthy.

Furthermore, it does not really matter whether the input comes from a human-bound source[1], a computer generated file or even in the form of parameters supplied to a specific supported API. All these items are examples of pieces of input that can be incorrect according to the expected pattern and, thus, require processing by a module that receives them and is able to both handle any sort of non-compliant information as well as transform it into secure and correct data structures.

Finally, one should never make the mistake of relaxing one's processing guidelines on input data simply because it was previously generated by one's own system as valid output. Sometimes, valid output can have distinct features that render it as invalid input which can compromise the system. Additionally, most of the times, that same output can be easily changed and, when sent back as input, it does not correspond to what was generated by the system, being, instead, a close and untrustworthy impersonation!

However, processing input data is not merely bound to the task of converting it into safe internal data structures. One must also be aware of the context under which it will be used, so as to ensure that all possible exploitation strategies can be minimized. To better understand this, take a careful look at the following items, usually responsible for creating problematic areas:

- Beware of input that is used to generate commands on external components, namely database servers or scripting engines; using it as direct input to generate SQL statements and scripting commands is always prone to generating unwanted effects,
- Beware of pattern substitution rules that create the opportunity to create sequences of data that are transformed into unwanted computational instructions,
- Beware of input that fails to adhere to the expected convention in terms of length and type.

2. **Always assume that any call on an external component can be dangerous.**

   All modern systems will use third party components that are integrated and, quite often, into unique binary components which execute within a unique securable environment. Simply put, many software components are built as the result of compiling into a single binary:

   - Source code that is native to the product,

---

[1] Such as an electronic form.

- Source code that is not-native to the product[1].

Thus, if both sets of code execute as a single binary item, no system provided securable boundary[2] guarantees any sort of added protection. Even if these two sets of code happen to be used to produce distinct binaries, should they be executed within the same atomic unit of independence and security provided by a modern operating system[3], one will have no real protection scheme that isolates them.

When possible, one should contemplate using an isolation policy, so as to ensure that suspicious binaries are isolated within whatever mechanism is supplied by the executing framework. This can include executing third party libraries in isolated surrogate processes as well as any other analogous mechanism.

This is especially important when the third party binary is built beyond one's control. Specifically, we are not alluding to libraries used in the product and, thus, tested to a reasonable extent[4]. Instead, we are mostly talking about systems that allow for or support pluggable components, which are materialized as binary items that implement some sort of predefined and agreed upon interface[5]. These are the primary candidates to be offloaded into surrogate processes, ensuring that the operation system's security context is upheld and malicious, or simply incorrect code, will not either bring down the system or compromise, albeit unintentionally, any data.

3. **Use frameworks that reduce direct memory manipulation.**

Managed execution environments are, sometimes, deemed to be safer than unmanaged ones, given that they enforce rules that prevent direct memory manipulation. The most common example of this is the infamous buffer overrun. This scenario allows one to supply more data than was expected and, additionally, for which enough memory had been reserved. Most situations of this type do come as a result of the desire to inject harmful instructions into the area that supersedes the reserved memory, while devising some schema to force their execution. This type of exploitation is considered to be impossible within a correctly managed environment, given that all memory boundaries are checked and protected by the system. Interestingly, the most common source of these memory overruns is, probably, code written in C or C++. Interestingly, while the execution environment does not validate the referred boundaries, it is fairly easy to confine these actions of direct memory manipulation to properly built types or

---

[1] And which, for this discussion, can be considered as third party.
[2] Such as a process in modern operating systems.
[3] Consider two dynamic libraries being executed within the same process.
[4] Although, in some cases, this might actually be applicable.
[5] Which one usually hosts in the product's own processes.

objects[1].Consequently, the same protection supplied by a managed system[2] is created, while also relieving software engineers from dealing with such complexity on a daily basis.

It is all about putting in place the proper framework, regardless of whether it is a managed or unmanaged one. If ensured that potentially dangerous actions in dedicated objects are adequately handled, it will be quite easy to build a correct system and, funny enough, even easier to fix any issues that eventually come along.

4. **Do not activate features that are not used.**

   Activation of product features should follow a just-in-time policy. One does not need to install and activate every single feature supported by the product simply because clients have acquired a license that entitles them to use it. Quite frequently, only a reduced set of features are used from the full software product and, exposing the whole breadth of its full potential mostly entails incrementing, in an unnecessary way, the existing attack surface. Therefore, the advice here simply boils down to avoiding activating the whole product upon installation and, additionally, clearly defining sets of features that are, somehow, bound together in a logical manner. By defining these itemized blocks of features, together with the creation of an autonomous mechanism so as to activate each one individually, one will minimize the attack surface and, thus, ensure that unused features cannot be exploited.

5. **Always configure the system, by default, to be as closed as possible.**

   Once a feature has been activated, one should still make it as restricted as possible regarding the available access to it. The sheer fact of installing and activating a specific feature should not imply that everyone can access it! Hence, one should, by default, actually take the opposite approach and deny all access to every single feature. Although this will force a bit more administration work[3], it will also ensure that no access is provided by means of omission. In turn, this means that no agent[4] will be able to supply a set of credentials that just happen to receive access to a specific feature because, by some management misfortune, access to it was not denied[5]!

   To prevent such occurrences, it must be ensured that, once a feature is installed and activated, it is configured so as to deny access to all credentials but those that are

---

[1] Many of which are available if using some of the available features of the latest revision of C++ or if using STL.
[2] In terms of overruns.
[3] On those who are expected to configure and managed the production environment.
[4] User or process.
[5] Instead of being truly entitled to it.

explicitly granted authorization, thereby mitigating the risk of accidental permission attribution.

6. **Lower execution privileges whenever possible.**

    Ensuring that every component executes at the lowest possible privilege set is key to delivering secure products. By lowering the execution privileges of all system components one reduces the risk of, accidently, giving rights to access certain resources to components that really do not need that sort of privilege. Though this will not ensure that unwanted actions are not executed *per se*, it does enforce that they will not be executed on unauthorized resources and that is, by itself, a great guarantee[1].

Item recap:

This item's fundamental guidelines can be succinctly systematized as follows:

- ✓ Diagnose the exact process data flows within your system. Treat all input as potentially malicious. Guarantee that all input is sanitized before being converted to internal data structures for further processing.
- ✓ Beware of any extension points that allow code or scripts to be executed within the context of your product. Always define an isolation policy so as to ensure that these elements are isolated in the strongest possible boundary. Should you support the execution of externally built binaries, ensure they execute effectively in surrogate processes. Furthermore, be equally defensive regarding interpreted scripts or dynamically generated code.
- ✓ Use managed or unmanaged frameworks that encapsulate direct memory manipulation. This can be performed even within languages like C or C++.
- ✓ Do not activate all features when installing them. Instead, allow activation to be made on a need to use basis.
- ✓ All activated features should, by default, deny access to all consumers, including both users and processes. Force an explicit authorization policy.
- ✓ Always execute with the lowest possible privilege level.

---

[1] As defined in item **32 Security is everything: make sure you know what privileges and accounts are used**.

34.   Invest in threat modeling

One of the major concerns that any enterprise capable software needs to address is the natural fear that surrounds security and, in particular, the different ways in which a solution can, potentially, be exploited by either a malicious user or software.

Therefore, creating a detailed and thorough threat model where one clearly identifies both the possible risks and how they can, eventually, be exploited, is absolutely mandatory. Furthermore, this type of analysis needs to be performed right from the early stages, when the overall architecture is being designed. Plus, it also needs to be constantly revisited as the different development cycles move along.

Thus, creating a good threat model requires looking into different features:

1.   **Review known attack methods.**

One of the great things about the maturity of the current software industry is the existence of an already vast history on which we can easily support ourselves. Within the latest half-century, give or take a few years, there have been loads of security holes being widely exploited and, therefore, from which we can easily learn valuable lessons.

Furthermore, recent technologies have been built with a firm purpose of providing security in depth and, hence, have steadily chased down problems that emerged within their predecessors' lifetime. As such, it makes nothing but sense to drink from this pool of knowledge, which can entail reviewing how similar existing solutions are being built, in terms of either supportive technologies or reference architectures.

By taking these elements and adding expert know-how from software security professionals, one will be able to easily identify the exact potential channels that can render one's solution vulnerable.

Having precisely identified both the common attack methods as well as entry points for known security holes within the technologies and architecture adopted, one can easily pinpoint the most efficient counter measures available.

Usually, these counter measures will take the form of different items, most notably:

- Architectural changes that will alter the exposed surface, so as to minimize the available targets of exploitation,
- Selection of different or alternative technologies that will deliver safer environments, where exploitation is less likely to be successful,
- Policies that need to be observed by developers in order to ensure that their code is created from the ground up under an intense security based driving force. Only through strong policies, considered security aware[1] regarding specific

---

[1] Thus, safer from exploitation.

191

software development patterns , will one's development team come to view this as a major goal and, consequently, embed their code with the relevant artifacts that will deliver the desired level and breadth of secure code,

- Policies that need to be observed by those creating testing procedures[1] which will specifically target security issues. These policies are vital in ensuring that the testing procedures will be directed towards an effective analysis of known security issues within the chosen technologies. It is also critical that testing procedures run all commonly known attack methods used to exploit the exposed attack surfaces.

2. Use existing tools to detect possible security holes.

It is said that buffer overruns are the single largest source of security issues that plague software in a way that enables malicious attacks. Although statistics vary, it is, nonetheless, true that buffer overruns have been traditionally used to perform security-related attacks on all sorts of systems and solutions. Interestingly, the good news is that there is a set of fairly comprehensive tools and techniques available that significantly cut down the chances of such problems.

Firstly, one can leverage the usage of tools that instrument the codebase and the solution so as to perform a static and dynamic analysis of buffer overrun issues. With tools in place, the vast majority of problems that the codebase has can be detected and, therefore, the risk of deploying a version that is wide open to such attacks can be avoided. Quite naturally, such tools exist not only to detect buffer overrun issues but also to identify a vast wealth of other types of possible security issues.

Secondly, one can also leverage existing tools to run attacks on the solution and, thus, effectively test how policies, chosen technologies and architecture, hold up against these known attack methods. Many of these methods are very well documented within the existing specialized literature, meaning that any interested engineer can quickly get up to speed and become a reasonable hacker. The real advantage in this is that there are a myriad of tools out there[2] that one can use to effectively run security tests on one's own solution, therefore ensuring that well-known exploitation holes have not been left wide open.

Thirdly, one can subscribe to security forums and other similar resources, where engineers are constantly discussing new and old security issues, including the optimum ways to address them. Having a keen eye to constantly scan through these resources will provide a great fast track so as to be constantly on top of the new emerging problems

[1] As defined in item **25 Having a formally defined development process does not imply adopting a formal process.**
[2] Many in the way of scripts or detailed how-to procedures.

being detected and exploited within the technologies one is using, as well as within the solutions that have some overlapping with the product we are building[1].

3. **Run simulated attacks.**

    Tools to test security features are great but, whenever one happens to have the chance, it is important to remember to bring, on board, a certified security professional who can really put the solution to the test by attempting to break into its safe boundaries using simulated attacks. These simulated attacks are nothing more than doing exactly what real hackers would perform, so as to diagnose whether it is possible to exploit the system or not and, therefore, to also detect what kind of damage can be inflicted. Most security attacks will either render the system totally or partially unusable for a given time period or generate the destruction of data that causes long term damage. Now and then, a real security bomb comes along when hackers take possession of confidential data, therefore allowing them to either extract direct gain from it or use it to conduct subsequent attacks that end up being even more damaging to organizations.

    Thus, running these simulated attacks in either the production environment[2], or within an exact duplication of it, can effectively bring out any issues that have survived all previous efforts to root them out[3].

    Additionally, it should not be forgotten that these simulated attacks need to be reviewed and re-executed from time to time, thus ensuring that:

    - Whenever a new public build is available, any changes made do not bring about new problems,
    - Existing and previously tested builds, on which no problems were initially found, cannot fall victims of either new techniques or new exploitation tricks that are constantly being created[4].

4. **Technology and feature selection.**

    The selection of a specific technology[5] is something that is conducted after reviewing lots of different issues, including security concerns. Some technologies are more prone to creating solutions that showcase a higher chance of including security holes, while others are naturally more resistant and, therefore, less likely to entail such deficiencies. Plus,

---

[1] In terms of architecture and usage patterns.

[2] Depending on whether these simulated attacks can be executed within a window of opportunity that does not jeopardize the system's availability.

[3] Ranging from a careful selection of technologies, a robust and security aware architecture, and a strong development effort, so as to ensure that an effective secure codebase is created from day one.

[4] Which will, naturally, be known by any good security professional that happens to be hired so as to perform these tasks.

[5] Such as a development language.

one needs to remember that no technology will be useful if handled improperly. As such, some technologies are often considered less safe, not because they truly are so, but merely because they were incorrectly used[1].

Finally, many technologies considered to be problematic are, usually, seen as such because of a limited number of features that, often, can either be disabled or simply not used[2].

Regardless of the exact situation being faced, that which should be kept in mind is that no technology is perfect and, most of the times, it really comes down to how one uses them[3].

As such, the most relevant guidelines surrounding this topic are:

- Select the best fitting technologies for whichever solution is being built and, afterwards, review which elements constitute the potentially greatest security issues within them,
- Implement all the required patterns and policies responsible for reducing the vulnerabilities inherent to these technologies,
- Forgo using any specific features present within these technologies that cannot be made safe by using reasonable patterns and policies,
- Disable any unused features that could be used to conduct attacks on the solution, even when the solution does not rely directly on them.

Summing up, threat modeling is an essential part of product development and, in this sense, relying on proven technologies is not enough. Since all technologies have strengths and weaknesses, it is up to software engineering teams to review where the problematic points reside and, afterwards, produce all the required best-practices so as to ensure that these areas are either not used[4] or are used in a way that effectively creates a reasonable security boundary around them.

Finally, one also needs to carefully review what the possible attacks and inherent techniques are and, by using either existing tools or expert man-power, verify that they can be effectively addressed[5].

---

[1] Here is where policies and patterns make all the difference!
[2] Therefore creating a scenario where such embedded vulnerabilities are, in fact, overcome.
[3] In the form of which features one decides to rely on and what patterns and practices are applied.
[4] Blocked in a way that prevents them from hindering the solution.
[5] In a way that no holes are left wide open.

Item recap:

This item's fundamental guidelines can be succinctly systematized as follows:

- ✓ To effectively deliver robust solutions, you need to invest in threat modeling. You need to identify which attack methods have been commonly used against the technologies you selected, as well as against architectures that are similar to the one your product has adopted.
- ✓ Ensure you have put in place the correct best practices and patterns so as to mitigate all exploitable areas.
- ✓ Run security screenings on both your code and product by using existing tools.
- ✓ Bring in security experts in order to run simulated attacks on your solution.
- ✓ Constantly review the potential threats and, consequently, continually test and verify your solution's robustness as you invest in building new versions of your product.

35. Define the recovery track: plan for backup requirements and restore steps

Every system exists in order to perform some sort of operation on given data. Additional, very few systems are pure functional execution engines that receive a set of inputs and produce a set of outputs by applying some sort of internal computing algorithms while, additionally, not requiring to store and persist any type of configuration data, processing data or any other kind of data whatsoever. When building such a truly stateless system, very few concerns will come about regarding either backup or restore procedures, since, as long as one knows where to get the binaries that compose the solution, it is easy to remain uncorrupted.

However, such a theoretically sealed system doesn't really exist, at least not that often. Instead, most systems deal with business data and produce side effects on them, while, furthermore, also requiring complex configuration policies in order to tweak their behavior so as to fit the desired computational pattern. One way or the other, it must be ensured that it is possible to create a backup point for the system and, subsequently, execute a restore from it.

What this backup/restore pair implies really depends on the system being built but, for the most part, there a few guidelines that should be regarded while designing a software product.

1. **Know what to backup.**

     In some systems it is quite easy to identify which parts need to be backed up. Whenever one thinks about backups the concept that immediately tends to pop up is that of information stored in solution data files[1], either under direct control of one's application or, possibly, controlled by another integrated product such as a database. Although all these types of elements need to be clearly identified to ensure one can build an operational guide that identifies that which needs to be saved, there are many elements that can be easily overlooked.

     Take, for example, the case of configuration data. Shouldn't the product's configuration be backed up so as to ensure that it is possible to restore the system in a distinct server at a later date? Although I imagine that most, if not all readers, will quickly answer positively, defining which items do make up each solution's configuration will surely be far less consensual. Are we simply talking about data that is directly defined in the product's configuration resources[2]? Or, alternatively, are there other key elements, potentially defining operating system behavior or constraining the behavior of any other integrated products?

---

[1] Or other persistent storage.

[2] As defined in item **29 Configuration is needed: minimize the options and use a centralized resource**.

Ultimately, it is a very blurry line that separates what needs to be backed up from what doesn't. The best advice I've heard on this issue is, quite frankly, as simply as saving any information on any level that will need to be changed so as to properly setup the system in a new server that is freshly installed with all the default options[1]. By achieving this, one will be very well positioned in order to create a truly complete backup procedure for one's software product. Nevertheless, it ought to be kept in mind that, within the data to be backed up, one can, potentially, include:

- Business data managed by one's product,
- The configuration data from one's own product,
- Environment configuration items[2].

2. **Determine whether you can accept an execution downtime while performing the backup or restore operations.**

Once all items that need to be safeguarded have been identified, one must address a complex issue related to how the backup procedure will execute. Most systems will allow the use of a short window of inactivity so as to execute and create a consistent backup, but what happens with systems that do not have windows of inactivity big enough to execute the backup routines?

This poses a very complex scenario where backups need to be created while, simultaneously, ensuring that the system continues performing its regular duties. Although this might seem relatively easy, it is quite complex, since one will need to, not only save data[3] while the system is still operating, but also ensure the consistency of all the backed up data, and the latter is far from easy. Just consider what would happen if, while performing a backup, an already backed up element of the data is actually subjected to a given change? Should we block the operation that is attempting to perform such a change while the backup procedure is on-going? Doing so could well do the trick, regarding backup consistency, however, the system would then be down until the backup routine is finished, which could take a fair bit of time and, therefore, would generate a backup procedure that would effectively bring down the server's availability.

Alternatively, we could question ourselves about allowing the system to move along with the data changing operation and applying it to the backed up data later on. Would this sort of replication create a consistent backed up item? Probably not! At least when performing a direct replication without really understanding the context of this change and what it implies.

---

[1] This includes installing any base products also using their own base defaults.
[2] Ranging from operating system configuration items that differ from the default installation, to other base product configurations such as those made on top of web servers, database engines, etc..
[3] Several types of data, as previously seen.

Hence, this is not an easy problem to solve and, believe it or not, the easiest way to fix it actually consists of minimizing the steps of the backup procedure so as to avoid receiving some sort of request that interferes with the backed up data while the system is executing. Plus, should such interference actually occur while executing the backup, it is possible to either cancel out the partially executed backup, so as to repeat it later in order to create a clean copy[1] or, alternatively, keep track of the changed data in order to reflect it within the backup. However, this latter option can only be performed safely if the contextual integrity of such a change is guaranteed.

Conversely, if the system can provide a window of opportunity that does allow for the backup to be executed without any other parallel tasks being performed, then this operation is nothing more than a kind of enhanced copy operation.

Additionally, what about the opposite part? Is the restore supposed to be executed while the system is down, or is it in any way viable to restore the system while allowing it to keep on running without any sort of stoppage?

In reality, I have never come across a system where it was actually a reasonable idea, or even an understandable requirement for that matter, to execute a restore while keeping the processing cycle from being interrupted. The closest thing I have seen in this regard have been systems which, by supporting side-by-side execution, allow for one executing instance to be restored while allowing the remaining ones to continue working without any impact. Nevertheless, this actually corresponds to a distinct scenario and, furthermore, it can only really work on top of pure side-by-side execution.

Finally, there is just one more point to consider, which pertains to partial and incremental backups. How are these affected?

As far as backing up data, nothing really changes. The big difference lies in restoring it. Performing a partial restore is, actually, something that can be aligned with a strategy that enables one to perform the restore without imposing any complete system downtime. It is just a matter of setting a limited boundary on what is to be replaced as well as on which operations are to be affected by the partial restore. Plus, within the features that are to be affected by the restore, we will have the same scenario as when performing a full restore, in the sense that keeping those running only makes sense within a side-by-side execution scenario.

3. **Identify the backup and restore tasks, as well as their execution plan and implications.**
   Executing a backup procedure and its counterpart restore operation needs to be based on a step-by-step map that:
   - Stipulates the order of execution of the required tasks,

---

[1] A viable solution, if the chances of this happening are deemed to be very slim.

- Predicts the impacts that each task will produce.

Though this is no different than any other computing routine, here one must identify, understand and plan for this sequence of tasks during an early product design phase. Otherwise, one may easily be overlooking critical dependencies and mandatory requirements that, later on, simply do not allow for the backup procedure to be performed, and even more so if one happens to be supporting a backup system that runs in parallel with the normal execution chores.

4. **Look into the impact of performing a backup or a restore on any other integrated system.**

   Alas, no one lives alone in this world and, in this case, it is equally unlikely that one's system will end up being an isolated and deserted island. Therefore, one needs to analyze carefully the impact of performing backup and restore operations from two distinct perspectives:

   - How one's system will impact others,
   - How other systems will impact our own.

   Performing a backup procedure, in the context of a solution that is integrated with other systems may force one to perform further integration steps, so as to ensure that it is indeed possible to create a complete contextual backup. Note that, by complete contextual backup, we are referring to one that, when restored, brings one's system back to a certain point in time in a consistent manner that enables integrated systems to continue functioning correctly. It is not difficult to imagine a scenario where one's solution is reverted to a previous state by virtue of executing a restore procedure, only to end up with an inconsistent environment given that other integrated systems fail to accommodate this reversal in time. Naturally, this really depends on how tight the integration between the systems is, meaning that the more loosely coupled a solution happens to be, the less likely it is that this will occur. However, should one fail to take this into consideration, it will surely come back to bite us when least expected.

   The execution of the backup operation *per se* is, usually, a less contrived problem, given that one is merely taking a snapshot of the system at a certain point in time. However, should one need to take into consideration integrated systems[1], there will be, quite naturally, added steps to execute when powering along with the backup tasks. The reason being that, inevitably, one will need to save more state that goes beyond one's own border and, thus, doing so enables one to, later on, bring back the whole solution into the saved point in time while maintaining a consistent view in all integrated systems.

---

[1] So as to ensure having a consistent state when performing a restore operation.

5. **Test the backup-restore cycle as early as possible.**

   Testing the backup-restore cycle should be performed as early as possible within the development cycle[1].

   As product development moves along, all supportive tasks and processes need to start being performed in parallel, so as to ensure that they cover the full breadth and scope of what one's product is capable off at each point in time[2].

   This will ensure that the backup and restore system being built is aligned with the rest of the product and, consequently, any existing dependencies between backup and restore tasks, as well as with other system operations, are:

   - Properly built from the ground up,
   - Effectively tested during the complete development cycle.

Item recap:

This item's fundamental guidelines can be succinctly systematized as follows:

- ✓ Precisely identify during the early design stages the exact items needing to be backed up. Define the step-by-step roadmap of all the tasks that need to be executed when performing backup and restore operations.
- ✓ Define whether you will support full and/or incremental backups.
- ✓ Define whether you need downtime to execute a backup and a restore. Should you attempt to perform these operations without downtime, you need to be especially careful during the backup stage, so as to ensure full consistency. Additionally, the restore procedure will, more than likely, demand a pure side-by-side execution scenario.
- ✓ Look into which dependencies will exist within the backup/restore procedures amongst external and integrated systems[3].
- ✓ Test your backup and restore procedures from an early point in the development cycle. Do not allow this to be an afterthought that is to be exclusively handled by operation teams, for it needs to be a core process of your product and, hence, defined by the product team.

---

[1] And not only when the product is either finished or close to it.
[2] This is equally true for other processes like installation process, as defined in item **27 For a product to be used, installed it must be!**
[3] Including the operating system.

36. Prepare for the unexpected: setup a proper symbol server

The surest thing in life is death and, likewise, the surest thing in software development is, sooner or later, having, at the very least, a given process either crash or hang. This should be taken as an absolute certainty that requires no mathematical or scientific proof[1]. It will simply happen and, to add insult to injury, usually at one of the worst possible times, such as:

- In a production system,
- On a high profile client,
- During some critical business period.

Therefore, planning ahead takes an absolutely crucial role. It needs to be assured that, when this does inevitably occur, one will have the proper tools already lined up and merely waiting to be used, so as to have a head start in the quest of tracing the root cause and, eventually, fixing the problem at hand. Thinking that one will, somehow, be able to analyze and fix this kind of issues without having the correct architecture in place, ends up being highly counter-productive and, thus, should be avoided at all cost. Additionally, one shouldn't consider the idea of setting up whatever infrastructure might be required upon being confronted with the problem given that the time it will take[2] will simply be unacceptable to clients and, furthermore, impossible to manage by the working team.

Thus, what exactly does one need to take into consideration so as to be effectively prepared for this type of catastrophic events? Funny enough, it is actually very easy these days. Almost every, if not all, professional compilers and enterprise operating systems already include the required features.

First, operating systems, with potentially low level software installed on top of them, will generate files known within the industry as dump files. These files are nothing more than a transposed image of the process's memory at a specific point in time, along with some additional information such as data stored in CPU registers. With the proper knowledge and tools, these dumps will allow software engineers to scavenge the remains and look for answers as to what was malfunctioning within the process. Common tasks that can be performed while analyzing these dump files include:

- Reviewing stack traces of existing process threads,

---

[1] History has shown this to be true!
[2] Assuming one can pull it off.

- Digging into specific memory areas, so as to determine which information was stored in specific areas/data structures,
- Quick analysis of common failure patterns, such as analyzing exceptions or locks.

Overall, this is usually comprehensively simplified by using debugging extensions especially built with the purpose of analyzing dump files that reflect a certain type of process or processing scenario.

For the most part, this layer of tooling is beyond one's reach. It will be terribly uncommon to end up writing either operating system code or low level debugging tools, including debugging extensions. All is usually provided by third party companies and, quite often, they happen to be the same vendors from which either the operating system or the development environment and associated frameworks were acquired. Hence, managing this first part is, essentially, a matter of knowledge and experience, meaning that it is fundamental to gain insight into the techniques that the environment being used supports in order to produce dump files, as well as which techniques allow for useful information to be extracted after they are produced. However, those who do not master this art can rest assured, since there are plenty of books out there exclusively dedicated to the mysteries of debugging dumps.

This brings us to the second part, which is that of debugging symbols. Debugging symbols are optionally produced by tuning some compiler options when creating one's binaries, or in other words, when compiling the source code. Symbol files have a wealth of information that, with the help of debuggers and debugger extensions, can be used to navigate through a dump file and, ultimately, correctly interpret and format areas within the extracted memory image. These symbol files have information about:

- Which functions reside in each binary,
- The data structures defined and used in source code and, furthermore, present during the process's execution.

There is a lot more stuff that could be mentioned but I shall not, given that its description is well beyond our scope. Nonetheless, overall, it boils down to information about source code and binaries that can help figuring out what the dump file portrays as the system's behavior prior to its generation.

Therefore, generating these symbol files is indispensable to allow debuggers to interpret call stacks and analyze memory data structures. Additionally, it is free, as it comes together with modern day compilers. Hence, that which one needs to perform is much reduced, and consists of:

- Certifying that the compiler is configured so as to generate these symbol files with every build that one performs,
- Wiring up the build process[1] and automating the task of dropping off these symbol files in a symbol server.

The symbol server can be nothing more than a shared location where the symbol files are stored. Adding symbol files to the store is, usually, as simple as issuing a scripted command through a platform utility that, often, comes along with all the rest of the debugging tools for the platform being used.

Afterwards, software engineers will simply need to configure their debuggers, so as to hook into this shared location. As a result, the debugger will extract the required files when needed, as long as they are in the shared store.

This process promotes a far better debugging experience, in the sense of generating a readable translation of call stacks and data structures. Although this seems to be quite simple to achieve, there are, maybe, a few other concepts that should be explored. Modern compilers can generate symbol files that can contain either a bit or a lot of additional information. The more information they have, the easier it will be to debug and, of course, the more exposed one's software product will be, should it be decided to make this information public.

In case one never sees any need to make these symbol files public, then this issue is actually irrelevant, given that one can pack as much information into them as possible while relying on the fact that they will only be used and accessed by one's own software engineers. If, on the other hand, one ends up needing to make symbol files available to either clients or partners, then creating two symbol servers ought to be considered, in the sense of having:

- One public symbol server, with public symbol files (i.e. symbol files with limited information),
- One private symbol server, to which access is tightly controlled and where one stores private symbol files (i.e. symbol files with far more information in them).

Additionally, one should also consider processing/embedding symbol files with information that will allow debuggers to quickly pull out source code that maps to specific points in the execution pipeline. Essentially, compiling tools may have the option of executing what is known as source indexing, thereby adding source information into the symbol files. Consequently, doing so allows

---

[1] As defined in item **23 Do not leave the build for last: invest in an automated build system from the very first** day.

debuggers to pull source code from its depot[1], as one navigates through the call stacks and delves into the generated binary code. This type of debugging experience allows one, not only to quickly review dumps[2], but also to add the ability of automatically accessing matching source code for a thorough analysis.

To wrap up this item, let us just focus for a bit on another perspective of debugging, which is that of live debugging. Symbol files and symbol servers are not just useful to process dump files. With the proper tools one can, on most platforms, perform some live debugging which, now and then, does prove handy in a production environment. In some situations, one will be faced with some unexpected behaviors within a software product and, it might be the case that it may be possible to hook into the process harboring the product so as to perform live debugging. Such a task essentially comes down to:

- Breaking into the execution as it happens in production,
- Setting breakpoints and exceptions traps as one feels relevant to do so during the debugging session, which itself entails looking into data structures and call stacks as the live execution evolves.

This type of debugging experience is rare, given that it may stall or kill the production execution environment. However, in sometimes in extreme cases, one may feel, together with the client, that it is the best, and possibly only, path to take. When this occurs, symbol servers are, once again, a priceless asset. The whole extended knowledge and experience gained from using them in dump analysis will also be used within a live debugging session. Nevertheless, though the techniques applied are very similar, one needs to keep in mind that the debugger has been attached to a live process. This usually means that one should not crash it, or even tweak its behavior in any way. Most often, one will cease this opportunity to inspect the behavior that is occurring within the execution boundary and, thus, acquire enough information to proceed and define the best solution to fix the unexpected behavior detected within the software product.

---

[1] Assuming one has configured debuggers to access the source depot and assuming one has adequate permissions to do so.
[2] Thus, getting a clear picture of what code was executing.

Item recap:

This item's fundamental guidelines can be succinctly systematized as follows:

- ✓ Remember to set up a symbol server that enables you to analyze dumps and perform live debugging.
- ✓ Consider setting up public and private symbol servers, should you need to supply clients or partners with access to symbol files.
- ✓ Consider using source indexing to quickly enable source access from the symbol files.
- ✓ Include these tasks within your build process in order to ensure everything is fully automated.
- ✓ Ensure that some of your engineers are masters in the art of debugging.

37.   Avoid guessing, know how your product is used!

Guessing games are great for kids but, when dealing with enterprise capable products a bit more than a mere hunch is in order. In this sense, knowing how one's product is used, as well as how changes affect users, is crucial to a successful evolution. Given this, relying purely on theoretical approaches so as to define the product's features ought to be avoided. Instead, it is wise to invest in a detailed analysis of how each product is used at each specific point in time, in order to benchmark such information against true A/B testing[1].

To really know how a product is used, data has to be gathered from a live production installation that enables the capturing of vast sequences of usage patterns, so as to reflect either the usage of the graphical user interface or the implied, behind the scenes, computational sequence.

When dealing with graphical user interfaces one needs to instrument the application to gather patterns of usage within the interface, and, even more so, should these patterns fail to relate directly to a specific backend action detectable through the analysis of standard logging and auditing features. The best graphical user interfaces out there successfully add value to a product by laying out their components in a way that maximizes end users' interaction with them. Depending on the context, this can be measured in utilization time, execution of specific actions, *etc.*. To acquire a deep commanding knowledge of the usage patterns that users are creating, the application needs to be instrumented so as to ensure it registers all interactions with the graphical user interface widgets[2]. Therefore, it must be diagnosed which elements are used, what areas of the graphical user interface are less explored and, more importantly, how these usage patterns evolve in response to a specific change in the interface.

Achieving this, warrants three things:

- Instrumenting the widgets so that they register all events related to them,
- Sending this data to a processing site,
- Performing A/B testing of new graphical user interfaces.

Thus, let us depict each one of these actions in greater detail.

Instrumenting widgets is fairly easy. Nevertheless, it ought to be performed in a way that does not interfere with the standard user experience. It needs to be assured that the way the interface works is not altered on account of this instrumentation and, furthermore, that both its inherent

---

[1] More on this later.
[2] Elements such as menu items, buttons, images, *etc.*.

performance and the established relation between existing widgets are not changed either. All instrumentation must be transparent to users as though it is not there[1].

Afterwards, once this information is gathered through instrumentation, one needs to feed it into whatever processing pipeline was established in order to analyze it. **Enter analytics!**

Analytics platforms are available from many different vendors, and, quite naturally so, with many distinct features and implied costs. Therefore, it needs to be ensured that it is possible to hook up into one of these platforms, should one decide to forgo building one's own platform[2]. Integrating with these platforms is, usually, done through standardized techniques, such as HTTP-based REST calls. Additionally, most analytics packages allow one to instrument the graphical user interface as well as feed the data to one or more different analytics engines.

Furthermore, one needs to understand how the instrumentation works within offline scenarios. Just because work is performed offline, it is no reason to lose interest in knowing how the product is used. In this regard, most analytics packages allow one to gather the instrumentation data, store it locally while offline and, later on, upload it to the analytics engine for processing. Actually, this feature is simply a particular scenario of the standard practice of asynchronous upload. Since one does not wish for the instrumentation layer to interfere in any way with the user experience, one needs an asynchronous pattern when uploading the collected data. This will ensure that the user interface experience is not stalled or changed in any way, just because one is interacting with the analytics engine.

Finally, once established how the graphical user interface is used, it is crucial to know how the usage patterns will be affected by a change in its design or layout. In this regard, the most critical question needing answering simply pertains to how the graphical user interface influences the product's value? More specifically, how will a change in the graphical user interface affect users' actions and, additionally, will it add or reduce the intrinsic value of the product? Will such a change diminish the product's overall usage? Will users start concentrating on features that generate less revenue? Will they, suddenly, start exploring the product in a different way and, as a result, actually start seeing more value in the product?

Though measuring the value itself might not be easy, at least establishing what the new usage patterns will be should be fairly manageable. Furthermore, this information will allow one to guide one's own product evolution according to such sound data. This is where A/B testing comes to the rescue. A/B testing is a technique whereby one changes some variables, in this case a part

---

[1] In most situations users must be aware that this behavior is being tracked. However, such legal constraints do not constitute our present focus.

[2] Which, at least during the early days of a product, will be the most common action.

of the graphical user interface, while making it available only to a limited part of one's existing universe. Afterwards, the instrumentation data from both versions[1] is collected, followed by a comparison of the results generated from the analytics evaluation. Once this data is in place, one can effectively realize how a change in the graphical user interface eventually affects the usage patterns. Furthermore, one can perform similar tests with different alternatives, thereby identifying which interface leads to whichever usage pattern deemed to work best for the product.

With these techniques in place, more power can actually be trusted into the hand of those who are designing the graphical user interface, given that, since it is possible to measure how they influence the perceived business value, it stops being an intuition based task!

Although these techniques are primarily used with graphical user interfaces, they can also be used, to some extent, on other backend features. Doing so merely requires the ability to:

- Gather usage/processing data,
- Upload it to a processing analytics site,
- Compare results generated by distinct versions.

Once this sort of reasoning is included within a product and embedded into the spirit of a development team, everyone will be hooked to it, since every change made will be based on some prior realistic analysis of what works and what doesn't.

It will not be a guessing game anymore and, although many great products have been created and many others have evolved over the years, based on their creators' sheer intuition and instinct, in most cases, a systematic approach to critical decision[2] making will, invariably, deliver far better results. If a reasonable sample of one's universe shows a specific usage trend when responding to either a new graphical user interface or a new usage scenario, one can safely bet that the overall pattern will not be too different[3].

---

[1] Version A, the previously existing one, and version B, the newly crafted one, hence the name A/B testing.
[2] In the sense that it will change the way people use the product.
[3] As long as one's sample group is sufficiently large and fairly representative of the whole population.

Item recap:

This item's fundamental guidelines can be succinctly systematized as follows:

- ✓ Instrument your product so as to acquire data on usage patterns and, particularly so, on graphical user interface usage patterns. Ensure that this instrumentation is transparent to users and that it works in offline scenarios. Ensure that all data uploads to an analytics site is performed asynchronously.
- ✓ Use the output from the analytics engine, in conjunction with A/B testing, to determine how users react to differences in the product. Guide your product design according to this information.
- ✓ Leverage existing analytics SDKs and engines so as to instrument your product as well as process the acquired data.

38. Problems are not solved by magic: create an operations guide

Unfortunately, one of the key elements I have seen missing in most products is a great operations guide. In fact, many products do not even provide an operations guide at all, let alone a great one. An operations guide is essential in ensuring that the product is properly managed once it is rolled out and put into a production scenario.

Once a product is in production, it needs to be constantly monitored and managed. Most products require regular maintenance actions so as to ensure they keep performing as effectively as they did when initially deployed. It is also quite common to find, within these periodic maintenance chores, tasks that will ensure the correct execution of a recovery process, should any major problems occur[1].

However, our discussion here is not about backup and recovery features. Instead, it is about all the other elements that an operations guide needs to address so as to guarantee that operation teams are, in fact, competent regarding the procedures that need to be undertaken.

As such, an operations guide should, at the very least, focus on these items:

1. **Architectural and data flow diagrams.**
    It is often said that a picture is worth a thousand words and, along these lines, when desiring to effectively convey the architectural essence of a product[2] to operation teams, it is important to avoid writing a bible-thick reference manual. Contrary to this, one should create a few simple diagrams that map out:
    - Each component,
    - How they relate to supporting software pieces,
    - How everything fits into existing infrastructures[3].

    Operation teams should not be left with simple and superficial ideas of what each system is. Instead, they should be made aware, in great detail, of each product's complete picture. They do not need, nor should they be expected to, know the gritty details of every line of code that is inherent to each component[4]. That which is, in fact, important for them to understand, is:
    - The modules comprising the solution,
    - Where they sit in the myriad of available servers,

---

[1] As defined in item **35 Define the recovery track: plan for backup requirements and restore steps**.
[2] Which components exist and how they relate to each other.
[3] Servers, network, firewalls, storage, *etc.*.
[4] That's the realm of developers!

- Which role they execute within the global picture,
- How they communicate with other elements.

Creating good block-type architectural diagrams is one step forward! Nevertheless, equally good diagrams of data flows need to be thrown in as well.

One of the key shortcomings of operation teams consists of their frequent failure to understand the flow of data between components. This lack of understanding, which prevents them from really comprehending how each distinct request is processed within the system, is really troublesome. Should they fail to understand which hops exist as data flows between components, they will be unable to, not only trace the flow, but also intercept it at key points where logging data is available. Without this know-how, it will be virtually impossible to diagnose issues correctly and, consequently, operation teams will, often, be self-limiting themselves to performing standard analysis that result in common and unfruitful diagnostics such as "the system is not working" or "there is some problem but we do not really know what it is".

Consequently, any great operations guide needs to, almost invariably, start with a bunch of clean and easy to understand diagrams that showcase the different components making up the solution, therefore identifying:

- Each component's purpose,
- How data flows through the system within each of the possible request types.

Without this knowledge operation teams will be unable to troubleshoot problems as well as understand whether a specific structural system-related decision has any impact on the solution.

2. **Periodic maintenance tasks in order to ensure overall health and performance.**

   Almost every single product needs to be regularly subjected to a few maintenance tasks. They may be either simple or complex, eventually, require a specific downtime and, occasionally, be executed online without any impact on the system itself. However, invariably, operation teams will need to execute them in order to ensure the system does not degrade over time.

   Additionally, we are not referring to the installation of new patches or updates[1]. Instead, we are referring to things such as:

   - Purging unneeded log files,
   - Rebuilding database indexes,
   - Recycling long running processes.

---

[1] That is another issue altogether, as defined in item **27 For a product to be used, installed it must be!**

Regardless of whatever is exactly required within a product, these tasks need to be clearly identified in a specific section of the operations guide. Otherwise, they will simply be overlooked by everyone and, eventually, failure to execute them can bring down the system altogether.

Hence, the operations guide[1] needs to precisely lay out:

- Which tasks need to be part of the regular maintenance plan,
- How they should be executed,
- In which order.

Additionally, it is crucial to avoid forgetting to document:

- Which dependencies exist,
- Which tasks have special impact on the system, such as:
  - Reducing its overall performance,
  - Blocking out certain types of requests,
  - Requiring some downtime.

Furthermore, one should also thoroughly document the positive impact of executing these actions while also documenting the reverse[2]. Warning operation teams of the dangers of omission, while also enlightening them on the rewards pertaining execution, will definitely place teams on the product's side and, therefore, improve the likelihood of having them being properly maintained.

3. **Known issues and workarounds.**

   Wouldn't it be great if one could create the first ever completely bug-free system? Though it definitely would, it is, however, highly unlikely to be accomplished. Therefore, and to be on the safe and more realistic side, a section on known issues should be added to an operations guide. One of the greatest things that operation teams can have aiding them while struggling with a crisis, is a map of some sort that effectively steers them away from stormy waters. Thus, as soon as systems start being used[3] and, therefore, bugs start creeping into one's issue tracking tool, it needs to be ensured that this section of the operations guide starts being built.

   Doing so should be comprised of having issues being described in a complete and detailed way, which includes identifying which key informational elements help diagnose each specific situation or issue. Afterwards, the overall picture needs to be described regarding both:

   - Why the issues exist,

---

[1] After the above-referred diagrams.
[2] The negative impact of not executing them.
[3] Even in a testing environment.

- What the impact on the overall solution will be.

Often, existing issues will constitute a minor inconvenience that can be managed by forgoing the usage of a specific feature or they can be sidestepped by changing the execution schedule of some concurrent tasks[1].

Should there be a workaround, it must be ensured that the exact way of implementing it is laid out, thus certifying that operation teams are, at least, able to reduce the seriousness of the problem.

Additionally, the build level to which the problem purports to must also be identified. As time moves on, and as new builds introduce both new features and a few bug fixes, many of the issues will be resolved. Thus, clearly knowing which problems may occur with the version installed is absolutely mandatory for a good troubleshooting session. Plus, if, on top of a temporary workaround, a new build that fixes the issue becomes available, such information also needs to be identified.

Operation teams will use this information to drive the product forward as well as push for updates that will help solve their own headaches, and a lot is to be gained from having most clients running on the more recent versions of one's product.

4. **Case-based troubleshooting.**

When a problem is detected, the first thing that any operation team must know is how to gain more insight about it, so as to, eventually, track down a root cause and, consequently, devise a solution[2]. Knowing how to troubleshoot a problem is absolutely critical for anyone who is managing a live production system and, furthermore, it is insufficient to have a reference guide that spits out all the different types of existing logging features.

When a crisis comes along something more direct is required. However, instead of knowing all the available choices, knowing about the immediate first steps that will assist in the first round of triage will suffice.

This is where a case-based troubleshooting section will be a great asset for the operations guide. By clearly documenting problematic situations that are either predictable or that have been previously experienced, the required time to diagnose the situations at hand will be shortened. Hence, when using a case-based approach, one needs to clearly identify the symptoms of each case, together with the troubleshooting elements to be used. Operation teams should, preferably, be guided through a workflow of possible alternatives, as one moves along the analysis potentially progressing from a

---

[1] Which will execute perfectly well if no overlapping exists.
[2] One which might be documented in the known issues section.

wider range of possibilities to a very narrow[1] path that is generating the existing problem. Upon reaching this stage, one should, in some cases[2], be able to refer back to the known issues section. However, and unfortunately so, one will be covering uncharted ground in other cases and, thus, needing to move towards a detailed data collecting phase. When no solution or workaround is available, operation teams can only gather as much data as possible, so as to, ultimately, allow for the issue to be registered within one's issue tracking tool. Afterwards, it will be up to the product team to further analyze the issue at hand.

Hopefully, in most cases, a new workaround will be found and relayed back to operation teams, which will then implement it and, thus, solve the issue until a permanent fix is made available on a subsequent build. In parallel, it must also be ensured that one's process guarantees that all this information is fed into the wheels turning the operations guide alive. It is wise to have both this new issue, as well as its workaround, being registered and included within a new version of the operations guide. Doing so may occur virtually immediately, when benefiting from the wonders of an online version.

A final quick suggestion is to advise operation teams to review the known issues section before the system heads off into production. Should they manage to go over the wide range of possible known issues, reacting to real problems will be quicker, since this information will already be, at least in part, in the back of their minds. This obviously allows them to, easily, relate occurring problems with documented scenarios and, thus, prompting both an immediate analysis of the situation and, hopefully the implementation of the corresponding existing solution or workaround.

---

[1] Ideally unique.

[2] In those lucky ones for which a known response or fix is available.

Item recap:

This item's fundamental guidelines can be succinctly systematized as follows:

- ✓ Create a detailed operations guide that contains clear cut diagrams of your architecture. Include diagrams that show how each flow is executed within the processing pipeline, thus illustrating how data hops between components and servers.
- ✓ Include a detailed section on known issues as well as existing solutions and workarounds. Supply detailed information on how to identify each issue and to which build level it applies.
- ✓ Include a section on case-based troubleshooting so as to guide operation teams regarding the required steps in order to diagnose and troubleshoot issues.
- ✓ Include a section on required maintenance tasks so as to maintain a healthy system. Clearly pinpoint the benefits of executing these tasks, which includes highlighting potential problems of failing to carry them out.

39.   Train operations teams using simulated scenarios

There is only so much one can learn from theoretical presentations and, ultimately, nothing really equals the amount of knowledge acquired through constant practice. Therefore, for operation teams to really succeed in managing products, it is crucial to invest in their training, since they cannot be expected to successfully learn the tricks of the trade[1] by merely reading a massive reference guide. That will simply not happen.

However, two very important concepts should oversee this whole training subject:

- It should not be looked at as an extra source of revenue for vendors,
- Training operation teams should not be an optional item that clients can choose to either buy or not. Instead, training should be made mandatory, and preferably covered by the product's base licensing fees. By creating this tandem, between acquiring licenses and mandatory training, every buyer will have, free of charge[2], a training session for their operation team.

By doing this, one also guarantees having the opportunity to really present the product to those who will, in fact, need to maintain it, therefore, passing along all the required practical information for them to be successful at it. If done correctly, one will also turn operation teams into best allies. By fully understanding the product's cornerstones they will feel comfortable with it and, furthermore, they will really comprehend how it works. Hence, whenever confronted with a problem, they will, hopefully, be able to successfully, as well as quickly, tackle it[3].

Nevertheless, though the concept of training operation teams is a very important one[4] in itself, the real revolution is, actually, in the way it is conducted, which should be by using simulated scenarios. Training sessions should never be merely limited to verbal, almost one sided presentations. Contrary to this all too common training strategy, it is fundamental to use simulated scenarios so as to effectively complement the mere introductory overview presentation of the product.

On this subject, here is a quick list of guidelines concerning simulated scenarios:

1. **Get their hands dirty.**

   As previously stated, nothing beats practice and, the best way to train operation teams, is really by making them have firsthand contact with the product. Doing so must include

---

[1] So as to properly maintain the product and adequately solve any surging problems.
[2] Yes, clients still love to be presented with these pseudo-free offerings!
[3] Instead of creating an internal aura of negativity that would, undoubtedly, jeopardize the product's image.
[4] And one that goes well beyond reference guides.

having them execute all the basic operations they will be performing with the product in a real production environment, namely:

- Base installation,
- Installing patches and upgrades,
- Reviewing logs,
- Changing product configurations.

Plus, these training tasks should not be run on perfectly sterilized environments! Quite often, these hands-on labs[1] are executed on what I call pristine and ideal environments. Within these pre-canned environments, all the pre-requisites are already nicely installed as well as configured and, the tasks at hand, usually run from start to finish without any mishaps[2]. Although this happy path has its merits[3] it is unwise to make all training labs this easy and clean. Instead, labs should be made to run into real life problems that can be easily prepared from real issues that actually did occur during the product's development stages. Early users will most definitely run into issues that will force the software development team to intervene! As such, it needs to be ensured that these labs are fed with whichever issues happen to be registered within one's own issue tracking tool.

Plus, labs should not be a mere step-by-step tutorial. Ensure that some "fill in the blanks" issues are included, so as to force discussion within the training session and, additionally, to force trainees to think for themselves while trying to discover the missing links. Engaging trainees in such a way will surely maximize their learning experience!

2. **Make them sweat.**

Competition is everywhere these days and, therefore, it is definitely important to consider spicing up training by running a few short competitive tasks. Doing so should include creating a few virtual machines that present trainees with broken scenarios. These broken scenarios can be easily constructed by searching one's own pool of items registered within the issue tracking tool. Afterwards, all one needs to do is put trainees head-to-head in a somewhat light contest geared towards solving the issues presented to them.

While this will force them to make use of all the knowledge acquired throughout their training[4], it will also have them fiddling around some of the product's troubleshooting tools.

---

[1] Common in many training sessions.
[2] As long as no one inserts a wrong input or skips a step of the prepared training script.
[3] Namely, to promote a positive first contact with the product.
[4] Including, both the initial presentation session and the lab type experiences.

Such contest will ensure that trainees are far more focused and dedicated to their training than if they were to be merely sitting around and running down the clock, as they were forced to endure mostly one sided presentations from the "software coach".

3. **Show them the troubleshooting tools and reasoning paths.**

    Within the context of the task presented in the previous item, it has to be ensured that trainees' efforts are closely monitored. Doing so is critical in order to ensure that, when needed, they receive the adequate guidance in finding the right path. This approach is key in ensuring that they really understand:

    - How to approach each distinct problem,
    - How they should analyze what is really happening,
    - Each issue's root cause.

    Helping them develop the appropriate reasoning path is essential, as it will enable them to face real production problems later on.

    Additionally, after establishing the right corrective approaches, one often needs to guide them through the existing tools, exemplifying how they can easily extract knowledge from them. Overall, the key thing really boils down to ensuring they use the tools while exploring them effectively, so that, when a production problem does occur, a few weeks or months later, they will know how to react!

4. **Review known issues.**

    Since training sessions need to be limited in time, it will be impossible to run every single known issue through simulated scenarios. Therefore, one should consider reserving a part of the training session to analyze and review as many known issues as possible. By using the issue tracking tool one can easily create a brainstorming session, where issues are presented and the audience is given a few seconds or minutes to line up potential troubleshooting paths[1]. Afterwards, one can quickly review what the solution really is and, by comparing it with what trainees ventured early on, it is possible to establish a parallel with what to do and what not to do in real life, therefore boosting, not only their overall know-how of the product, but also their problem solving techniques.

---

[1] Which, quite naturally, includes throwing in some guesses as to what the problem might be.

Item recap:

This item's fundamental guidelines can be succinctly systematized as follows:

✓ Create specific training protocols for operation teams and make them mandatory for all clients that purchase licenses to use your product.

✓ Ensure that these training protocols are based on simulated scenarios. Force attendees to really get their hands dirty, in the form of being presented with real life professional challenges.

✓ Create some friendly competition within training sessions, so as to ensure that attendees remain focused and engaged.

✓ Show them what the correct reasoning paths are and how existing tools can help them reach the right solution.

✓ Review known issues and give attendees the chance to brainstorm suggestions pertaining to the most adequate routes for solving the presented challenges.

40.   Always ensure that you have segregated environments

All enterprise capable products end up needing a set of different environments so as to support their daily existence. A very common scenario consists of having, at least, two distinct environments:

- One for production,
- Another for testing.

However, in many situations, even more autonomous and distinct environments will be needed, so as to respond to all distinct requirements.

Having a testing environment is, almost always, mandatory with the purpose of being able to try out all changes to be applied to the solution, in the form of either a software upgrade or a configuration change. Plus, it is common to also have a development environment, particularly in cases where the base product supports a set of extensibility features on top of which, in-house or external teams, end up creating custom tailored components.

Regardless of the exact number of distinct environments one has and supports, segregation barriers meant to prevent cross access between them have to be created. Creating these barriers can be accomplished on different levels, which are not necessarily exclusive. In some cases setting up access control policies based on credentials can be enough, however, in other cases, enforcing isolation at a more physical level, which includes setting up servers without direct network bridging, can do the trick.

Regardless of the methods chosen, the segregation barriers will help achieve a safety and compliance threshold that successfully addresses the following issues:

1. **Prevent access to sensitive data.**
   Most enterprise capable systems will store a given amount of sensitive data that cannot be accessed by an unauthorized account. Unfortunately, in many cases, there are credentials that are used on quality or testing environments that end up having access to production systems, therefore creating a possible security loophole. Sometimes, this unintended access to production systems occurs after a troubleshooting effort, where temporary access was granted to certain specific accounts but, ultimately, never revoked after its completion. In other circumstances, certain credentials, rightfully given access to quality and development environments, maintain access over production systems after a specific procedure is executed. A common example is the execution of an upgrade in production after having previously tested it within other environments. In other cases,

specific user accounts or service accounts are added to a privileged group, thereby inheriting the access authorization.

Thus, actually ensuring segregation of environments based on credentials is not as easy as it first seems. Plus, there is a risk that, over time, a few additional holes are actually created. Therefore, one needs to, periodically, review which credentials are actually given access to each environment, including carefully reviewing all layers of access granting options[1].

2. **Protect against errors.**

Having no environment segregation can lead to having operations being executed inadvertently within the wrong environment, thus causing catastrophic results. Should it be possible to use the same set of credentials to access different environments, the door will be wide open to errors. This circumstance creates the possibility of executing a specific action, either manually by the operation teams or by a miss-configured software component, which, ultimately, can destroy valuable data and render the system unusable. As such, it is of great value to ensure that no accidental access can occur between environments, thereby effectively protecting systems from misusage[2].

It is quite common to see solutions that reference resources, such as web service hosts or databases, from within their configuration. In many instances, these configurations are copied between environments and then changed manually by operation teams. Should any of these configurations be left unchanged[3], a scenario where a system would try to reference an incorrect resource would come about. The only real protection against this is segregation of the environments enforced and controlled at different layers, namely by preventing direct network access between them.

Hence, a final question remains, which pertains to whether there should be any real possibility of performing cross environment access? Though the answer is simple, it is, nonetheless, composed of two elements:

- There should be no direct access between environments in order to prevent the above mentioned problems,
  - There might be situations where accessing two environments simultaneously from a unique point might be required, which entails perhaps needing to access more than one environment from an external point that does not really belong to either. Within

---

[1] Namely, if groups or profiles are used in order to create a more manageable set of rules for managing access.

[2] Especially unintended misusage.

[3] Typically, by force of human error.

these limited scenarios[1] access should be allowed from the external point, though using a limited set of credentials as well as privileges. Nevertheless, the key point is to have no direct access between them[2].

Item recap:

This item's fundamental guidelines can be succinctly systematized as follows:

- ✓ Always ensure you segregate the distinct environments that you support for your product: production, testing, development, *etc.*.
- ✓ Segregating environments ensures protection against misusage as well as unauthorized access and, additionally, also creates a barrier so as to avoid errors.
- ✓ Beware of configurations that give temporary access to certain sets of credentials meant for specific administrative or maintenance tasks.
- ✓ Beware of configurations that migrate between environments and which may compromise the system.
- ✓ Consider using different layers to support segregation, such as access credentials and network bridging.

---

[1] Commonly used to perform specific tasks such as data transference between environments using routines specifically built and thoroughly tested for this purpose.
[2] Forcing one to go through an access point external to both.

41. Support mainstream scripting tools for management features

Scripting has been here for a very long time and, despite all the nice features of fancy graphical user interfaces, the reality is that, when it comes to management operations, everyone expects that all required actions can be performed as well as automated through mainstream scripting tools.

Therefore, it is important to cater for this common expectation that most clients share. Even if products come along with a powerful graphical user interface[1], one simply cannot do without support for scripting tools. Operation teams will need, at one point or another, to automate a set of tasks, often integrated within a management plan that spans over several applications and different solutions.

To do so, one definitely needs to have support for scripting tools and here are a few guidelines with this in mind:

1. **Automation is everything.**

    When it comes to managing platforms[2], every single management task must be automated or, otherwise, these tasks will not be executed[3] or will drive the maintenance costs through the roof[4].

    Furthermore, currently, there is simply no place for constant manual intervention as a replacement for tasks that are, inherently, repetitive and predictable. Manual interventions need to be exclusively reserved for the most unexpected scenarios, where it is impossible to automate any procedure and, thus, the human mind's flexibility is required. Other than that, modern data center technologies and topologies, together with cost-reducing policies, will force the adoption of as many automated management tasks as possible.

2. **Management tasks need to be orchestrated.**

    Alas, products do not live in a remote and isolated island. Thus, operation teams are expected to successfully coordinate the management tasks, which happen to be needed to maintain a solution's good health, together with other tasks performing similar deeds

---

[1] Regardless of whether it is web-based or using a client-server approach.

[2] Especially production platforms which are, often, comprised of several servers, spread out through different datacenters.

[3] Jeopardizing the chances of having successful products.

[4] As one is forced to either create an alternative way of delivering such automation or manually execute these tasks.

for other existing, and sometimes integrated, solutions. Therefore, to allow operation teams to build such integrated and cohesive orchestrations, one needs to follow market trends by supporting the most common tools used in such scenarios. There are situations in life where innovating will not bring any additional benefits, and the present case perfectly fits the bill. Should these common management scripting features be absent from one's product, those eventually adopting such product will have to create wrappers that deliver this same functionality. In the end, this strategy will simply create an additional barrier and, obviously, additional related costs, which may well hinder the widespread adoption of one's own solution.

3. **Operations teams are not developers.**

Operation teams do not usually have developers within them. Plus, since GUI-based approaches fall short when automation and orchestration are required, it is important to privilege scripting features over full blown API-based solutions that require a true programming language environment. Operation teams are not developers and therefore, they cannot be expected to craft code on top of management APIs.

Nevertheless, and interestingly so, over the years, operation teams have turned to scripting languages[1] in order to create all automated tasks needed to maintain healthy systems. Through this amassed level of knowledge, a fully developed trend has emerged where one simply cannot survive without supporting these scripting tools[2].

4. **Ensure complete scope.**

Supporting scripting tools is simply not enough, meaning that delivery of a complete and broad support, covering every single product feature, must be ensured. Supporting only the most commonly used items in these scripting tools will not suffice. Instead, it needs to be ensured that the whole set of possible management tasks can, in fact, be successfully executed through these scripting tools.

Hence, it is crucial to get feedback from one's group of beta testers[3]. Although most required features can be foreseen and anticipated during the design phase, there is definitely a set of operations that can only be detected and understood[4] when starting to use products in their respective production environments. Ultimately, the risk of sending out a product lacking certain key features should to be avoided at all costs. Therefore it is imperative to get as much feedback as possible from one's beta testing group as early as

---

[1] Which, historically, have been the bread and butter of operating system shells.

[2] Unless of course one wants to clash with operation teams and simply risk having a solution that cannot be properly maintained in its production environment.

[3] As defined in item **44 Get early feedback from beta-testers spanning all possible roles**.

[4] As to their purpose.

possible. Doing so, allows one to add whichever critical items happen to be missing from the management pack and, thus, ensure that a complete and capable experience can be delivered to operation teams.

Item recap:

This item's fundamental guidelines can be succinctly systematized as follows:

- ✓ Always support mainstream scripting tools for management features. Operation teams will need to automate several tasks in order to maintain your product healthy.
- ✓ Additionally, they usually need to orchestrate these tasks in conjunction with other similar ones required by other solutions.
- ✓ Do not provide an API-based approach, given that operation teams are not developers. Though they are used to scripting tools, such tools are way different from a full-blown development language.
- ✓ Provide the full breadth of features within these scriptable management packs. Take in feedback from early beta-testers and users so as to ensure that you are not missing critical elements.

42. Have a great support process and an equally great support team

It is imperative to invest in having a great support process so as to generate satisfied customers. Whenever a problem comes about, customers will be a lot more tolerating should they know exactly what to do in order to get help in resolving the issue.

Putting aside all financial and contractual aspects that may surround the sheer existence of direct customer support, it is relevant to bear in mind that, when customers purchase software products, they expect them to run without any glitches, just as any person expects from the car they buy. Should problems occur, the very minimum that they demand, is access to a professional support service that will successfully fix the existing problems, particularly if they are inherent to the acquired asset.

Given this, why should it be any different with software products? It shouldn't, and it actually isn't. Enterprise capable systems need to be as problem-free as possible but, should any unwanted bugs appear, there ought to be a support process in place that is not only available but truly accessible. Here are a few relevant guidelines that need to be observed when setting up such support services:

1. **The availability of the support channel should be appropriate to the importance of the solution.**

   Having a support channel that runs 24x7 is a costly operation and such extreme is not necessarily required in all scenarios. That which needs to done is to clearly understand the timeframe in question when one's solution is used by the existing client base. Some solutions are used during working hours, while others are operated only during specific daily timeslots. Thus, the support service's availability needs to be aligned with the product's specific usage timeframe. Furthermore, customers need to be adequately informed of the reasons behind such a policy.

   Although this may seem easy at first, when taking into consideration things like varying time zones as well as different cultural elements[1] between regions, it all starts getting rather gloomy.

   However, and more often than not, such a complex scenario will not be the starting point. When starting to build software products one will only be targeting a few initial clients, which will, nonetheless, require a good support channel that is available when needed. Consequently, despite all the resources entailed[2], this cannot, in any way, be left out of one's operational plan.

---

[1] Such as different calendar working days and distinct rest days.
[2] From extra people to added cost.

2.	**The initial response time and triage should be as short as possible.**

One of the greatest things that can be offered to customers is the ability to quickly establish contact with support engineers when problems occur. Plus, ensuring that engineers are able to perform an effective triage and, thus, clearly understand both the scope and the severity of the reported incidents, is absolutely vital. Investing in this initial sort of short response time[1] is something that can really work wonders in one's favor.

First of all, one successfully manages to appease customers by showing deep concern in immediately establishing a direct two-way communicating relationship. I can safely vouch for customers behaving a lot more amicable after this initial contact, and especially so should they really feel that they were able to interact with an engineer who showcased adequate expertise, given that this enhances their confidence in seeing their problem being handled appropriately.

Secondly, by determining, first-hand, the severity of the incident, one will be able to gather information on the business impact[2] as well as on the technical nature of the issue[3], and the latter allows one to successfully manage the incident internally by pushing it into the appropriate internal queue, according to one's own policies.

This triage really needs to be as efficient as possible and, having a first line of support made up of people who are insufficiently trained and poorly skilled, must start to be regarded as something of the past.

3.	**The level of supporting engineers' technical expertise should not be overlooked and needs to match the importance established within the triage step.**

Following suit with the previous item's last few statements, one needs to treat both the support process and its engineers with the same level of relevance conferred to one's development team. The days where support engineers were below par[4] must become a thing of the past. Clients simply want and expect more. Consequently, one needs to certify that support engineers really know all the details about the product they are supporting, so as to ensure they can, effectively and quickly, solve surging issues.

A great way of achieving this consists of promoting direct contact between support engineers and the development team[5]. This can usually come about by having support engineers going through formal training that is supplied by engineers from the product

---

[1] With information that clearly goes beyond the typical automated emails that, often, seem to be merely meant to meet certain legal requirements of an existing SLA.

[2] Usually supplied by the customer.

[3] Usually supplied by the technical engineer.

[4] In terms of their technical expertise and depth of knowledge regarding the product they are supporting.

[5] Which allows for knowledge to be effectively transferred between teams.

team, while also allowing for support engineers to work directly in the development cycles and, therefore, contribute to either testing or design tasks.

Additionally, having development engineers sporadically working on support teams can also be quite positive, given that the following two things will, usually, also take place:

- Development engineers will gain new insight and respect for the work delivered by supporting teams, since they are able to feel first-hand the pressure and stress that comes from being directly faced with clients struggling to fix issues pertaining to the solution. This experience will, usually, lead development engineers to enhance their concerns about overall product supportability, therefore leading to products far easier to troubleshoot and debug.
- Development engineers will also pass along key information to support engineers while they work together in this cross-collaboration model. Usually, this direct relationship eases the task of establishing future contact between support teams and development groups[1].

4. **The overall incident time[2] needs to be in line with its severity and impact.**

One of the worst things that can happen is to have critical issues dragging on for several days, causing massive problems[3] to clients. As such, it is fundamental to ensure that each incident can be resolved within a timeframe deemed appropriate according to the issue's severity. Again, this is easier said than done! Consider the following:

- What if one requires non-accessible information so as to successfully troubleshoot the problem[4]?
- What if the required data wasn't collected and one simply can't troubleshoot the problem's origin and root cause?
- What if one's support engineer is simply unable to establish the required level of communication with its peer on the client side?

The reality is that, from time to time, all these issues will come up in a few, though hopefully isolated, incidents. In such cases, the approach to them should rely on:

- Firstly[5], one needs to have a proactive support team that effectively reaches out to clients and is able to work alongside each client's team in quickly and diligently taking whichever steps are required so as to unravel the incident's critical elements.

---

[1] Which, in the end, is vital in delivering great customer service.
[2] And, consequently, the time spent in resolving issues
[3] Including, possibly, substantial financial losses.
[4] That can only be collected with either the help or effort from the client.
[5] For the vast majority of cases.

- Secondly, one needs great support managers who effectively review the emerging cases and successfully make direct interventions whenever specific incidents happen to be getting out of hand. Support managers need to properly diagnose problems that really are showstoppers and, therefore, they also need to effectively intervene in overcoming any communication issues that may have emerged[1]. It should be avoided, at all costs, ending up in a position where one can be induced to start blaming customers for either the inefficiencies of the support process or the inability to timely resolve incidents. One needs to, at the very least, share the burden and the blame. Such reasoning will stem an internal culture of responsibility within one's team that effectively fuels a strong desire to solve the existing problems while keeping clients pleased.

5. **Support incidents need to be integrated into the knowledge base.**
One definitely needs to fully document all incidents, so as to ensure that future problems can be quickly tackled and resolved. We will restrain from dwelling again on this topic, given that we consider that enough has already been said concerning it in previous items[2].

6. **Have great people with the right skill sets.**
Having great people on the support team is not simply about having great technical engineers. Support engineers need to be different from those working on development teams, given that they may need to face clients, either directly or indirectly. Additionally, they most definitely need to:
    - Establish communication with other people whom they really do not know,
    - Master the art of understanding the essence of problems, including their degree of seriousness, while being often constrained in the dialog they are able to establish with the existing counterpart.

In this sense, they will act precisely as pediatricians, who need to diagnose illnesses by analyzing the available symptoms, while being incapable of always maintaining objective dialogs with patients[3]. Hence, this is, quite definitely, an art dependent on skills that go well beyond purely technical expertise, meaning that it branches out by including human management skills.

---

[1] Thus guaranteeing that support engineers are able to move along and deliver the expected results.
[2] As defined in item **22 Store and share know-how: create an internal global knowledge depot**.
[3] Should they manage to maintain any dialog at all.

Item recap:

This item's fundamental guidelines can be succinctly systematized as follows:

- ✓ Ensure that you have adequate support with direct and easy access.
- ✓ Ensure that the support channel is available at appropriate times, according to the product's usage by your client base.
- ✓ Ensure that you deliver a timely response that solves incidents within the timeframe deemed appropriate according to each incident's severity.
- ✓ Ensure that support engineers have a deep technical knowledge of the product together with sound human management skills that enable them to successfully interact with clients.

Section V – Miscellaneous

This section will present and discuss eight diverse elements that do not revolve really around any technical issues. They are mostly concerned with your team, your product plan and the surrounding environment. Despite being far away from the technical arena, they are nonetheless critical to ensure that you can create an effective and successful software product.

43. Do not accept impossible challenges

One of the most critical issues in software development consists of the incredibly high tendency to focus on delivering the impossible. It is without surprise that, doing so, invariably results in disaster. Unfortunately, it is very common to create unrealistic project development plans which utterly fail to effectively contemplate the time and tasks required to create a solution of great quality.

More often than not, such movements towards the abyss are brought about by either the need/desire to market a product too quickly or simply due to blunt inability of those managing development projects. Regardless of the exact reasons behind these impulses, it is vital to avoid making these same mistakes. A development project needs to progress at an adequate pace, where all necessary tasks are executed diligently, from design to coding, testing or documenting. Little is to be gained by leapfrogging important steps and, failing to respect this premise is, ultimately, a recipe for miserable results.

Consequently, one needs to be extremely careful in juggling the three main variables that will define each project:

- Its features,
- Its cost,
- The time needed for its execution.

It is a well-known adage that, regarding software development projects, clients or sponsors should be allowed to define any two of these three variables, as long as development teams are able to manage the remaining one. Although metaphoric in sense, this idea does effectively relay the correct mindset, meaning that it is impossible to ask for too many features in a very short time and still expect for the cost to be low[1].

Therefore, defining project goals needs to be conducted quite carefully, namely in the sense of ensuring the creation of realistic plans. Given this, it is obviously extremely unwise to set out expecting miracles to occur and, thus, one should never assume that development teams will run cycle after cycle without hitting a few problems along the way.

Considering that software development is not an exact science, if there is one thing that one can be absolutely sure of, is that unexpected things will happen along the way. Such occurrences will take many forms, so beware of the following potential mishaps:

---

[1] Overall, one cannot expect to attain any other theoretical perfect combination of these elements.

1. **Scope creep.**

   One of the most common reasons for failing software development projects is a change of scope. Usually, this comes about as a result of seemingly innocuous small changes that, over time, pile up and end up creating an uncontrollable monster. Whenever changes are made to a project's scope, it must be ensured that their impact is carefully evaluated, and such an analysis should never be rushed. Quite often, a small change that initially seems to have very little impact on either the solution or the development plan, can really spur a slew of problems. Hence, it is crucial to get input from all the different parties involved[1], so as to ensure that the review of the real impact of the change is performed in its full breadth.

   Some formal development processes[2] argue that adding a new feature in a development cycle can only be performed in case another of equal weight is removed. Although, sometimes, this is not as straight forward as it seems, it is, nevertheless, a good way to set one's base battleground. Whenever a new feature is requested[3] one should immediately start evaluating the type of compensation that is to be expected. For the most part, it can come either in the form of removal and elimination of other features from the project plan or through added time and cost.

   Regardless of how one manages it, constant change in scope cannot be allowed to transform a viable and well defined project into an unsuccessful nightmare!

2. **Unforeseen issues with underlying technology.**

   There are very few development projects where people will deal exclusively with mature technology they fully master. Obviously, this is not to say that one should go out and start adopting every new piece of technology that is out there[4]. Instead, it is very much the opposite. It is fundamental to ensure that the bulk of one's solution is built on mature technology that one understands quite well. However, despite this foundational mindset, it is inevitable to, eventually, be faced with situations where certain expectations about the underlying technology fail to materialize.

   Quite often, one will to resort to certain mixtures of technologies that, in this process, will inevitably lead to hitting the wall here and there. As such, it is extremely important to reserve both specific tasks and time, to research these areas where there is greater potential for technical issues.

---

[1] From architects to developers and testers.
[2] As defined in item **25 Having a formally defined development process does not imply adopting a formal process.**
[3] Or a change in an existing feature for that matter.
[4] As defined in item **21 Observe the 10.000 hour principle: be a specialist in the technology you are using.**

By having these tasks included in one's plan[1], it will be possible to experiment with all fuzzy areas one is unsure of, so as to, ideally, avoid late reengineering efforts. This reasoning can be linked with the overall idea of prototyping the solution[2]. Furthermore, without it, one will be an easy target for a complete project collapse, given that critical parts of the solution may fail to work as expected, thus leading to either successive project delays[3] or successive unreliable builds[4].

3. **Team reshaping.**

Wouldn't it be great to drive a project forward knowing that the team will always be ready, always able to deliver at the precisely needed and expected velocity, while also imposing no unforeseen overhead towards accommodating new elements?

Though it would surely be wonderful, it almost never happens[5]. Unfortunately, catering to a changing team is a must and, this being so, one needs to be on the lookout for any situations that call for team reshaping to be performed.

Such a change within one's team can take place for many different reasons. Sometimes, people just decide to move on. Other times, that decision is made for them. Additionally, every now and then, it is realized that a given critical piece of knowledge or manpower is missing which, naturally, calls for the addition of new elements[6]. However, regardless of the exact circumstances surrounding these episodes, one can be sure that they will definitely happen and, when they do, they will have to be addressed. Therefore, it is wise to, not only contemplate some margin of error from the very early start, but also assume that these rotations will happen and that, invariably, they will have an initial negative impact that is, hopefully, followed by a positive compensation in the long run.

4. **Reengineering forced by early review and feedback.**

Perfect plans are always an illusion and, thus, the cold and naked reality is that, once feedback starts coming in[7], there will be a set of features that needs changing and another set that must be added as it simply had not been thought of[8].

Hence, it is very likely to have the project plan requiring adjustments after the first wave of reviews. This feedback is critical to reach the level of features and usability required by

---

[1] And, consequently, by having them trickle down to the development cycles.
[2] As defined in item **18 Prototype everything**.
[3] If one is lucky.
[4] Hopefully, not published as public ones.
[5] Even in small projects.
[6] Although, usually, this does come after a change of scope.
[7] Either from clients or beta testers – as defined in item **44 Get early feedback from beta-testers spanning all possible roles**.
[8] Though vital in ensuring the solution's broad acceptance and adoption.

successful solutions. Nevertheless, it is also quite common to have these changes forcing one into performing unpredicted reengineering efforts.

Naturally, the stronger one's design happens to be, the better it will adapt to changes. However, in the end, reengineering is unavoidable and, therefore, it is vital to be prepared to make the best of it. Whenever faced with this need it is advisable to make every attempt towards making it as positive and productive as possible. This should be done by, namely, ensuring that one will, not only address whichever direct issues were raised by incoming reviews and feedbacks, but also by streamlining any related technical issues that have emerged as the development effort progresses.

Fixing up these issues, sometimes known as technical debt, will, sooner or later, come to be a necessity. Thus, the sooner it is done, the better. Therefore, it is advisable to seize the opportunity and attempt to benefit from whatever synergies that might emerge from a slightly deeper reengineering[1] and, thus, eliminate other technical problems detected throughout the development cycle.

Item recap:

This item's fundamental guidelines can be succinctly systematized as follows:

- ✓ Do not set out to do the impossible. Do not expect miracles.
- ✓ Carefully review the balance between features, timeline and cost.
- ✓ Avoid scope creep. Balance new features and changes according to the overall plan, while maintaining a reasonable delivery goal.
- ✓ From the very first day, include, in your project plan, time to be used in solving unexpected problems[2].
- ✓ Cater to your team's reshaping needs. New team elements will start by impacting your production rate negatively.
- ✓ Always consider that you will need to perform some reengineering as you start getting feedback from beta-testers.
- ✓ Also consider that, somewhere along the way, you will need to change certain technical decisions that were previously taken. Set aside time for these tasks within your initial project plan.

---

[1] Than what is strictly demanded by the issues raised from the reviews and feedback.
[2] Including technical issues.

235

44. Get early feedback from beta-testers spanning all possible roles

Beta-testers are a key element in the chain of events that leads to successful software products. However, despite their usefulness in ripping out bugs, their value actually goes well beyond this element. Getting feedback from beta-testers, and doing so as early as possible within the development cycle, is critical in identifying major missing features as well as elements needing redesigning.

Since it is a given that no one wishes to market software products with bugs, the value of getting feedback from beta-testers on these issues is, by itself, of immense value. Though beta-testers skillfully generate feedback based on unforeseen[1] usage patterns, letting them use early builds of the solution will also generate a very good and precise notion of how the general public will perceive the overall quality and completeness of the product.

Through beta-testing one will quickly learn about the following critical types of issues:

1. **Identify missing features.**

    Perhaps one of the most interesting elements of beta-testing feedback is the ability to quickly acquire new ideas on new features to equip the developing product with. Plus, even if including, or attending to, every single user request happens to be impossible, at the very least the critical items that, if not implemented, can drive clients away from the product, should be carefully reviewed.

    Occasionally, a few missing features can really turn users away and, therefore, it is a huge and unnecessary mistake to risk having one's massive development effort failing on account of a few extra missing features that could easily have been included in the overall project plan[2].

2. **Identify breaking changes[3].**

    Whenever creating a new product version[4], maximum possible retro-compatibility must be ensured. Consequently, any breaking changes are to be avoided. Alternatively, should any breaking changes exist, it needs to be ensured that, by using the default configuration, the solution will, at least, behave in a way that reflects the non-breaking behavior. This will relegate the usage of such breaking changes to new optional modes, activated by explicit configuration.

---

[1] By even the most experienced quality assurance teams.
[2] Either at a little extra cost or by replacing some rarely used features of low business value.
[3] From previous versions.
[4] Regardless of being a major version or a simple patch.

Therefore, beta-testing can be extremely valuable in detecting any unintended breaking changes, as well as in acquiring feedback on any deliberate breaking changes[1].

3. **Identify new features not favorably accepted by users.**

   Sometimes, new features that seem to be a great step forward are badly received by users. Such occurrence should motivate a careful review of one's design decisions which, eventually, may lead to either reengineering those enhancements or simply admitting that the existing client base is just not favoring the new paradigm[2]. History is filled with examples of so-called enhancements to software products that were simply rejected by users. In such cases, it is just preferable to step back during a beta-testing cycle, so as to avoid paying the price that comes with persisting with such mistakes.

Hence, considering that this great feedback can be invaluable in creating successful software products, the final question really boils down to who should be deemed an adequate beta-tester?[3] Beta-testers ought to include all sorts of different actors interacting with the solution[4], thus ensuring that a relevant sample of profiles is included. Doing so is the best way to cover the usage of the full wealth of features supported by one's product, thus enabling one to determine, within every component, which items require either an adjustment or major reengineering.

Taking into account that one will be creating regular builds during the development cycle, the value of user feedback can be maximized by allowing beta-testers to use different selected builds as time marches on.

Doing so will spur a greater contact between the client base and the product being developed, therefore contributing to the goal of nurturing the ecosystem. Additionally, it will also allow one to get several rounds of feedback before the product is fully developed, therefore enabling one to even get feedback on reengineered features, which can, possibly, enable the evaluation of how user feedback is evolving as the product gets tweaked over the development cycles.

---

[1] Including their impact on the existing installed base.
[2] Bringing about the retraction of these ideas, followed by the reinstatement of the previous scenario.

[3] Which constitutes the key element to success.
[4] Instead of merely focusing on one specific user group.

Item recap:

This item's fundamental guidelines can be succinctly systematized as follows:

- ✓ Get feedback as early as possible from beta-testers.
- ✓ Use beta-testing on all product releases. Identify bugs, breaking changes and missing features.
- ✓ Understand when beta-testers are not comfortable with either new features or product enhancements and, if needed, retract from this path.
- ✓ If possible, use beta-testing in different cycles of your development effort, so as to acquire a sense of how they view the product's overall evolution.
- ✓ Ensure that your beta-testers include all different actors able to interact with the product. This will deliver a complete analysis of features and usage patterns.

45. Nurture the ecosystem

Any successful living organism requires an adequate and healthy ecosystem to survive, and software is no different. Creating successful software products requires constantly monitoring our ecosystem together with feeding it, so as to allow this symbiotic relationship to grow in perfect harmony.

It is a huge mistake to think that either new or even established products can really evolve and survive in an adverse environment. Like any other living organism, successful software products need to be in perfect balance with their environment and, therefore, it is our obligation to nurture the growth of all surrounding elements that, one way or another, contribute to the success of this equation.

Currently, this entails having a strong foothold within all types of social networking vehicles, along with the more traditional internet presence.

On the traditional internet presence's side, it is important to take into account that:

- This should include an organized and informative website through which users will be able to search and browse all items registered in the issue tracking tool and considered to be of public access. This immediate access to an issue database, with possible workarounds or references to existing patches, is vital in ensuring a quick and effective maintenance.
- Additionally, the website should also allow users to gain immediate access to upgrades to which they are entitled[1].
- Furthermore, an effective website, geared towards promoting a product, needs to bring the community together by enabling easy contact between all sorts of clients and professionals who, one way or another, interact with the product. Thus, it is strongly recommended putting together interactive and moderated forums, where different types of threads can be created so as to discuss either technical or commercial issues.
- Bringing both the product development team as well as the product support team closer to the actual users[2] is also vital in helping those struggling with specific issues.
- Doing so will equally allow one to gather insight as to what the market thinks of the product, which ignites an objective and well informed perspective pertaining the product's evolutionary options.

Now, moving towards the new breed of social networking, one should:

[1] Based on the existing licenses and software assurance contracts.
[2] Regardless of their respective roles, such as true end users or as members of an operations team.

239

- Ensure having a presence in the best well known social networks while allowing for people, groups and existing communities, to link themselves up to one's product. The main difference between this type of presence and the more traditional internet scenario pertains to the speed and frequency of events as well as changes and updates of the available information.

- Bear in mind that the traditional internet presence[1], only calls for a news feed when there is truly new information to spread around, which is not that frequent. To this exception, I would add the need to respond promptly to the forums' threads, although having a good ecosystem surrounding the product helps in having many entries actually coming directly from external sources, which means that questions and answers can usually flow without the required intervention of the development team[2].

- Inversely, the common trend in social networking calls for a high degree of events per time unit. Thus, should one fail to add new posts regularly[3], visibility will be lost. Social networking cannot be about publicizing new versions. Instead, it must be about ensuring a constant flow of information that keeps users interested and aware, thus, making one's presence really felt. This can be achieved by allowing anyone on the team to post non-confidential information on such modern communication vehicles.

Given this, the main take home message is that it is crucial to make people aware of one's product[4] in order to scale up the user base. Naturally, the degree of relevance of this marketing element depends on the type of product being built but, in most cases, assuring its competent execution will be far more helpful than detrimental.

Finally, a word of caution in that there is still a market segment out there keen on more classic events, where direct human presence and contact take place. Hence, it is very important to remember to promote the ecosystem by creating periodic events where clients, partners and/or team members, get together to either talk about forthcoming versions of the product or exchange knowledge and experience. Effort should be made in order to get every possible type of actor involved and, ultimately, to promote direct contact between them, without one's own mediation. Doing so will, not only drive the ecosystem forward, but also put in place a self-feeding structure that will continue growing without requiring one's constant presence and direct intervention.

---

[1] Through a standard website.
[2] Although a quick and effective moderation is vital in maintaining quality and spurring its long term usage.
[3] These days, almost at an hourly basis!
[4] Even if one happens to gain a dominant stance on the market.

Item recap:

This item's fundamental guidelines can be succinctly systematized as follows:

- ✓ A successful product needs a good surrounding ecosystem.
- ✓ You need to ensure that people can access information about your product as well as establish communication channels with peers.
- ✓ You need to bring development and support teams closer to end users.
- ✓ You need to leverage and balance a traditional internet presence, based on a standard website, where you can get information on known issues, where you can discuss problems in moderated forums and where you can acquire latest builds and patches.
- ✓ You also need to make your product known and talked about using social networking.

46. Be alert and understand the surrounding environment

One of the most crucial things in developing software products is to have a very good and broad understanding of what is happening in the surrounding environment. Having a clear and precise view of the key forces shaping up the contextual environment where one's product is to make a stand is mandatory in ensuring that one will not be shooting in the dark.

Thus, what are the main issues one needs to be on the lookout for? Though several will come to mind, the following are, by far, the most important ones:

1. **Know your market.**

    Understanding what the market really is for a product should probably constitute the number one concern. It is quite relevant to identify what markets are looking for as well as the key drivers that will ignite any future shifts. Markets cannot be seen as static entities, given that they end up changing over time and, usually, make choices, regarding preferred products, according to a very small set of key features. Sometimes, all it takes for products to be successful is the ability to address one specific business problem, thus creating great value for those using it. On other occasions, products' success comes from a small group of combined factors, such as one or two key innovative features and a compelling price.

    Regardless of the precise market goal of one's own product, current options already available must be fully understood, given that such information will help figuring out how one's product will be able to differentiate itself from the competition[1]. By being successful in clearly identifying those non-tackled areas, it is easier to develop a product that provides those missing elements which, in turn, vastly increases the chances of having a product with great market value.

2. **Know the competition.**

    Although one's main goal should be to deliver something that, so far, has not been addressed by other products, the reality shows us that it is highly likely that one's product will need to complement certain truly innovative features with a whole set of standard traits shared with several other existing solutions. Despite this, developing such standard features still needs to be performed with the utmost care and professionalism, which is made easier by studying the competition and knowing how their own products work.

---

[1] In the form of understanding the existing market gap, more specifically that which the market needs and is currently not being addressed by any available product.

Performing such a detailed study of the competition also enables one to detect their weaknesses which, afterwards, can be turned into an advantage[1].

A constant review of the competition, the technologies they use and where they aim to progress to, is something that is well beyond the art of software engineering. However, it is, nonetheless, required, in order to have very favorable odds of developing successful products that come to enjoy a long lasting life.

3. **Know the market trends.**

Knowing, at each point in time, where markets are leaning towards and, consequently, trying to anticipate where they are headed to, is an art that can definitely boost one's chances of creating successful products.

However, apart from this general concept, the specific field of software development also warrants being highly aware of how the underlying technologies will evolve. In this regard, there are two key scenarios that can ruin one's plans:

- Firstly, having the chosen underlying technologies[2] being either deprecated or abandoned by the companies owning them. The last thing one needs is to spend a significant effort, as well as money, building a software product, only to discover that the technologies used are going to be discontinued. Such an occurrence will, sooner or later, cause a massive reengineering effort[3]. Although many companies do hide their game plan, by constantly monitoring upcoming news from the underground[4], one is, for the most part, able to pick up on rumors pertaining to the policies that lay at the core of companies' decision to, sometimes, abandon certain technologies in favor of more recent and more evolved ones. Hence, it is wise to pick the main supportive technologies, which define the foundation for the product being built, from vendors regarded as big players[5].
- Secondly, no one wants to invest heavily in basic plumbing technology[6], and even less so at the risk of seeing other far bigger players producing their own similar technology[7].

---

[1] Namely, by engineering a solution that outplays them in these exact spots.
[2] To build one's product.
[3] Given that it is very unlikely that one will be able to sit on top of discontinued technologies for a long time.
[4] Forums, chats, *etc.*.
[5] Since, usually, these have very well defined support plans and deprecation policies.
[6] Even if, in the short run, it entails a competitive edge.
[7] Given that it is likely to have it undermining one's efforts as well as overwhelming one's creation, once they manage to introduce far better and more evolved features.

- Creating base plumbing technology is a very risky business, given that there is a high risk of being eaten up by big companies which enjoy the benefits that come from having a major presence in the market. Hence, those who still happen to choose to go down this avenue should, at the very least, try to secure such investment by tying them up to some specific business features that other companies, aiming at far wider markets, are unlikely to match.

4. **Know what makes you unique.**

When able to establish a new product and, consequently, conquer a relevant client base, it becomes very important to focus on ensuring that the product sticks out. Successfully doing so can be accomplished by being very aware of what makes each product unique. It is of the utmost importance to be constantly passing along this message to the market! Always reinforce the unique traits and features of a product, so that the whole environment starts warming up to the message and, over time, starts automatically associating the product with it.

In this regard, even existing clients need to be frequently remembered of these unique features, otherwise, sooner or later, it is possible that other vendors will successfully take over one's territory. Hence, it is crucial to be constantly and relentlessly trying to innovate and improve one's product, which should include investing a significant portion of the development effort towards these unique features that make the product a success. By constantly attempting to improve these features, one minimizes the risk of losing the edge which, in turn, is key in keeping ahead of the competition.

Item recap:

So from this item we can distil the following main guidelines:

- ✓ Research the market and understand what your product will be delivering that is valuable for your potential clients.
- ✓ Know exactly which unique features your product has and how they provide added value to clients.
- ✓ Know where the competition is and where they will be likely moving towards.
- ✓ Understand where the technology panorama is moving towards, and be very careful not to adopt technologies that will soon become deprecated, unsupported or obsolete. Be very careful if you decide to build low-level technology that is far from any business need (it is a very risky endeavor!).
- ✓ Constantly invest in enhancing the unique features that your product has, to keep yourself ahead of the competitors.

47. Hire the best and have a complete and heterogeneous team

Trying to create a great software product with a mediocre team is simply impossible! I can testify firsthand that one either has a really good team to work with or the intended goals will not be achieved.

Developing software is hard, and only by combining the talent and skill of several engineers will it be possible to, ultimately, create great products. Hence, the first major guideline within this item pertains to hiring the best, since one should never be content with bringing in average personnel. When looking to hire certain sets of skills, it is wise to commit to bringing someone in only when convinced the engineer in question will excel and deliver high valued work. Otherwise, one will be better off continuing searching until the right person comes along.

The time and effort teams require in order to onboard a new hire is not small. Therefore, it is important to be betting on a sure thing, as much as one can be. As such, the process of building teams has to be conducted with great care, which includes not rushing, and much less bringing in a somewhat unreliable extra set of hands on account of an aggressive deadline. It is unrealistic to think that someone who joined one's team only recently will be the difference in making a critical deadline. In fact, in most cases, hiring new people will, initially, actually reduce overall work rate[1]. Hence, as already stated, one golden rule to live by is never to rush recruitment processes.

Having established that a final decision concerning recruitment processes will only be favorable upon finding engineers who fully meet one's criteria, it means that it is fairly relevant to know how to define such criteria. Doing so requires careful thought about the mix of skills that one wishes to see in the new hire, which includes analyzing, to name just a few, the relative importance of:

- Technical skills,
- Past experience,
- Inter-personal abilities.

Therefore, the recruitment process has to be comprised of enough steps that ensure being able to get objective and reliable evaluations.

Speaking of evaluations, it is also crucial to gather a wide array of opinions and, above all else, it is a huge mistake to merely rely on one's own views. Whenever possible, certain members of the current team should be involved by actively participating in the technical and non-technical

---

[1] Given that the effort of bringing new workers up to speed will hinder overall productivity.

screening. Hopefully, someone who gets a positive and consistent review from all those involved in the selection process will pop up. All things considered, the final decision is to be exclusively about high quality, since achieving it will generate new and added benefits in a very short time.

Another important topic that also needs addressing is that of a team's completeness, which includes the need to be heterogeneous. Having a broad set of skills is an absolute must-have, given that it ends up being useless to have great developers and poor architects. It is even quite ineffective to invest highly in most technical profiles, only to miss out on other complementary roles, such as good managers[1].

Failing to have a complete and broad set of skills will surely lead to a negative outcome. Thus, the team that offers greatest chances of success is that which can really excel in all different aspects, both technical and non-technical.

Additionally, it is very important to avoid making the ultimate mistake of thinking that technical people will, somehow, be able to deliver great quality should they be assigned to non-technical tasks[2]. Strangely enough, examples of attempting to assign technical tasks to non-technical resources are far less common, though such experiences have been unsuccessfully performed as well.

Finally, team managers should actively and deliberately look to create heterogeneous teams, though this has actually nothing to do with either skills or roles. Teams ought to even showcase diversity within the same roles, given that diversity will propel distinct ways of thinking and, thus, different approaches. Such healthy clash of views will bring about strategies that are more adaptable and, consequently, the best possible results. Having different people with vastly distinct personalities and backgrounds will lead to different approaches to problems and, usually, teams will gain from reviewing these alternative solutions. Quite often, the path taken is a mixture that brings together the best features of different ideas.

Additionally, promoting such critical thinking that spurs team members to really think independently, profoundly and outside the box, will even bring about a greater awareness of both one's weaknesses as well as possible alternative routes.

Consequently, the real key lies in motivating constructive criticism, where peers respectfully and cordially:

- Analyze each other's ideas,

---

[1] Product, project or program managers.
[2] Even if just to compensate a budget limitation or to temporarily stand in while the recruitment process moves along.

- Identify weaknesses,
- Suggest improvements.

Finally, given that what goes around comes around, and with everyone having their ideas being scrutinized, all should expect to experience both good and bad days and, ultimately, remain focused on the only relevant goal, which is of constantly having the team, as a whole, moving forward in the direction of successfully building great software products.

Item recap:

This item's fundamental guidelines can be succinctly systematized as follows:

- ✓ Hire the best people. Do not rush the staffing process when hiring a new team element and be sure to gather input from different people from within your team.
- ✓ Ensure you have all required sets of skills. Do not think that you can develop great products if missing a given key expertise, including both technical and non-technical ones.
- ✓ Ensure you have great diversity within your team, even within each role. Diversity will ignite different ways of thinking, distinct approaches and, quite naturally, a healthy professional debate that will bring about the best possible solutions.

---

48.   Do not outsmart yourself

Einstein once said *"Make everything as simple as possible, but not simpler."* and, in software engineering, these are words to live by, given that one will be made to pay a high price when failing to control products' complexity. However, controlling complexity is just one side of the equation, since one also needs to avoid pursuing avenues that are just beyond one's grasp.

Trying to use technologies that are either not fully understood[1] or with which one lacks experience, is a recipe for disaster. Additionally, disaster will also strike should one attempt to use algorithms that are not fully comprehended either, with things inevitably becoming really chaotic[2] and, ultimately, generating solutions that are overly engineered and provide insufficient value[3].

Unfortunately, avoiding this capital sin is, sometimes, easier said than done. Many software engineers seem to be highly engaged in feeding their ego, with such being usually done through the creation of obscure solutions that lead to layers of virtually unmanageable code. Plus, quite often these components simply fail to meet the existing requirements, introducing subtle bugs that prove extremely difficult to tame.

However, failure also comes through the hands of common trends. Usually, once a specific technology becomes fashionable, a horde of engineers can easily be seen eager to follow in the footsteps of the enlightened crowd, while being completely oblivious to the fact that they are, actually, in over their heads.

I remember participating once in a project where there was a clear guideline and strong orientation towards making use of template meta-programming in C++. Unfortunately, as history and time ended up proving, it was a clearly misguided concept, given that virtually none of the team's engineers understood the ins and outs of template meta-programming in C++. Additionally, and regarding this particular project, the benefits that could stem from using such technology are still a mystery to me[4]. Anyway, the reality is that we tried to be too ingenious and ended up having to backtrack, in the form of dropping all the template meta-programming ideas and simply going back to reengineering those components that had, initially, been created using this paradigm.

---

[1] As defined in item **21 Observe the 10.000 hour principle: be a specialist in the technology you are using**.
[2] Should one fall victim to the trap of using one's own engineering skills for one's intellectual self-amusement.
[3] Considering their development and future maintenance costs.
[4] Though it might be the case that I am still not able to fully grasp template meta-programming in C++.

This episode was a clear example of trying too hard to be smart and utterly failing in doing so. Overall, I view this episode's morale to be equally applicable to all technical tasks, though it is not just about choosing a specific technology that one does not fully understand or with which one lacks experience. Instead, it is about applying the same principle in any given task. Software engineers need to ensure they effectively understand all the intricacies pertaining to the tasks they are assigned, so as to avoid failing to comprehend the full impact of the decisions they end up making as well as of the code they write.

Hence, it is crucial to be both smart and humble enough so as to ask for either more information or help when one is not comfortable with the level of detailed information possessed. Again, it is unfortunate that, too often, engineers fail to speak out on account of thinking that they are expected to know everything and prohibited to ask for assistance.

Furthermore, this happens to be especially true with new team members. Consequently, it is extremely important to ensure being able to supply new engineers with proper coaching and mentoring. Doing so is vital in avoiding problems that, for the most part, come about when workers try to do something they do not fully understand.

Nevertheless, and going back to the principle of not outsmarting oneself, it is fundamental to focus on devising really simple solutions from the very early stages of the design phase. The simplest solutions are the less costly ones to implement and, usually, the ones that end up being implemented with far fewer problems. Implementing something that is low on complexity and limited in scope allows engineers to quickly understand the impact of every aspect of it. Consequently, they can quickly gain a full view of their working space. When, on the other hand, they go for a really complex problem, with far reaching consequences, problems are sure to trickle in.

Hence, as Einstein said, keep everything as simple as possible while not running away from warranted complexity when absolutely needed. When those few situations do come up, one needs to rely on a vast wealth of engineering techniques, from encapsulation to testing, as well as from architecture blueprints to code reviews, so as to be sure of delivering great quality, despite the complexity of such elements.

Item recap:

This item's fundamental guidelines can be succinctly systematized as follows:

- ✓ Keep every task as simple as possible.
- ✓ Do not over-engineer your solution. Do not go for complex solutions when simple ones will deliver the exact same results.
- ✓ Do not adopt technologies, algorithms or solutions that you do not fully understand and master.

49.   Be flexible and have a flexible team

I have never heard of a single software development project, successfully running from start to finish, without experiencing either significant problems, detours or simply changes in scope and timeline. The reality is that developing software products is not an exact science and, this being so, many different factors can influence and change the plan initially laid out.

Therefore, not only is being flexible quite useful, but it also needs to be instilled within the team members[1]. However, finding a balance between the flexibility required to deal with changing targets and the discipline needed so as to ensure that assignments, schedules and deadlines are followed[2], is key.

Nevertheless, flexibility does not equal lack of direction, nor should it suggest being deprived of a steady development rhythm. It simply means showcasing the ability to adapt when, every now and then, something comes along that really justifies a major change in the project. Plus, since any major change will force a review of the project plan, it can be taken for granted that the vast majority of the team[3] will be affected by it in one way or another.

Despite this, it must be ensured that the team focuses on the reason why the change is needed together with why it will benefit the product in the long run. People need to understand that the change is, actually, a positive and well thought out move. Furthermore, it is quite relevant to highlight how, any negative impact the change happens to have on tasks either already finished or under way, will be easily compensated by the long term positive impact it will bring about.

Therefore, the key lies in accentuating the positive and ensuring that morale is not hit by the change in a way that would deeply affect the team's commitment, quality or productivity. However, is there a way to really prepare one's team so as to ensure that they are able to be flexible? My take on that is somewhat mixed. Overall, I consider that some people and certain societies are, culturally, less guided by strict planning and, therefore, more used to change. Hence, such workers experience greater ease in coping with unexpected twists in the project. Others, on the other hand, by being keener on having very tight plans and processes, meet any change with a demeaning posture. Given this, having a heterogeneous team can also work in one's favor when dealing with such particular circumstances.

While some elements of a team can react less favorably to change, by having others being capable of adapting easily, those less keen on changing will, eventually, come round and tag

---

[1] Naturally, some people are just more naturally capable of coping with change and, though everyone can learn to be more flexible, not all team members will showcase the same degree of improvement.
[2] While still delivering the quality required.
[3] If not the whole team.

along. Overall, most software engineers are somewhat used to change and, unless it entails a major hurdle regarding either the skills or experience they possess, the vast majority will easily survive the process.

Therefore, this means that the biggest issue lies with changes which either force the adoption of new technologies or warrant some type of previous experience that is lacking, and both these cases require extreme care. Adopting technologies that one does not fully master leads to trouble and, additionally, expecting people to deliver high quality work when suddenly assigning them tasks beyond their experience[1] is also a recipe for disaster.

Most people will be flexible up to a certain point but, upon reaching it, they will start feeling uncomfortable and, while a few engineers are always keen to take on new challenges[2], most people will not react like that. Hence, it needs to be ensured that this breaking point is not reached and, as stated thus far, achieving this warrants making sure that demands placed on software engineers are:

- Acceptable,
- Reasonable,
- Doable.

Impossible challenges usually do not have happy endings and, even flexibility, must be looked upon as having an upper limit.

Item recap:

This item's fundamental guidelines can be succinctly systematized as follows:

✓ Try to have a flexible team which showcases an open mindset regarding potential necessities to readjust the development plan.
✓ Do not confuse flexibility with lack of direction. Being flexible still requires strong direction and a clear understanding of what the targets are.
✓ Do not push people beyond what they accept as being reasonable change.

---

[1] As well as against the role they were expecting to have to fulfill.
[2] Regardless of whether they fully comprehend what they are signing up for or not.

50. Use your instinct to drive the product and do not forget to have fun

Despite all the theories behind product development, marketing strategies and a myriad of equally important concepts that must be contemplated when any product is under development, there will always be a part of the creational process that really boils down to belief. Everyone involved must believe in the project, although doing so does not offer any assurances of success.

However, and regardless of this absence of any real assurances, part of the team's driving force must come from belief and instinct. It is crucial to believe that one is on the right track and about to create something of true value. Plus, every now and then, one's instincts have to be allowed to drive some of the decisions when going for certain paths that may seem doubtful to many.

It is this instinctive belief that some options are worth pursuing that, usually, leads to significant innovation and relevant breakthroughs. History is filled with stories of entrepreneurs who succeeded when most thought they would fail. Furthermore, there are even a few known cases of products that were a huge success, despite the fact that there is still a certain dose of mystery as to the real reasons that led to such a remarkable outcome.

Who hasn't heard tales of young creative minds responsible for creating hugely successful products[1] which broke almost every possible and conceivable rule about what is considered to be the correct way of conducting product development?

Therefore, the bottom line boils down to understanding that, though following known practices and proven guidelines can be of great value, there must always be some room for throwing a bit of caution to the wind and letting wild horses run free. It is from this, sometimes reckless creational force, that great ideas come along. Thus, without losing track the 99% of the work must be performed by following rules as well as standard processes and patterns, it is important to allow both oneself and one's team that 1% of creative freedom to do or to think as they please, while creating the next big thing!

Additionally, by doing so, one will, almost inadvertently, come to the last point of the day: **having fun!** Very few people seem to be able to deliver their absolute best when not really enjoying themselves. Given this, one needs to ensure that everyone on the team feels a sense of purpose from their daily routine and, additionally, that they are actually enjoying the ride[2].

---

[1] Followed by successful companies.

[2] Enough to have it constitute a driving force that has them getting up excited and eager to work.

Having fun in the workspace is incredibly valuable, since, at the end of the day, nothing is more motivating, irrespective of either money or any other material compensation. These latter items will motivate people to move only so much and for a limited time period. After a few months[1], either people are truly happy with what they are doing or they will opt between leaving or staying put while lowering their productivity rate considerably[2].

Therefore, having fun is not just a marketing hype concerning great companies. It is, in fact, the force that can bring one's team together by ensuring that day after day, month after month and year after year, engineers will continue working hard as a result of still being fueled by the passion that is absolutely indispensable in guaranteeing that one's product stays on top. Only those who are truly motivated and happy with what they are doing, will continue pushing forward so as to innovate, create new things, come up with brand new ideas that will, ultimately, generate the differences needed so as to distance oneself from the competition and, ultimately, stay on top by exhibiting a great software product!

Item recap:

This item's fundamental guidelines can be succinctly systematized as follows:

- ✓ Balance sound judgment and theoretically proven processes and techniques, with a mild dose of risk and instinct.
- ✓ Do not be afraid to take a few doubtful paths. However, do not make it your "way of life".
- ✓ Ensure that people on the team enjoy their work, for only those who are having fun will continuously deliver their best possible creative work.

---

[1] Or years, in a best case scenario.
[2] And, not surprisingly, even the quality of what they do.

Final notes

So this is it! If you have come this far I have only to thank you for the time you have dedicated to reading this book and the perseverance you showed to deeply analyze its content.

I'm sure that there were a few things you have not agreed with and others that you felt that are simply missing. Despite that, I hope that the majority of the items and their inherent content presented valuable ideas that will help you create better software products.

Obviously, this book could have twice as many items and no two readers will ever agree on which ones would be the 50 most important ones. I guess, even I, a few months or years from now, will have a slightly different opinion as I learn new things and gain new insight while hard at work building yet a new set of software products.

Despite that, I truly believe that this content will help those that are actively working in software engineering, as it gives a broad view of different types of things we need to consider if we are to create a great and successful software product!

And let's have even more fun by doing it once again!

Item List

> **Coding and execution runtime**
> 1. An unavoidable reality: errors and exceptions will happen
> 2. Juggling the retry logic conundrum
> 3. Coding rules: are we back in elementary school?
> 4. Document you source code: follow the proximity rule
> 5. Beware of abstraction layers that generate code
> 6. Minimize the impact of slow operations
> 7. Interfaces and mock objects
> 8. Algorithm complexity and optimizations
> 9. Maximizing efficiency
> 10. Think globally from ground up
> 11. Be defensive: choose the safest techniques
> 12. Linking code: the static vs. dynamic option
> 13. Do's and don'ts of APIs
> 14. Leverage the full power of the IDE and all related add-ins and tools

> **Development environment and technologies**
> 15. Use as many enterprise building blocks as possible and refresh common design patterns
> 16. Use in-memory distributed caching systems to enhance performance and scalability
> 17. Achieving scalability: scale-out and reduce resource consumption
> 18. Prototype everything
> 19. Shoot for the sky: leverage cloud-based services to provision temporary environments

> **Development process**
> 20. Nothing works better then test driven development
> 21. Observe the 10.000 hour principle: be a specialist in the technology you are using
> 22. Store and share know-how: create an internal global knowledge depot
> 23. Do not leave the build for last: invest in an automated build system from the very first day
> 24. Time is precious: invest wisely in worthwhile features
> 25. Having a formally defined development process does not imply adopting a formal process
> 26. Testing and quality assurance procedures

Item List (cont.)

> ## **Deployment and supportability**

27. For a product to be used, installed it must be!
28. Upgrades will happen: ensure you have an effective upgrade strategy
29. Configuration is needed: minimize the options and use a centralized configuration resource
30. Strange unexplainable behaviors are inevitable: create a detailed and systematic tracing feature
31. Generate performance data and pave way for proactive alarms
32. Security is everything: make sure you know what privileges and accounts are used
33. Know thyself: reduce the attack surface
34. Invest in threat modeling
35. Define the recovery track: plan for backup requirements and restore steps
36. Prepare for the unexpected: setup a proper symbol server
37. Avoid guessing, know how your product is used!
38. Problems are not solved by magic: create an operations guide
39. Train operations team, use simulated scenarios
40. Always ensure that you have segregated environments
41. Support mainstream scripting tools for management features
42. Have a great support process and an equally great support team

> ## **Miscellaneous**

43. Do not accept impossible challenges
44. Get early feedback from beta-testers spanning all possible roles
45. Nurture the ecosystem
46. Be alert and understand the surrounding environment
47. Hire the best and have a complete and heterogeneous team
48. Do not outsmart yourself
49. Be flexible and have a flexible team
50. Use your instinct to drive the product and do not forget to have fun